READERS' GUIDES TO ESSENTIAL CRITICISM

CONSULTANT EDITOR: NICOLAS TREDELL

Published

Lucie Armitt	George Eliot: *Adam Bede – The Mill on the Floss – Middlemarch*
Simon Avery	Thomas Hardy: *The Mayor of Casterbridge – Jude the Obscure*
Paul Baines	Daniel Defoe: *Robinson Crusoe – Moll Flanders*
Richard Beynon	D. H. Lawrence: *The Rainbow – Women in Love*
Peter Boxall	Samuel Beckett: *Waiting for Godot – Endgame*
Claire Brennan	The Poetry of Sylvia Plath
Susan Bruce	Shakespeare: *King Lear*
Sandie Byrne	Jane Austen: *Mansfield Park*
Alison Chapman	Elizabeth Gaskell: *Mary Barton – North and South*
Peter Childs	The Fiction of Ian McEwan
Christine Clegg	Vladimir Nabokov: *Lolita*
John Coyle	James Joyce: *Ulysses – A Portrait of the Artist as a Young Man*
Martin Coyle	Shakespeare: *Richard II*
Justin D. Edwards	Postcolonial Literature
Michael Faherty	The Poetry of W. B. Yeats
Sarah Gamble	The Fiction of Angela Carter
Jodi-Anne George	Chaucer: *The General Prologue to The Canterbury Tales*
Jane Goldman	Virginia Woolf: *To the Lighthouse – The Waves*
Huw Griffiths	Shakespeare: *Hamlet*
Vanessa Guignery	The Fiction of Julian Barnes
Louisa Hadley	The Fiction of A. S. Byatt
Geoffrey Harvey	Thomas Hardy: *Tess of the d'Urbervilles*
Paul Hendon	The Poetry of W. H. Auden
Terry Hodgson	The Plays of Tom Stoppard for Stage, Radio, TV and Film
William Hughes	Bram Stoker: *Dracula*
Stuart Hutchinson	Mark Twain: *Tom Sawyer – Huckleberry Finn*
Stuart Hutchinson	Edith Wharton: *The House of Mirth – The Custom of the Country*
Betty Jay	E. M. Forster: *A Passage to India*
Aaron Kelly	Twentieth-Century Irish Literature
Elmer Kennedy-Andrews	The Poetry of Seamus Heaney
Elmer Kennedy-Andrews	Nathaniel Hawthorne: *The Scarlet Letter*
Daniel Lea	George Orwell: *Animal Farm – Nineteen Eighty-Four*
Sara Lodge	Charlotte Brontë: *Jane Eyre*
Philippa Lyon	Twentieth-Century War Poetry
Merja Makinen	The Novels of Jeanette Winterson
Matt McGuire	Contemporary Scottish Literature

Jago Morrison	The Fiction of Chinua Achebe
Carl Plasa	Tony Morrison: *Beloved*
Carl Plasa	Jean Rhys: *Wide Sargasso Sea*
Nicholas Potter	Shakespeare: *Antony and Cleopatra*
Nicholas Potter	Shakespeare: *Othello*
Steven Price	The Plays, Screen plays and Films of David Mamet
Andrew Radford	Victorian Sensation Fiction
Berthold Schoene-Harwood	Mary Shelley: *Frankenstein*
Nick Selby	T. S. Eliot: *The Waste Land*
Nick Selby	Herman Melville: *Moby Dick*
Nick Selby	The Poetry of Walt Whitman
David Smale	Salman Rushdie: *Midnight's Children – The Satanic Verses*
Patsy Stoneman	Emily Brontë: *Wuthering Heights*
Susie Thomas	Hanif Kureishi
Nicolas Tredell	F. Scott Fitzgerald: *The Great Gatsby*
Nicolas Tredell	Joseph Conrad: *Heart of Darkness*
Nicolas Tredell	Charles Dickens: *Great Expectations*
Nicolas Tredell	William Faulkner: *The Sound and the Fury – As I Lay Dying*
Nicolas Tredell	Shakespeare: *Macbeth*
Nicolas Tredell	The Fiction of Martin Amis
Matthew Woodcock	Shakespeare: Henry V
Angela Wright	Gothic Fiction

Forthcoming

Pascale Aebischer	Jacobean Drama
Annika Bautz	Jane Austen: *Sense and Sensibility – Pride and Prejudice – Emma*
Matthew Beedham	The Novels of Kazuo Ishiguro
Jodi-Anne George	*Beowulf*
Sarah Haggarty Jon Mee	William Blake: *Songs of Innocence and Experience*
Matthew Jordan	Milton: *Paradise Lost*
Timothy Milnes	Wordsworth: *The Prelude*
Stephen Regan	The Poetry of Philip Larkin
Mardi Stewart	Victorian Women's Poetry
Michael Whitworth	Virginia Woolf: *Mrs Dalloway*
Gina Wisker	The Fiction of Margaret Atwood

Readers' Guides to Essential Criticism
Series Standing Order ISBN 1–4039–0108–2
(outside North America only)

You can receive future titles in this series as they are published by placing a standing order. Please contact your bookseller or, in the case of difficulty, write to us at the address below with your name and address, the title of the series and the ISBN quoted above.

Customer Services Department, Macmillan Distribution Ltd, Houndmills, Basingstoke, Hampshire RG21 6XS, England

---

Charlotte Brontë

Jane Eyre

SAR...

Consultant editor: Nicolas Tredell

palgrave
macmillan

First published 2009 by
PALGRAVE MACMILLAN

Palgrave Macmillan in the UK is an imprint of Macmillan Publishers Limited,
registered in England, company number 785998, of Houndmills, Basingstoke,
Hampshire RG21 6XS.

Palgrave Macmillan in the US is a division of St Martin's Press LLC,
175 Fifth Avenue, New York, NY 10010.

Palgrave Macmillan is the global academic imprint of the above companies
and has companies and representatives throughout the world.

Palgrave® and Macmillan® are registered trademarks in the United States,
the United Kingdom, Europe and other countries.

ISBN-13: 978-0-230-51815-5 hardback
ISBN-10: 0-230-51815-X hardback
ISBN-13: 978-0-230-51816-2 paperback
ISBN-10: 0-230-51816-8 paperback

This book is printed on paper suitable for recycling and made from fully
managed and sustained forest sources. Logging, pulping and manufacturing
processes are expected to conform to the environmental regulations of the
country of origin.

A catalogue record for this book is available from the British Library.

Library of Congress Cataloging-in-Publication Data

Lodge, Sara.
      Charlotte Brontë – Jane Eyre / Sara Lodge.
         p. cm.—(Readers' guides to essential criticism)
      Includes bibliographical references and index.
      ISBN 978-0-230-51815-5—ISBN 978-0-230-51816-2 (pbk.)
         1. Brontë, Charlotte, 1816–1855. Jane Eyre. 2. Governesses in literature.
      3. Women in literature. I. Title.

PR4167.J5L54 2009
823'.8—dc22
                                                              2008038428

In memory of my grandmother,
Jane Theodora Fairlie (1914–2004)

Contents

Acknowledgements   x

Introduction   1

CHAPTER ONE   4

Victorian Responses: Power and Popularity;
Coarseness and Criticism

This chapter covers critical assessments of *Jane Eyre* in the Victorian period. The first section looks at the earliest reviews of the novel, when the identity of the author was unknown, showing that the plot, style, and influence of *Jane Eyre* were, from the first, the subject of politicised debate between admirers and detractors. The chapter then looks at how *Jane Eyre*'s reception changed after mid-century, when Charlotte Brontë's tragic personal history became widely known. It closes with late nineteenth-century assessments that assimilate *Jane Eyre* into their accounts of literary history, often with a mixture of admiration and condescension.

CHAPTER TWO   30

Jane Eyre's 'I': From Humanism to Deconstruction

This chapter, divided into three sections, explores the twentieth–century movement from humanist, through formalist, to deconstructive readings of *Jane Eyre*. It examines changing approaches to Brontë's prose style and to a central critical challenge that *Jane Eyre* poses, the intense subjectivity of its first person narration. The chapter details the increasing attention paid to the formal construction of the text, its imagery and verbal art. It shows how critical trends shifted in the course of the century from regarding Jane's viewpoint as identical with Charlotte Brontë's and her history as a triumph of self-determination, to regarding Jane as a potentially unreliable, unstable, and elusive figure, whose 'self' remains shadowy.

CHAPTER THREE   62

An Iconic Text: Feminist and Psychoanalytic Criticism

This chapter discusses the rich history of feminist readings of *Jane Eyre*. It starts with Virginia Woolf's treatment of Charlotte Brontë in *A Room of One's Own* (1929). It then explores seminal feminist accounts of the novel from the 1960s and 1970s by figures including Adrienne Rich, Helene Moglen, Maurianne Adams, Elaine Showalter, and Sandra Gilbert and Susan Gubar, outlining the debate between those who consider Jane a heroine of liberation and those who view her as a compromised character, reflective of women's limited opportunities and divided selfhood. The chapter explores ways in which psychoanalytic criticism and feminist criticism have often informed one another. Finally, it considers how recent feminist critics negotiate potential tensions between feminist reading and other critical approaches to the text and how modern accounts of gender and sexuality in the novel have incorporated work on Victorian masculinities, race, and class.

CHAPTER FOUR   90

Caste Typing: Marxist and Materialist Criticism

This chapter looks at Marxist and materialist responses to *Jane Eyre*. Beginning with Raymond Williams's account in *The English Novel from Dickens to Lawrence* (1970) of *Jane Eyre* as part of a literary movement pitting social passion against the heartlessness of industrial capitalism, it examines Terry Eagleton's *Myths of Power: a Marxist Study of the Brontës* (1975), with its influential counter-argument that *Jane Eyre*'s plot marries bourgeois with aristocratic values, cementing, rather than challenging, existing power structures. Looking at inheritors of this debate about class, power, and ideology in the novel from Nancy Pell (1977) to Chris R. Vanden Bossche (2005),the chapter explores issues such as *Jane Eyre*'s treatment of France, its handling of working women, and its depiction of advertisement and the marketplace, considering whether the text works to criticize or consolidate the Victorian class system, and asking what has historically been at stake in identifying the politics and allegiances of a text that is alternately characterised as radical and conservative.

CHAPTER FIVE   109

Bertha's Savage Face: Postcolonial Concerns

This chapter considers the growing number of postcolonial readings of *Jane Eyre*. Beginning with Jean Rhys's provocative 'prequel' *Wide Sargasso Sea* (1966) and Gayatri Spivak's 'Three Women's Texts and a Critique of Imperialism' (1985), which argues that Jane Eyre's triumph is achieved at the expense of the colonised subject (Bertha), it surveys a variety of works that analyse the novel's approach to race, nation, and imperialism. Later sections deal with readings that argue for the influence of the Brontës' Irish heritage on the presentation of colonial issues within the text and one reading, by Erin O'Connor (2003), that challenges Spivak's focus on imperialist ideology in *Jane Eyre*.

CHAPTER SIX   125

New Historicism and The Turn Toward History

This chapter looks at readings of *Jane Eyre* since 1980 that display the influence of the New Historicism and the critical turn toward situating *Jane Eyre* within nineteenth-century social, cultural, and political contexts, reading it alongside forms of contemporary representation, from missionary tracts to treatises on madness, that would once have been considered separate from literary endeavour. It devotes sections to considering 'Jane Eyre: Phrenology, Psychology, and Economics', to the politics of visuality and reading the body in the novel, and the place of evangelical thought and education in Jane Eyre's narrative. It then examines works that place *Jane Eyre* within the history of the novel as a form and, deploying John Sutherland's entertaining piece of detective dating of the novel's action, *Can Jane Eyre Be Happy*? (1997), asks whether there are limits to the use of historical evidence to interpret the novel.

CHAPTER SEVEN   143

Jane Eyre Adapted

This chapter discusses some of the different forms (including stage play, fiction, and film) into which *Jane Eyre* has been adapted over the years. It charts the modern trend toward analysing these many versions and reworkings of *Jane Eyre* and examines some of the critical issues that they raise, asking whether *Jane Eyre* now exists as much as a set of cultural connotations as it does as a nineteenth-century novel.

Conclusion   152

Notes   155

A Brief Guide to Further Reading   168

Select Bibliography   172

Index   179

Acknowledgements

I am deeply grateful to David Evans of the School of Modern Languages at the University of St Andrews, who supplied a fresh translation from the French of Eugène Forçade's 1848 review of *Jane Eyre*, which is reproduced in Chapter One, and to Jon Ralls, who cheerfully undertook the laborious task of proofing my manuscript and word-counting the quotations. Any remaining errors are, of course, my own. Heartfelt thanks are also due to Gavin Boyter, Sam Daws, and Tom and Erin Moore for their generous hospitality while I was consulting material in the British Library and to Elizabeth Henderson, Susan Manly and Angus Stewart, Annabel Talbot Rice, and Mike Stocks for their company and encouragement during the writing process.

Introduction

Everybody reads *Jane Eyre*. Charlotte Brontë's story of a rebellious orphan who survives a harsh school, becomes a governess in a mysterious mansion and falls in love with the owner, only to discover a secret that forces her to escape and forge a new life before returning to him, has gripped a remarkably diverse audience from its publication in 1847 to the present day. Queen Victoria (1819–1901; reigned 1837–1901) read it, recording in her journal that it 'is really a wonderful book very peculiar in parts, but [...] such a fine tone in it, such fine religious feeling, such beautiful writing. The description of the mysterious maniac's nightly appearances awfully thrilling'.[1] The young American poet Emily Dickinson (1830–86) pronounced it 'electric'.[2] The all-male crew of HMS Discovery on the polar expedition of 1901–4 led by Captain Robert Falcon Scott (1868–1912) borrowed it repeatedly from the ship's library. The literary historian Prince Dmitri Mirsky (1890–1939), fighting in the Russian Civil War in 1918, remembered coming across *Jane Eyre* in an Armenian town during the white army's retreat and experiencing 'the intense thrill of the first reading'.[3] In 1947, a speaker to the Brontë Society recalled that *Jane Eyre* had recently been serialised on the radio and had attracted more than 6,000,000 listeners for eleven successive weeks: in the sombre post-war climate 'the tale shone through these grey days, when we seem almost afraid of emotion, like [...] a live coal.'[4] More recently, in 2004, listeners to the BBC Radio programme 'Woman's Hour' voted *Jane Eyre* second in an all-time list of books that had changed their lives.

Critical opinion of *Jane Eyre*, however, has varied as wildly as sales have remained steady. While some of its first reviewers thought the novel unrivalled among modern productions for 'its power of thought and expression'[5] and praised its passion, which, 'rises at times to a height of tragic intensity which is almost sublime',[6] others pronounced it 'coarse', 'an Anti-Christian composition' which displayed 'the tone of mind and thought which has overthrown authority and violated every code human and divine abroad, and fostered Chartism and rebellion at home'.[7] One American reviewer objected loudly to Rochester's 'profanity, brutality, and slang' and the animal energies of Jane and Rochester's 'courtship after the manner of kangaroos'.[8] Heated debate continued in the twentieth century. Lord David Cecil (1902–86), a critic and biographer who would become Goldsmiths' Professor of English Literature at Oxford in 1949, regretted in 1934 that *Jane Eyre*, while galvanised by Brontë's

1

'volcanic' imagination, was formless, humourless, and exaggerated. In 1948 F.R. Leavis (1895–1978), then the most influential literary critic in England, dismissed Charlotte Brontë as a minor talent. Formalist critics in the 1960s rebelled against such scholarly sneers, asserting that *Jane Eyre* was impeccably well crafted and an organic whole structured through compelling patterns of symbol and image. Later in the twentieth century, poststructuralists would prefer to see *Jane Eyre* as an unresolved and indeterminate text, challenging and even 'plotting against' the reader with plural interpretive possibilities. Feminists have hailed *Jane Eyre* as a novel about the travails of womanhood; Marxists have weighed its class allegiances; postcolonial critics have interrogated the place of empire and the question of slavery in the text. After almost two centuries of critical readings, basic questions about *Jane Eyre* still stimulate violent disagreement. Is it a radical novel or a conservative one, a realist novel or a tissue of wild improbabilities, a distinctively female novel or a novel that disrupts assumptions about gender? Critical opinion even remains undecided about *Jane Eyre*'s literary merit: the novelist Angela Carter (1940–92) has suggested, with affection, that 'of all the great novels in the world, *Jane Eyre* veers the closest towards trash'.[9]

This guide traces the history of critical responses to *Jane Eyre* from its first publication to the present day, offering an account of the key figures, ideas, and movements that have shaped analysis of this extraordinary book. It aims both to summarise significant texts and ideas in an accessible fashion, providing a thorough introduction to the field, and to offer a bibliographic base from which readers will feel inspired to launch their own critical reading and writing.

Chapter One presents the early history of *Jane Eyre*'s reception from the first newspaper reviews to the end of the nineteenth century. It uncovers the controversy between those who hymned the praises of the novel and those who found it immoral, irreligious, and politically subversive. It then describes how responses to *Jane Eyre* changed once the author's gender and life history became common knowledge and how *Jane Eyre* was gradually assimilated into the literary canon – a mixed blessing. Chapter Two looks at a particular issue that has beset interpretations of *Jane Eyre* – the intense subjectivity of Jane's narrative voice. It traces the differing views of *Jane Eyre*'s narrative method, tone, and style that were current in the early, mid, and late twentieth century, showing how critical trends from formalism to deconstruction have produced wholly different interpretations of Jane: as a mouthpiece for Charlotte Brontë; a figure in an elemental allegory; an unreliable, even vengeful narrator; or an unknowable construct, a vanishing point in the text. Chapter Three discusses the rich history of feminist responses to *Jane Eyre*, explaining how the novel came to be regarded as a 'cult text' of feminism, with 'The Madwoman in the Attic' – a reading of Bertha as Jane's angry double by Sandra M. Gilbert (born 1936) and Susan Gubar (born 1944) – becoming a short-hand for female repression under systems of patriarchal power. It airs disagreements between feminists about whether *Jane Eyre*'s ending delivers the heroine to self-fulfilment, or not, and modern feminist responses to the critical accusation that traditional celebratory feminist readings ignore the politics of class and race in the text. Chapter Four examines Marxist and materialist interpretations, highlighting the history of conflict between readings of *Jane Eyre* as a novel that consolidates the relationship between the middle classes and the gentry and readings that see it as a novel of radical protest that allies itself with workers, rebels, and the oppressed. Chapter Five introduces post-colonial criticism, which argues for the submerged but crucial role of discourses of race and Empire in *Jane Eyre*, while Chapter Six treats the 'turn towards history' in *Jane Eyre* in the wake of New Historicism. This chapter explores readings that are particularly attentive to the social and cultural context of which *Jane Eyre* is part, emphasising the text's embeddedness in contemporary debate about topics including the new science of psychology, the ideology of evangelical education, and the role of the female artist. Chapter Seven looks at recent analysis of Jane Eyre's 'afterlives' – its history of re-production and adaptation in multiple media.

Hundreds of books and articles have been written about *Jane Eyre* and this guide is necessarily not exhaustive. Rather, it selects, summarises, and contextualises the most significant and illustrative readings produced by each era and critical methodology, highlighting trends in *Jane Eyre*'s reception and interpretation and significant issues and areas of debate. One of the qualities that ensures *Jane Eyre*'s perennial appeal is its passion. Jane speaks directly to the reader: 'Many will blame me, no doubt', she provocatively announces, and, later, 'Reader, I forgave him on the spot'. Lucasta Miller feels that 'Jane must be the most irresistible first-person heroine in literature'.[10] To Doreen Roberts, however, she is 'a fiercely Protestant, chauvinistic, and self-righteous heroine', whose discourse is marked by distortion.[11] Jane's voice, with its fiery ardour and cool antagonism, moves critics to equally heated praise and icy detraction, often bringing out their best lines. This book samples and discusses the many dialogues that *Jane Eyre* has inspired over the years. I hope that the reader will find listening to and joining in these critical conversations as surprising, entertaining, and illuminating as I have done.

CHAPTER ONE

Victorian Responses: Power and Popularity; Coarseness and Criticism

The novel we now know as *Jane Eyre* was first published, in three volumes entitled *Jane Eyre. An Autobiography. Edited by Currer Bell*, in London on 16 October 1847. It was immediately and resoundingly popular. The first edition sold out within three months. A second edition, with an authorial preface, was issued in January and a third in April 1848. Thomas Wemyss Reid (1842–1905) mused in 1877 that 'Those who remember that winter of nine-and-twenty years ago know how something like a "Jane Eyre" fever raged among us.'[1] The novel was widely reviewed in newspapers and magazines and discussed by readers including the novelist William Makepeace Thackeray (1811–63), whose own literary masterpiece, *Vanity Fair*, was appearing in monthly numbers during 1847–48. Thackeray, to whom Brontë's publishers had sent a complimentary copy, thanked them for a gripping and emotionally intense experience:

> ■ I wish you had not sent me Jane Eyre. It interested me so much that I have lost (or won if you like) a whole day in reading it [...] Who the author can be I can't guess – if a woman she knows her language better than most ladies do, or has had a 'classical' education. It is a fine book though – the man & woman capital – the style very generous and upright so to speak [...] Some of the love passages made me cry [...] St. John the Missionary is a failure I think but a good failure there are parts excellent I dont know why I tell you this but that I have been exceedingly moved & pleased by Jane Eyre. It is a womans writing, but whose?[2] □

The novel was all the more intriguing to its first audience because it had appeared out of the blue, without fanfare or any information about the author. The novel called itself 'an autobiography'; the first edition announced that it was 'edited' by Currer Bell, the second that it was 'by Currer Bell'. But who was Currer Bell? And were the experiences related in *Jane Eyre* autobiographical in the sense that they reproduced some elements of the author's life? Even Charlotte Brontë's publishers – Smith, Elder & Co – did not know the true identity of *Jane Eyre*'s author until July 1848, when Charlotte presented herself in person at their London office. In 1847, all they knew was that, having rejected the manuscript of a novel called *The Professor* by Currer Bell, they had encouraged the author to submit new work when it was ready; within a month they received the manuscript of *Jane Eyre*, which they promptly accepted and published six weeks later. A book of poetry by Currer, Ellis, and Acton Bell had been published by Aylott and Jones in 1846, but had sold only two copies and excited little curiosity. In December 1847, eager to profit from *Jane Eyre*'s success, the unscrupulous publisher, Thomas Newby (1797/8–1882), published Ellis Bell's *Wuthering Heights* and Acton Bell's *Agnes Grey*, which he had accepted that summer, announcing them as 'by the Bell brothers' and thus deliberately fuelling confusion about whether Currer Bell (Charlotte Brontë's pseudonym), Ellis Bell (Emily Brontë; 1818–48), and Acton Bell (Anne Brontë; 1820–49) might in fact all be the same person. *Jane Eyre* piqued early readers' interest not only because it was an extraordinary book, but also because its mystery did not end when the final page was turned. Criticism of the novel's merits and flaws was interlaced with speculation about the gender, social position, and character of the person who had written it.[3]

Early reviewers in general shared and spread the public's enthusiasm for *Jane Eyre*. George Henry Lewes (1817–78) announced that it was 'decidedly the best novel of the season'[4] and others concurred in praise for 'a story of surpassing interest, riveting the attention from the very first chapter', which was 'sure to be in demand'.[5] Favourable reviews stressed the novel's fresh and energetic approach to language and subject matter, the intense way in which it engaged the reader, and the emotional reality it conveyed. A handful of strongly worded critiques, however, accused the novel of faults including vulgarity, moral impropriety, and politically inflammatory and even antichristian tendencies. These reviews reacted negatively to a number of aspects of *Jane Eyre* that often escape the modern reader. The language of the novel struck some contemporaries as 'coarse' – or at least unusually vigorous and direct; Rochester, in particular, used 'slang'[6] and the first-person narrative voice of Jane Eyre herself was peppered with 'Northern' and 'provincial' expressions. Behaviour in the novel also struck some readers as coarse; Jane was an undutiful, thankless, and irreverent child. Rochester, during his courtship of Jane, admitted the fact that his ward, Adèle, was the illegitimate daughter of a French opera dancer who had been one of his mistresses. Jane sat on Rochester's knee and frankly confessed her passion for him to the reader. Finally, Rochester attempted bigamy and Jane forgave him. More subtly, to some commentators Jane Eyre's anger about her upbringing and determination to improve her lot smacked of the same rebellious political spirit that had brought about the French revolution; impatient of authority, Jane Eyre lacked Christian humility and feminine softness.

This chapter considers in detail both the positive and negative critical response to *Jane Eyre* from the first reviews to the end of the nineteenth century. It divides broadly into three sections. 'The First Reviews' considers the early response to *Jane Eyre*, between 1847 and 1849, when the debate began between those who deemed the novel a triumphant success and those who thought it morally and technically flawed. '*Jane Eyre*'s Reception after 1850' discusses the changes that accompanied the revelation of Currer Bell's true identity and the enormously influential biography of Charlotte Brontë by the novelist Elizabeth Gaskell (1810–65), which led to a tradition of biographical readings of *Jane Eyre* and the inseparability of the 'Brontë story' from criticism of the novels. This section also looks at readings of *Jane Eyre* as a prototype of the 'sensation' novels of the 1860s, many of which featured mad, bad, and upwardly mobile women. 'A tribute-wreath of flowers: *Jane Eyre* after 1870' identifies a new phase in nineteenth-century criticism of *Jane Eyre*, where Charlotte Brontë's place in the literary canon was carved out and critics looking back over a half-century of Victorian novels sought to position *Jane Eyre* within national, regional, and European contexts.

THE FIRST REVIEWS: 1847

'Soul speaking to soul': Early Enthusiasts

The *Atlas* was among the first newspapers to review *Jane Eyre* in the autumn of 1847 and its verdict was overwhelmingly positive:

> ■ This is not merely a work of great promise. It is one of absolute performance. It is one of the most powerful domestic romances which have been published for many years. It has little or nothing of the old conventional stamp upon it; none of the jaded, exhausted attributes of a worn-out vein of imagination, reproducing old incidents and old characters in new combinations; but is full of youthful vigour, of freshness and originality, of nervous diction[7] and concentrated interest. The incidents are sometimes melodramatic, and, it might be added, improbable; but these incidents, though striking, are subordinate to the main purpose of the piece, which depends not upon incident, but on the development of character; it is a tale of passion, not of action; and the passion rises at times to a height of tragic intensity which is almost sublime. It is a book to make the pulses gallop and the heart beat, and to fill the eyes with tears [...] The action of the tale

is sometimes unnatural, but the passion is always true. It would be easy to point out incidental defects; but the merits of the work are so striking that it is a pleasure to recognise them without stint and qualification.[8] □

'Power' and 'powerful' were words that ran through most of the reviews.[9] Henry Fothergill Chorley (1808–72), in the literary review, the *Athenaeum*, also noted that parts of *Jane Eyre* were improbable and melodramatic – particularly towards the end, where Thornfield burns down and Rochester and Jane are reunited – but that this scarcely mattered as there was 'so much power in this novel'[10] as to make the reader overlook them.

Several reviewers expressed relief that *Jane Eyre* was not like many fashionable novels, which dwelt on the dress and manners of upper-class society. The *People's Journal* observed that 'the very selection of so homely a name for the heroine is an omen of good. It indicates a departure from the sickly models of the Minerva Press'. (The Minerva Press was famous for publishing lurid Gothic thrillers and sentimental romances aimed at the female reader). The *Era*, comparing *Jane Eyre* with the work of the Renaissance painter Raphael (1483–1520), whose figures were 'not elaborately executed, but true, bold, well-defined, and full of life', was struck by the unique quality of the story:

■ This is an extraordinary book. Although a work of fiction, it is no mere novel, for there is nothing but nature and truth about it, and its interest is entirely domestic; neither is it like your familiar writings that are too close to reality. There is nothing morbid, nothing vague, nothing improbable about the story of Jane Eyre [...] We have no high life glorified, carica-tured or libelled; nor low life elevated to an enviable state of bliss; neither have we vice made charming. The story is, therefore, unlike all that we have read, with very few exceptions; and for power of thought and expres-sion, we do not know its rival among modern productions. Bulwer [Edward Bulwer Lytton (1831–91)], [G.P.R.] James [1799–1860], [Benjamin] D'Israeli [1804–81] and all the serious novel writers of the day lose in comparison with Currer Bell, for we must presume the work to be his. It is no woman's writing. Although ladies have written histories, and travels, and warlike nov-els, to say nothing of books upon the various arts and sciences, no woman *could have* penned the 'Autobiography of Jane Eyre'.[11] □

Guesses about the gender of *Jane Eyre*'s author frequently brought out the critic's assumptions about typical female subject matter and writing style: the *Era*'s assertion that *Jane Eyre* must be by a man reflects the review-er's perception that it is unlike other contemporary novels by women. Charlotte Brontë was particularly pleased by the *Era*'s account, which laid emphasis on *Jane Eyre*'s moral tendency to improve the reader: 'you are receiving a delightful and comprehensible lesson, and you put down the volume with the consciousness of having benefited by its perusal [...] The obvious moral thought is, that laws, both human and divine, approved in our calmer moments, are not to be disobeyed when our time of trial comes'[12] Jane Eyre's time of trial was Rochester's invitation, after their cancelled wedding, to elope with him as his mistress; her refusal was a moral victory and eventual legitimate marriage was her reward.

A.W. Fonblanque (1793–1872) in the *Examiner*, a politically liberal journal, agreed with the *Era*'s reviewer that *Jane Eyre*'s author was probably male and that one of its strengths was that: 'It is anything but a fashionable novel. It has not a Lord Fanny for its hero, nor a Duchess for its pattern of nobility. The scene of action is never in Belgrave or Grosvenor Square [expensive areas of London]. The pages are scant of French and void of Latin'.[13] He drew, however, a somewhat different moral from the story:

> ■ Without being professedly didactic, the writer's intention (amongst other things) seems to be, to show how intellect and unswerving integrity may win their way, although oppressed by that predominating influence in society which is a mere consequence of the accidents of birth or fortune.[14] □

Fonblanque congratulated Currer Bell on writing a story that, far from aping aristocratic life, showed the triumph of the social underdog. The style was occasionally 'rude and uncultivated' but it was also pleasingly 'resolute, straightforward, and to the purpose'. Interestingly, Fonblanque argued that *Jane Eyre* was 'as a novel or history of events [...] obviously defective'. It was unlike the novels of Sir Walter Scott (1771–1832) and Charles Dickens (1812–70) and should instead be compared with the works of William Godwin (1756–1836), the radical philosopher and father of Mary Shelley (1797–1851), whose 'autobiographies' were 'an analysis of a single mind [...] an elucidation of its progress from childhood to full age'. Since Godwin's novels are designed to illustrate his ideas about human development and the need to resist the tyranny of government and social injustice, Fonblanque's comparison hints that *Jane Eyre* may have similarly political overtones.

One of the most sensitive early appreciations of *Jane Eyre* came from George Henry Lewes, journalist, philosopher, and partner of the novelist George Eliot (1819–80), who was also intrigued by *Jane Eyre* but was less fulsome in her praise.[15] Lewes wrote two glowing reviews, one in the *Westminster Review* and the other in *Fraser's Magazine*. In the latter, he painted a memorable picture of the passionate and intimate reading experience *Jane Eyre* created:

> ■ The story is not only of singular interest, naturally evolved, unflagging to the last, but it fastens itself upon your attention and will not leave you. The book closed, the enchantment continues [...] You go back again in

memory to the various scenes in which she has figured; you linger on the way, and muse upon the several incidents in the life which has just been unrolled before you, affected by them as if they were the austere instructions drawn from a sorrowing existence, and not merely the cunning devices of an author's craft. Reality – deep, significant reality – is the great characteristic of the book. It *is* an autobiography, – not, perhaps, in the naked facts and circumstances, but in the actual suffering and experience [...] This gives the book its charm: it is soul speaking to soul[16] □

Lewes, like Fonblanque, noted that the style of *Jane Eyre* – with specific reference to its language and phrasing – was 'peculiar', judging that there were too many 'Scotch or North-country phrases', but argued that 'although by no means a fine style, it has the capital point of all great styles in being *personal*, – the written speech of an individual, not the artificial language made up from all sorts of books.'[17] Lewes perceptively registered the novel's skill in accurately representing 'the material aspects of things' – characters, the natural world, houses, rooms, and furniture – but also 'of connecting external appearances with internal effects – of representing the psychological interpretation of material phenomena'. He quotes as an example the young Jane's confinement in the Red Room, where the 'faculty for objective representation' of the cold and gloomy furnishings is united to 'a strange power of subjective representation', in which the reader sees Jane's state of mind reflected in the surroundings, particularly the mirror in which Jane's alienated self-perception and description of the strange, abandoned chamber coalesce.[18] In noting this effect Lewes anticipates later psychoanalytic critics who would, in the twentieth century, similarly explore the connections between representations of external objects and internal states in *Jane Eyre*. Like other enthusiastic reviewers, Lewes stresses the difference between the standard of art represented in a novel such as *Jane Eyre* and the level attained by run-of-the-mill novels; the novel in 1847 was still a medium associated with light reading, which demanded literary defence as a serious art form; *Jane Eyre* was among the works that paved the way for a new perception of the novel as a central literary achievement of the Victorian age.

One of the 1847 reviews, an anonymous notice in the *Spectator*, was noticeably cooler than the rest. It compared *Jane Eyre* to medieval sculpture, in which 'considerable ability both mechanical and mental was often displayed upon subjects that had no existence in nature, and as far as delicacy was concerned were not pleasing in themselves'.[19] There was, the reviewer admitted, no literal grotesqueness in *Jane Eyre*, no foxes in monks' clothing, yet the effect was 'unnatural', with too much attention to the 'minute anatomy of the mind' and too much contrivance in the plot. The *Spectator*'s complaint about the convenient coincidence whereby Jane inherits her uncle's money and discovers that the

Rivers family are her cousins was not unduly damning – other, more favourable critics noted this as a weakness – but it objected to the courtship between Jane and Rochester, 'a course of hardly "proper" conduct between a single man and a maiden in her teens', and concluded that:

> ■ There is a low tone of behaviour (rather than of morality) in the book; and, what is worse than all, neither the hero nor the heroine attracts sympathy. The reader cannot see anything loveable in Mr. Rochester, nor why he should be so deeply in love with Jane Eyre; so that we have intense emotion without cause.[20] □

Charlotte Brontë worried, having read the *Spectator*'s negative comments, that 'the way to detraction has been pointed out, and will probably be pursued'.[21] She was right; 1848 would bring further evidence of *Jane Eyre*'s popularity, but also some less favourable reviews.

THE FIRST REVIEWS: 1848–49

'Pre-eminently an Anti-Christian Composition': Doubters and Detractors

A variety of factors may have contributed to the critical climate of 1848, in which *Jane Eyre* received both praise and blame. The novel was now an established hit: reviewers felt free to handle it with gloves off.[22] The appearance of *Wuthering Heights* and *Agnes Grey* in December 1847, moreover, led some critics to make unpleasant comparisons between the challenging subject matter and treatment in all three novels. Politically, 1848 was also a troubled year. After a poor harvest and economic depression that had caused widespread hardship, a series of revolutions exploded across Europe. In Paris in February, following mass unrest, the King Louis-Philippe 1 (1773–1850; reigned 1830–48) abdicated and a Second Republic was declared; in March Hungary followed with demands for representative government that were quickly echoed by revolutionary mobs in Germany, Austria, and Italy; violence, uncertainty, and political upheaval across Europe preoccupied the newspapers. In Britain, the Chartists – a workers' movement calling for the extension of the vote to all men and a charter of other electoral reforms – held mass meetings and submitted petitions to Parliament. Elizabeth Rigby (1809–93) in the *Quarterly Review* would specifically link the spirit of *Jane Eyre* to the contemporary background of political agitation and protest.

Anne Mozley (1809–91) in the *Christian Remembrancer*, a High Church Anglican magazine, published a review of *Jane Eyre* in April 1848, which, while acknowledging the novelist's 'depth and breadth of thought', 'painter's eye and hand', and 'great satiric power', also launched some barbed criticisms:

■ we, for our part, cannot doubt that the book is written by a female, and, as certain provincialisms indicate, by one from the North of England [...] Yet we cannot wonder that the hypothesis of a male author should have been started, or that ladies especially should still be rather determined to uphold it. For a book more unfeminine, both in its excellences and defects, it would be hard to find in the annals of female authorship. Throughout there is masculine power, breadth and shrewdness, combined with masculine hardness, coarseness, and freedom of expression. Slang is not rare. The humour is frequently produced by a use of Scripture, at which one is rather sorry to have smiled. The love-scenes glow with a fire as fierce as that of Sappho [the ancient Greek poetess], and somewhat more fuliginous [smutty]. There is an intimate acquaintance with the worst parts of human nature, a practised sagacity in discovering the latent ulcer, and a ruthless rigour in exposing it, which must command our admiration, but are almost startling in one of the softer sex.[23] □

The free use of language of *Jane Eyre*, its passionate treatment of Jane and Rochester's attraction, and its coolly detached observation of scenes such as Sarah Reed's deathbed, struck Mozley as unladylike and cynical. Correctly intuiting that the scenes at Lowood School (based on Brontë's sufferings at Cowan Bridge School) and the passages about ill-used governesses were drawn from real experience, Mozley charged the author with bearing a grudge that suffused the book with resentment:

■ Never was there a better hater. Every page burns with moral Jacobinism. 'Unjust, unjust,' is the burden of every reflection upon the things and powers that be.[24] □

The Jacobins were French revolutionaries who believed in the abolition of the monarchy, the levelling of class distinctions, and the universal vote. In accusing *Jane Eyre* of burning with 'moral Jacobinism', Mozley was identifying the novel with protest against the social order. Moreover, she argued, Currer Bell was quick to attack social and religious hypocrisy, but slow to offer religious consolation. Indeed, Mozley felt that 'the feeblest character in the book is that of Helen Burns, who is meant to be a perfect Christian' and that:

■ In her [...] the Christianity of Jane Eyre is concentrated, and with her it expires, leaving the moral world in a kind of Scandinavian gloom, which is hardly broken by the faint glimmerings of a 'doctrine of the equality of souls,' and some questionable streaks of that 'world-redeeming creed of Christ,' which being emancipated from 'narrow human doctrines that only tend to elate and magnify a few,' is seldom invoked but for the purpose of showing that all Christian profession is bigotry and all Christian practice is hypocrisy.[25] □

Mozley admired the force with which *Jane Eyre* satirised the hypocritical Brocklehurst and self-torturing St John Rivers, but worried that the book supplied no positive Christian exemplars to counterbalance them. She concluded that 'to say that Jane Eyre is positively immoral or antichristian, would be to do its writer an injustice. Still it wears a questionable aspect.'

Elizabeth Rigby (1809–93), writing in the conservative *Quarterly Review* of December 1848, was much harsher in her verdict on *Jane Eyre*'s irreligious and politically inflammatory tendencies:

■ Altogether the auto-biography of Jane Eyre is pre-eminently an Anti-Christian composition. There is throughout it a murmuring against the comforts of the rich and against the privations of the poor, which, as far as each individual is concerned, is a murmuring against God's appointment – there is a proud and perpetual assertion of the rights of man, for which we find no authority either in God's word or in God's providence – there is that pervading tone of ungodly discontent which is at once the most prominent and the most subtle evil which the law and the pulpit, which all civilised society in fact has at the present day to contend with. We do not hesitate to say that the tone of mind and thought which has overthrown authority and violated every code human and divine abroad, and fostered Chartism and rebellion at home, is the same which has also written Jane Eyre.[26] □

Strikingly, Rigby connects Jane Eyre's angry determination to escape or better her circumstances with the spirit of 'ungodly' political discontent that has produced class conflict and demand for social reform across Europe. Rigby's allusion to 'the rights of man' recalls the famous 1790 radical political treatise of that name by Thomas Paine (1737–1809), which declared that every generation had the right to determine how it was governed. Jane Eyre, in this view, is a social and political rebel, resisting authority and insisting on her 'right' to rise to a position of equality with her upper-class employer. Rigby's review directly compared Jane Eyre with Becky Sharp, the selfish, gold-digging heroine of Thackeray's *Vanity Fair*, who also spends time as a governess and marries into the class of her employer. Jane's actions were not as obviously immoral as Becky's, but they asserted the same proud independence of social origins and a refusal to see them as god-given and hence just:

■ It is true Jane does right, and exerts great moral strength but it is the strength of a mere heathen mind which is a law unto itself. No Christian grace is perceptible upon her [...] It pleased God to make her an orphan, friendless, and penniless – yet she thanks nobody, and least of all Him, for the food and raiment, the friends, companions, and instructors of her helpless youth [...] On the contrary, she looks upon all that has been done for her not only as her undoubted right, but as falling far short of it [...] It is by her own talents, virtues, and courage that she is made to attain the summit of human happiness, and, as far as Jane Eyre's own statement is concerned, no one would think that she owed anything either to God above or to man below. □

Rigby objects to Jane's 'self-made' narrative and destiny in the novel: Jane is neither humble, nor thankful as a Christian should be, but 'the personification of an unregenerate and undisciplined spirit', who promotes herself to the reader, but does not endear herself. Rigby, who on her marriage in 1849 became Lady Eastlake, wife of the first Director of the National Gallery, Sir Charles Lock Eastlake (1793–1865), also accused both *Jane Eyre* the novel and Jane Eyre the character of 'vulgarity'; the book displayed 'coarseness of language and laxity of tone'. Like other critics, she homed in on the depiction of Blanche Ingram and the other aristocratic visitors at Thornfield, to show the novelist's 'total ignorance of the habits of society', from correct morning dress to the polite fashion in which a lady would address a host's servant. Rigby had encountered *Wuthering Heights* and saw a 'decided family likeness' between the 'Jane and Rochester animals in their native state' and Catherine and Heathcliff, although *Wuthering Heights* was 'too odiously and abominably pagan to be palatable'.[27]

Despite the strength of her objections, it is clear that Rigby, like Mozley, was partly moved to discuss *Jane Eyre* because she recognised that it was 'a very remarkable book', with 'passages of beauty and power', which rendered it 'impossible not to be spellbound with the freedom of the touch'. Her article is worth reading in full to appreciate the tension in it between admiration and irritation. Rigby closed with a plea to address the plight of real governesses, whom low pay and an awkward social position between servant and gentlewoman rendered vulnerable to isolation and poverty in old age; her sense of the difference between the lives of these women and the unusual fate of Jane Eyre aggravates the tone of her review. Charlotte Brontë was stung to the quick by Rigby's remarks and responded to them angrily in writing.

Elizabeth Rigby was not the only critic to reflect on the connections between *Jane Eyre* and the other books by the mysterious 'Bell brothers', Emily Brontë's *Wuthering Heights* and Anne Brontë's *Agnes Grey*, and Anne's second novel, *The Tenant of Wildfell Hall*, which appeared in summer 1848. E.P. Whipple (1819–86) in the *North American Review* insisted that he could detect 'the marks of more than one mind and one sex' in *Jane Eyre*, suggesting that the Bells' novels were collaborative efforts involving both male and female members of one family. As we have seen, critical opinion was divided about whether *Jane Eyre*'s author was male or female. Whipple's review is interesting for its identification of those aspects of the novel that seemed to him the product of a masculine hand and those that seemed feminine:

■ The leading characteristic of the novel [...] and the secret of its charm, is the clear, distinct, decisive style of its representation of character, manners, and scenery; and this continually suggests a male mind. In the earlier chapters, there is little, perhaps, to break the impression that we are reading the autobiography of a powerful and peculiar female intellect; but when the admirable Mr. Rochester appears, and the profanity, brutality, and slang of the misanthropic profligate give their torpedo shocks to the nervous system, – and especially when we are favored with more than one scene given to the exhibition of mere animal appetite, and to courtship after the manner of kangaroos and the heroes of Dryden's plays, [by the dramatist John Dryden (1631–1700)] – we are gallant enough to detect the hand of a gentleman in the composition. There are also scenes of passion so hot, emphatic, and condensed in expression, and so sternly masculine in feeling, that we are almost sure we observe the mind of the author of *Wuthering Heights* at work in the text.[28] □

In Whipple's account of Jane Eyre's shockingly 'masculine' depiction of the combative and passionate relationship between Rochester and Jane, one senses disapproval mixed with pleasure. Likewise, James Lorimer (1818–90) in the *North British Review* hovered between admiration and admonition. He acquitted *Jane Eyre* of 'conventional vulgarity' and recognised the novel's attractions, but argued that there were 'latent' objections to its tendency:

■ In Jane [...] there is a recklessness about right and wrong which is very alarming, and although in the great action of her life, that of leaving Rochester, she valiantly resists a very powerful temptation, and her general conduct is not very reprehensible, the motive by which she is actuated is seldom a higher one than worldly prudence.[29] □

Jane Eyre's both cavalier and pragmatic approach to morality, Lorimer felt, were faults magnified a thousand-fold in *Wuthering Heights* and *The Tenant of Wildfell Hall*.

Other reviews of 1848 were much more complimentary, defending *Jane Eyre* from the attacks it had received. John Eagles (1783–1855) in *Blackwood's Magazine* reproduced the current debate about whether *Jane Eyre* violated social propriety in the form of an imaginary dialogue between a lady and a gentleman:

LYDIA. – I think every part of the novel perfect, though I have some doubt many will object, in some instances, both to the attachment and the conduct of Jane Eyre.

AQUILIUS. – It is not a book for Prudes – It is not a book for effeminate and tasteless men; it is for the enjoyment of a feeling heart and vigorous understanding.

Eugène Forçade (1820–69) in a French journal, the *Revue des Deux Mondes*, offered a long and appreciative review in October 1848, which pleased Charlotte Brontë, who commented that Forçade, unlike some critics, had 'understood and enjoyed' *Jane Eyre*, and that his 'censures are as well-founded as the commendations'.[30] Forçade, like Elizabeth Rigby, related *Jane Eyre* to the current political context, but his analysis was wholly different. He had just lived through the violent upheavals of the February Revolution in Paris, where street protests against limitations on the right of assembly and suffrage led to an invasion of the Chamber of Deputies and its replacement with a reformist provisional government. Socialists and moderate Republicans then contested the future of the French state, the former proposing radical new labour rights such as guaranteed employment and income for casual workers, and a new government was elected on the basis of universal adult male suffrage. Forçade was not a socialist and he presents *Jane Eyre* as a book whose moral and political tendencies provide a healthy antidote to Utopian socialism:

■ What is the sickness of our time? Utopia, this sham poetry, makes of man an absurd and false ideal. [...] What is that people look for in this utopia? A social mechanism which spares men from life's struggle, which spares them from suffering, that is to say from effort, from work, from action, moreover, from what makes human virtue and glory. The socialist utopia, therefore, represents the expression of and the desire for an indolence of the mind, a degradation of the imagination and a weakness of character. The socialist utopia must appeal, above all, to those men who are capable of attempting an uprising in the hope of ridding themselves at once of life's battle, since they are scared of this battle which patiently begins again each day; to those men who pursue an illusory rest beneath the leveller of humanitarian tyranny, in order to free themselves from the proud, laborious duties of freedom and personal responsibility; to those men who, after and in spite of revolutions, under republics as well as monarchies, will always remain subjects and [...] will always be slaves in their souls. Poetry, that flame of human liberty, which would be extinguished by the geometric and mechanical humanity which the utopians construct with ruler and compass; poetry, which needs men of flesh and blood, ardent souls, characters of infinite diversity, indefatigable wills, in short: real men, those who accept and maintain their duel with destiny; poetry, to the same extent as society, is involved in refuting the impossible ideal of the socialists. Poetry herself holds the most powerful weapon in the philosophy of the passions, whose intimate depths she alone can fathom, and which she alone can express with her irresistible eloquence. This, therefore, is the role of the novel, this form of poetry devoted to the individual history of human emotions; above all, it is the novel which must formulate against socialism the protest of society and of art, and knock down the humanitarian dummy with the pulsating man of reality. *Jane Eyre* is not a literary work of great scope; but it is a highly curious and endearing moral study for those who, like me, cannot, despite being French, accept becoming socialists. It is an entirely English book, English in the moral sense of the word. You sense the spirit of that Saxon race, as crude as you like [...] but it is male, hardened to suffering, tireless against pain [...] They firmly implant in their children the feeling for freedom and responsibility; they have given the world no Saint-Simon and Fourier but William Penn, Daniel Defoe and Benjamin Franklin.[31] □

Comte Henri de Saint-Simon (1760–1825) and François-Marie-Charles Fourier (1772–1837) were both French Utopian socialists who believed in the possibility of a transformed society, where existing hierarchies and hardships would be replaced by a good community that served the interests of all. Forçade negatively contrasts them with the Americans, William Penn (1644–1718), the Quaker founder of Pennsylvania, and Benjamin Franklin (1706–90), inventor, statesman and architect of the Declaration of Independence, whose libertarian and entrepreneurial vision he finds more sympathetic. Forçade associates socialism with 'indolence of mind' and 'weakness of character', a failure of the individual to take responsibility for fighting their own way in life's necessarily competitive struggle. *Jane Eyre*, to him, is an anti-socialist text, in that it asserts the freedom and responsibility of the individual to shape their own destiny. Interestingly, although he himself is inclined to believe the author female, he reports that it has been seriously suggested to him that the author is Sir Robert Peel (1788–1850). Peel was a reformist Conservative, who had led his party for two terms as Prime Minister (1834–35, 1841–46), passing legislation including the creation of the Metropolitan police (1829), the Factory Act (1844) and the repeal of the Corn Laws (1846). To the French eyes of Forçade and his friends, then, *Jane Eyre* looks more like a moderate conservative text, which, though it may be by a woman, endorses 'virile', 'active', 'robust' Anglo-Saxon values, and explores 'regular events taken from real life' in contrast to the typically 'effeminate' French novel, which explores 'depraved instincts, corrupt affections, monstrous events'.[32]

Forçade praises the characterisation and situation of *Jane Eyre,* but finds the plot at times far-fetched and disjointed: it could, he suggests, be simpler. Nonetheless, the novel is admirable: it 'vibrates with feeling' which sometimes has the tone of personal confession, but is a 'sober' and 'serious' tale. It does not deal with high society, but with the interesting and numerous needy middle-class of women who, unlike men, have no opportunity via 'political, colonial and mercantile activities' to earn the money that would resolve the 'inner conflict' caused by the disharmony between their 'birth, education and fortune'. If there is class struggle in the *Jane Eyre*, then, it is not for Forçade the struggle of the worker against the state, but that of the middle-class libertarian against the limits of her fate.

Already in these early reviews there are elements of debates that persistently resurface in criticism of *Jane Eyre*. In political terms, does it lean towards revolution or away from it? Is there 'nothing but nature and truth [...] nothing improbable about the story of Jane Eyre' or is it 'unnatural', melodramatic, and far-fetched? Is it pre-eminently a woman's novel, or is there a 'masculine' quality to the text: vigorous, direct, even coarse? Does Jane Eyre display moral propriety or impropriety, piety or impiety, heroic self-control or pragmatic self-interest? These very debates, naturally, helped fuel the fire of public interest that made the novel a runaway success.

JANE EYRE'S RECEPTION AFTER 1850

After the death from tuberculosis of her sisters Emily, at the end of 1848, and Anne, in 1849, Charlotte Brontë felt less need to maintain the secrecy of the Bell pseudonym, which Emily had been particularly passionate about preserving. At the end of 1849, Charlotte appeared openly in London as the author of *Jane Eyre* and the respectable and melancholy family history of the Brontës gradually became public. This knowledge markedly changed the reception of *Jane Eyre*. Those who had suspected a 'sternly masculine hand' of penning the novel and accused the 'firm of Bell & Co' of having 'a sense of the depravity of human nature peculiarly their own'[33] were disconcerted by the revelation that *Jane Eyre* had been written by a chaste spinster daughter of the perpetual curate of Haworth in Yorkshire, who had lost a mother and five young siblings to incurable illnesses. Charlotte's own sudden and early death in 1855 brought a flood of tributes. In March 1857 Elizabeth Gaskell's *Life of Charlotte Brontë* appeared. Gaskell's biography was a popular bestseller, which brought the details of the Brontës' authorship to many who did not yet know them. From Gaskell, pitying readers learned to identify Helen Burns with Charlotte's sister Maria Brontë (1813–25), who, with another sister, Elizabeth Brontë (1815–25), had died at Cowan Bridge School – an institution that bore a distinct resemblance to Lowood. The romantic portrait Gaskell drew of Charlotte, as a saintly and heroic figure, suffering under the strains of an overbearing father, dissolute brother, sick sisters, and rural isolation, was, however, opinionated and often misleading. Itself a critical reading of Charlotte's achievement,

Gaskell's *Life of Charlotte Brontë* was enormously influential, fostering a newly biographical mode of interpreting *Jane Eyre*.

Biographical Readings

As Margaret Sweat put it in the *North American Review* of October 1857, 'looking at these novels in the strong daylight cast upon them by our study of the hearts and brains in which they had their birth [...] they come to us as the very outpouring of pent-up passion, the cry of fettered hearts, the panting of hungry intellects restrained by the iron despotism of adverse and unconquerable circumstance.'[34] In this reading, Jane Eyre's sufferings under unsupportable domestic regimes echo Charlotte Brontë's. Sweat suggested that public judgement remained 'somewhat undecided as to the tendency of "Jane Eyre," ' viewed simply in its moral aspect', but argued that there were several points where 'our present knowledge of the author decidedly modifies, and others in which it totally changes, opinions passed upon it in the absence of such knowledge'. Pictures of masculine excess in the Brontës' work were now taken to reflect their experience of their brother Branwell Brontë (1817–48) and to a lesser extent their father, Patrick Brontë (1777–1861), whom Gaskell had handled unsympathetically. It was now evident that *Jane Eyre* was not literally autobiographical, although the passages set at Lowood reflected personal experience. In this context, the opening phase of the novel, describing Jane's childhood, came in for renewed praise. Sweat felt that Charlotte Brontë had seen with 'a kind of literary clairvoyance' that 'the time was ripe' for the kind of minute analysis of character development that the early part of *Jane Eyre* provided. Modern novel readers 'are not satisfied with pictures of external and social life, however brilliantly colored'. Brontë, in her account of Jane's growth into womanhood, anticipated public desire for the novelist to dissect 'heart, brain and nerve, to lay them before the reader for examination and analysis'. Sweat shows the detailed character analysis *Jane Eyre* promotes by giving her own reading of Jane, Rochester, and St John Rivers as 'studies' of character in which personal will and adverse circumstances produce striking conflict. Sweat's reading of Charlotte's biographical 'struggle' between self and circumstance colours her account of *Jane Eyre* as a novel of contest between Jane, Rochester, and St John in which 'victory we are sure must be with her'.

Émile Montégut (1825–95) in the *Revue des Deux Mondes* for July 1857 similarly made the connection, irresistible since Gaskell's biography, between Charlotte's life and the history of Jane Eyre:

■ The life of Charlotte Brontë is the very substance of her novels [...] In Jane Eyre she depicted her imaginative life [...] Jane Eyre has been reproached with being an immoral book and although no good reason for the accusation has been given, it is not entirely unfounded. The author has struck only one chord of the human heart, the most powerful it is true, and has set it vibrating alone, to the exclusion of all the rest [...] Jane Eyre is a passionate dream, a perfect castle in Spain. In this book [...] Charlotte Brontë imagines for us the life she might have had and [...] tells us how she would have liked to love and whom she could have loved.[35] □

Eugène Forçade at the *Revue des Deux Mondes* nine years earlier had dubbed *Jane Eyre* a healthy, realist novel capable of exerting important socio-political influence in countering the false ideals of utopian socialism. Montégut, knowing the history of the author, sees *Jane Eyre*, however successful, as an escapist fantasy, whose origins are personal and whose scope is limited. This shift is typical of the changed approach to *Jane Eyre* after mid-century. The novel remained popular and highly regarded, but it was assimilated into the realm of women's fiction and its social, political, and religious dimensions were no longer subjects of heated controversy. Critical voices instead turned to perceived linkages between Charlotte Brontë's biography and the development of her novels – readers could now compare *Jane Eyre* with Charlotte's later novels *Shirley* (1849) and *Villette* (1853) and with her apprentice work, *The Professor*, which was published posthumously in 1857.

Setting a Trend: Jane Eyre as a 'Sensation' Novel

Increasingly, as *Jane Eyre* became an established model of novelistic success, critics also analysed the influence it exerted on contemporary fiction. The novelist and biographer Margaret Oliphant (1828–97), writing in *Blackwood's Magazine* in 1855, saw *Jane Eyre* as having begun a revolutionary (and worrying) trend in the presentation of romance between men and women. Where, previously, ideal male suitors were 'humble and devoted' in chivalrous fashion and beautiful women consented to be wooed, modern romance was depicted as a skirmish in which both parties proved their strength and passion in single combat. The 'little fierce incendiary, doomed to turn the world of fancy upside down' was Jane Eyre:

■ She stole upon the scene – pale, small, by no means beautiful – something of a genius, something of a vixen – a dangerous little person, inimical to the peace of society. After we became acquainted with herself we were introduced to her lover. Such a lover! – a vast, burly, sensual Englishman, one of those Hogarth men, whose power consists in some singular animal force of life and character, which it is impossible to describe or analyse. [Oliphant alludes here to a certain kind of male figure represented in the paintings of William Hogarth (1697–1764)] Such a wooing! – the lover is rude, brutal, cruel. The little woman fights against him with courage and spirit – begins to find the excitement and relish of a new life in this struggle – begins to think of her antagonist all day long – falls into fierce love and jealousy – betrays herself – is tantalised and slighted, to prove her devotion – and then suddenly seized upon and taken possession of, with love several degrees fiercer than her own [...] Such was the impetuous little spirit which dashed into our well-ordered world, broke its boundaries, and defied its principles – and the most alarming revolution of modern times has followed the invasion of Jane Eyre.[36] □

Oliphant is one of the first critics to read *Jane Eyre* as a feminist novel. Brontë's presentation of Jane and Rochester jousting fiercely with one another, in Oliphant's view, expounds a doctrine, 'startling and original' but since adopted by 'hosts of imitators', that regards contest between men and women as proof of their equality, where the 'pretty fictions of politeness' from male suitors condescending toward women are degrading because they reinforce women's actual subjection. When *Jane Eyre* was published:

■ Nobody perceived that it was the new generation nailing its colours to the mast. No one would understand that this furious love-making was but a wild declaration of the 'Rights of Woman' in a new aspect.[37] □

Oliphant is by no means sympathetic to the feminist ideology she perceives *Jane Eyre* as propagating; she portrays the idea of romance as a duel between man and woman in comic terms. She also retains the idea that Jane Eyre is 'indelicate', especially in the conversations between Jane and Rochester, but admits that:

■ When all this is said, *Jane Eyre* remains one of the most remarkable works of modern times – as remarkable as *Villette*, and more perfect. We know no one else who has such a grasp of persons and places, and a perfect command of the changes of atmosphere, and the looks of a country under rain or wind [...] We feel no art in these remarkable books. What we feel is a force which makes everything real – a motion which is irresistible. We are swept on in the current, and never draw breath till the tale is ended. Afterwards we may disapprove at our leisure, but it is certain that we have not a moment's pause to be critical till we come to the end.[38] □

A few critical voices remained. A sermon preached and later printed, by a Scottish minister, George Campbell, in 1861, examined *Jane Eyre* from a doctrinal point of view and found that, despite its many beautiful passages, it was an 'infidel' book. Campbell was especially bothered by the suggestions implicit in the novel that there is no hell, and that all souls are judged and admitted to heaven on the basis of morality rather than faith. Like Anne Mozley, he found the novel's religious quotations and allusions unsatisfactory; Brontë seemed to lay little emphasis on church worship and Christ saving the sinner; rather she emphasised the individual's pursuit of their own moral truth. In her preface to the second edition of *Jane Eyre*, Brontë spoke out against 'Phariseeism'. A pharisee, in this context, is someone who is self-righteous or hypocritical in maintaining religious purity, adhering to the letter, rather than to the spirit, of religious law. Campbell suggested that Brontë, in invoking the superiority of religious spirit to religious doctrine, was pursuing her own quasi-Biblical mode of argument, defining her terms to suit herself.

■ Those of you who have seen her writings will have observed that her style is distinguished by a repetition of statement, like the Hebrew parallelism. The one clause answers to the other, and when she says that Christianity is not Phariseeism, she means the same thing as when she says morality is not conventionality; that is to say, Christianity is morality, and *vice versa*.[39] □

Campbell accused *Jane Eyre* of substituting its own view of morality for Christian orthodoxy. But he was prescient enough to see that *Jane Eyre* was not alone in this among contemporary texts: the work of Thomas Carlyle (1795–1881) and the long poem *In Memoriam* (1850) by Alfred Tennyson (1809–92) also attract his criticism.

From the 1860s, *Jane Eyre*'s plot, in which bigamy is averted, began to look comparatively tame next to the scandalous happenings in the 'Sensation' novels currently popular. For example, in *Lady Audley's Secret* (1862) by Mary Elizabeth Braddon (1835–1915), the female protagonist was not only a governess who married an aristocrat, but also committed bigamy, attempted murder and arson, and became insane: rolling all the objectionable qualities of Jane Eyre, Mr Rochester, and Bertha Mason into the career of one person. Margaret Oliphant, writing in 1867, suspected that *Jane Eyre* had set the novel on the slippery slope toward 'Sensation':

■ The change perhaps began at the time when Jane Eyre made what advanced critics call her 'protest' against the conventionalities in which the world clothes itself. We have had many 'protests' since that time, but it is to be doubted how far they have been to our advantage [...] all our minor novelists, almost without exception, are of the school called sensational.[40] □

Sexual impropriety and violence, crime, and revelations of sordid scandal beneath the surface of polite, domestic life were all features of the 'sensation' novel. *Jane Eyre* did not contain all these elements, but some felt that it provided a model that inspired the genre. Indeed, reviewers of the 1850s and 1860s were struck by the pervasive influence of *Jane Eyre* as a model for popular fiction in general. One pithily remarked that: 'The governess in an autobiographical novel is pretty sure to be the heroine and authoress thereof. She is the family dissector – the social anatomist: she is a manager of women, and of men [...] We confess for ourselves, that we do not greatly care for these ladies in books. In actual life they are admirable; in books they are tedious, morbid, distasteful. They have a terrible deal of temper, too. They can "fire up," and, upon occasion, fire off [...] Of these heroine-governesses, one can only wish that England may have more of them, and the circulating libraries less'.[41]

In 1863, Bret Harte (1836–1902), an American humorist, published a parody of *Jane Eyre* in a series called *Sensation Novels Condensed*, making the same link as Margaret Oliphant between Brontë's novel and the 'sensation' school of the 1860s. The parody, entitled 'Miss Mix' 'by CH-L-TTE BR-NTE' is fascinating and still very funny. The fact that it assumes the reader's familiarity with the plot and characters of *Jane Eyre* shows how well established the novel had become in America, as well as in Europe, in the fifteen years since its publication. Harte's eleven-page parody provides a genial critique of *Jane Eyre* that can usefully be read alongside more conventional contemporary critical responses. 'Miss Mix' features a prim, plain, but vain governess who arrives at the Gothic mansion, Blunderbore Hall, to teach the illegitimate child of Mr Rawjester. Like Jane Eyre, she saves Rawjester from being burned in his bed by a demonic figure, one of the three mad wives Rawjester keeps in captivity. Rawjester, who resembles a gorilla, is comically rude to Miss Mix, wiping his feet on her dress and calling her 'Carrothead', behaviour that serves only to inflame her admiration for his radical contempt for the 'artificial restraint of society'. In the end, Rawjester appears at his own party disguised as a highwayman (a parody of the gypsy scene in *Jane Eyre*), robs and restrains all his guests except Miss Mix, who recognises him, then sets fire to Blunderbore Hall, which disposes of the three wives and leaves him free to run off with the governess.

Harte spoofs aspects of *Jane Eyre* that other contemporary critics also queried. The improbability of the plot is highlighted by multiplication. The Byronic hero, Rawjester, is an exaggerated version of Rochester's animalistic, violent, and morally dubious energies. Miss Mix combines primness and laxity, self-assertion and submissiveness, ('He seized a heavy candlestick, and threw it at me. I dodged it submissively but firmly'[42]), parodying apparently contradictory aspects of Jane Eyre's character. The combative courtship between Jane and Rochester, her calm reception of the news about his sexual indiscretions, and her instant forgiveness of his attempted bigamy are all neatly critiqued in Harte's send-up. Perhaps most interestingly, the parody raises issues concerning the racial identity of Rochester's wife. In 'Miss Mix', the wife who sets fire to Rawjester's bedclothes is 'a large and powerful negress, scantily attired, with her head adorned with feathers

[...] dancing wildly, accompanying herself with bone castanets [...] like some terrible *fetich*'. Harte has grasped the central role that Bertha's Creole identity plays in her depiction in *Jane Eyre*; his parody version, while ludicrous, points to racial and sexual frissons in the relationship between Rochester, Bertha, and Jane that would not be raised seriously by postcolonial critics until the late twentieth century.

'A TRIBUTE-WREATH OF FLOWERS': *JANE EYRE* AFTER 1870

Late nineteenth-century critical approaches to *Jane Eyre* reflect a growing desire to canonise the Brontës: to establish the important status of their works within English literature. The 1870s and 1880s saw publication of a number of works that paid tribute to the Brontë sisters: *Charlotte Bronte. A Monograph* (1877) by T. Wemyss Reid (1842–1905) described itself as 'a tribute-wreath of flowers culled from her own letters' laid on the altar of her memory. The gushing *A Note on Charlotte Brontë* (1877) by the poet and critic Algernon Charles Swinburne (1837–1909) quickly followed and in 1881 Peter Bayne (1830–96) published *Two Great Englishwomen: Mrs Browning and Charlotte Brontë*. The Brontë Society was founded in 1893 and created a museum of memorabilia in Haworth, which in 1896 was already drawing 10,000 visitors annually. Reid compares *Jane Eyre* favourably with the work of Shakespeare; Swinburne asserts that Charlotte Brontë's work is better than that of George Eliot and other more recent female authors. Reid, in 1877, lamented that *Jane Eyre*, like the other Brontë novels, was not read as often as it had been in the 1850s and 1860s, but trusted that the lapse would be temporary:

■ It is true that in some respects these books are not attractive. Though they are written with a terse vigour which must make them grateful to all whose palates are cloyed by the pretty writing of the present generation, they undoubtedly err on the side of a lack of literary polish.[43] □

Reid, however, distinguishes between the technical staging of *Jane Eyre*, which he regards as showing Charlotte Brontë's inexperience, and the human drama, which is worthy of comparison with the work of William Shakespeare (1564–1616):

■ In 'Jane Eyre' there was much painting of souls in their naked reality; the writer had gauged depths which the plummet of the common story-teller could never have sounded, and conflicting passions were marshalled on the stage with a masterful daring which Shakespeare might have envied; but the costumes, the conventional by-play, the scenery, even the wording of the dialogue, were poor enough in all conscience. The merest playwright or reviewer could have done better in these matters [...][44] □

Reid, like other late nineteenth-century critics, was amazed by the accusations of impropriety and immorality that *Jane Eyre* had provoked earlier in the century. Times had changed; *Jane Eyre* no longer breached standards of social or literary decorum. Swinburne, in *A Note on Charlotte Brontë* suggested that Elizabeth Rigby – the critic who had written in 1848 that the author of *Jane Eyre*, if a woman, must be one who had justly forfeited the company of her own sex – deserved to be strung up like a polecat.

Swinburne asserted that 'unfashionably' he rated Charlotte Brontë's work more highly than that of George Eliot and other contemporary women writers. While Eliot's work was the product of 'intellect', Charlotte Brontë's work was the product of 'genius': Adam Bede [the hero of George Eliot's 1859 novel of that title] was a 'construction', Rochester was a 'creation'.[45] Swinburne's romantic account of *Jane Eyre* emphasises depth and ardour of feeling and spiritual force that works below the conscious level of knowledge and culture to make readers feel an 'inevitability beyond reason' in the narrative that the novels of Sir Walter Scott and William Thackeray cannot match:

> ■ Whatever in 'Jane Eyre' is other than good is also less than important. The accident which brings a famished wanderer to the door of unknown kinsfolk might be a damning flaw in a novel of mere incident; but incident is not the keystone and commonplace is not the touchstone of this. The vulgar insolence and brutish malignity of the well-born guests at Thornfield Hall are grotesque and incredible in speakers of their imputed station [...] So gross and grievous a blunder would entail no less than ruin on a novel of manners; but accuracy in the distinction and reproduction of social characteristics is not the test of capacity for such a work as this. That test is to be found in the grasp and manipulation of manly and womanly character. And, to my mind, the figure of Edward Rochester in this book remains, and seems likely to remain, one of the only two male figures of wholly truthful workmanship and vitally heroic mould ever carved and coloured by a woman's hand.[46] □

Contrastingly St John Rivers, in Swinburne's view, is not one of Brontë's most successful portraits:

> ■ the central mainspring of his hard fanatic heroism is never quite adequately touched; her own apparent lack of sympathy with this white marble clergyman (counterpart, as it were, of the 'black marble' Brockenhurst, who chills and darkens the dreary dawn of the story) seems here and there as though it scarcely could be held down by force of artistic conscience from passing into actual and avowed aversion; but the imperishable passion and perfection of the words describing the moorland scene of which his eyes at parting take their long last look must have drawn the tears to many another man's that his own were not soft enough to shed.[47] □

Swinburne draws attention to the poetic qualities and analogues to Charlotte's writing and to the influence of French novels, especially the works of George Sand (pseudonym of Amandine Aurore Lucie Dupin (1804–76)). He also draws positive connections between Emily Brontë's work and Charlotte's; both writers have an 'instinct' for the 'tragic use of landscape'. While Reid still considered Charlotte as 'naturally holding the foremost place' above her sisters, Swinburne deems *Wuthering Heights* in certain respects superior to *Jane Eyre*: 'there was a dark unconscious instinct as of primitive nature-worship in the passionate great genius of Emily Brontë, which found no corresponding quality in her sister's'.[48] Swinburne's judgement marked a turning of the tide towards admiration for Emily's work vis-à-vis Charlotte's. Where *Jane Eyre* had, earlier in the century, been thought a challenging novel and *Wuthering Heights* a barbaric one, to an audience newly appreciative of symbolism and decadence, *Wuthering Heights* had the charm of wildness, where *Jane Eyre* seemed comparatively limited and traditional in its moral structure.

Just as Reid's monograph had stimulated Swinburne's response, Swinburne's *A Note on Charlotte Brontë* stimulated a reply from Leslie Stephen (1832–1904), future director of the *Dictionary of National Biography* and father of the novelist Virginia Woolf (1882–1941). Stephen (*Cornhill Magazine*, December 1877) disputes Swinburne's preference for Charlotte Brontë's passion over George Eliot's intellectualism. He laments the 'comparative narrowness of the circle of ideas in which [Charlotte Brontë's] mind habitually revolved' – which he attributes to her provincial 'imprisonment' in Haworth – and contends that 'we cannot sit at her feet as a great teacher, nor admit that her view of life is satisfactory, or even intelligible. But we feel for her as for a fellow sufferer who has at least felt with extraordinary keenness the sorrows and disappointments which torture most cruelly the most noble virtues'.[49] Stephen praises Brontë's distinctive realism:

> ■ The specific peculiarity of Miss Brontë seems to be the power of revealing to us the potentiality of intense passions lurking behind the scenery of everyday life. Except in the most melodramatic – which is also the weakest – part of *Jane Eyre*, we have lives almost as uneventful as those of Miss Austen, and yet charged to the utmost with latent power.[50] □

Unlike Swinburne, however, he finds that Rochester 'though he does his very best to be a man' is really a figment of woman's fantasy, who expresses one side of the author's own personality. Moreover, Stephen detects in Brontë's writing an unresolved inner conflict, which sometimes results in stylistic contortions and a fretful sense of 'aspiration after more than can be accomplished'. This intellectual and emotional struggle is between passion and duty, protest against social convention and self-sacrifice to it:

■ One great aim of the writing, explained in the preface to the second edition of *Jane Eyre*, is a protest against conventionality. But the protest is combined with a most unflinching adherence to the proper conventions of society; and we are left in great doubt as to where the line ought to be drawn. Where does the unlawful pressure of society upon the individual begin, and what are the demands which it may rightfully make upon our respect? At one moment in *Jane Eyre* we seem to be drifting towards the solution that strong passion is the one really good thing in the world, and that all human conventions which oppose it should be disregarded. This was the tendency which shocked the respectable reviewers of the time. Of course they should have seen that the strongest sympathy of the author goes with the heroic self-conquest of the heroine under temptation. She triumphs at the cost of a determined self-sacrifice, and undoubtedly we are meant to sympathise with the martyr. Yet it is also true that we are left with the sense of an unsolved discord.[51] □

Leslie Stephen admires *Jane Eyre*, but finds its uneasy compromise between protest and conformism intellectually dissatisfying. Charlotte Brontë is awarded a high place in 'the great hierarchy of imaginative thinkers', which Stephen would do so much to establish, but 'she is not in the highest rank' in a literary canon based on the extent of a writer's contribution to the history of ideas.

While full of admiration for its subjects, Peter Bayne's *Two Great Englishwomen: Mrs Browning and Charlotte Brontë* (1881) also provides evidence that *Jane Eyre* now lagged behind current critical debate on social mores. Bayne argued that modern readers, with a new view of women's rights and opportunities, would not approve of Rochester's egotistical treatment of Jane and her acceptance of it:

■ The length to which he protracted his persecution of Jane was, next to his hypocrisy, the worst thing in his conduct. No man could have a right to bait and badger a woman like that; and if Jane had been a little more strong and a little more proud, she would never have favoured him with another look of her face. Am I right here, ladies?[52] □

Bayne also reflects on the inequality present in the fact that Jane accepts Rochester's admission of sexual dalliances, whereas Rochester would not have accepted a similar confession from her:

■ It is worth while, in these days of vociferous debate concerning the place of women in the social system, when perfect equality between men and women is indignantly claimed as a right, or asserted as a fact, by a thousand voices, to take note of Jane Eyre's mode of allusion to Rochester's career of dissipation during his wife's lunacy. She does not quite approve of his successive *liaisons*, but her rebuke is the mildest of upbraiding glances [...] it seems never to have occurred to Charlotte Brontë, as a possible way of viewing the case, that Jane might have said to him, "Now suppose, Mr. Rochester, that I had conducted myself as you have done, and had then bestowed on you so frank a series of confidences [...] how would you have taken it?"[53] □

Jane Eyre remained a well-known and popular text in the changing climate of the late nineteenth century but the critical script was being rewritten in subtle ways: on the one hand, *Jane Eyre* was becoming an established part of the literary canon, with monographs devoted to analysis of Brontë's achievement; on the other, the very fact that Charlotte Brontë was now a 'Great Englishwoman' and the story of *Jane Eyre*'s publication and early reception belonged to history, underlined the distance between the views and conduct depicted in the novel and more modern literary approaches. Next to the novels of George Eliot, *Jane Eyre* might look nostalgically romantic (to Swinburne) or sadly unscientific (to Stephen), but its manners and mindset unquestionably belonged to an earlier era.

Jane Eyre in the 1890s

Mary Augusta Ward (1851–1920) undertook substantial introductory commentaries to each volume in the *The Life and Works of Charlotte Brontë and her Sisters* (1899–1900), which form a landmark at the end of nineteenth-century Brontë criticism. Ward, the niece of the prominent Victorian poet and critic Matthew Arnold (1822–88) and herself, as Mrs Humphry Ward, a successful novelist, well-read in several languages, situates *Jane Eyre* in an unusually wide historical and international perspective. She emphasises the personal relationship between the Brontës, their works, and their readers: 'Charlotte Brontë *is* Jane Eyre [...] You cannot think of her apart from what she has written, and everything that she wrote has the challenging quality of personal emotion or of passion, moving in a narrow range among very concrete things'. Ward criticises *Jane Eyre*'s loose plot construction, however: 'it abounds with absurdities and inconsistencies'.[54] Nonetheless, she concludes that, as a 'study of feeling' and an expression of personality, it is spellbinding. Looking back over 50 years since the novel's first publication, Ward stresses the influence of French novels – by authors such as Victor Hugo (1802–85), Alfred de Musset (1810–57),

and George Sand – on Charlotte Brontë's intellectual development
and identifies *Jane Eyre* as 'linked in various significant ways with the
French romantic movement':

■ One may almost say of it, indeed, that it belongs more to the European
than to the special English tradition. For all its strongly marked national
and provincial elements, it was very easily understood and praised in
France [.]⁵⁵ □

Mary Ward does not see *Jane Eyre* as the work of a social rebel –
'Charlotte Brontë's main *stuff* is English, Protestant, law-respecting,
conventional even' – but she suggests that the influence of contemporary French novels, which challenged social and moral conventions,
seeped unconsciously into Charlotte's work and 'for all her revolt from
them [...] they fertilised her genius'.⁵⁶

This is an interesting refinement of the debate in the first decades
of *Jane Eyre*'s reception between those who thought it a socially defiant
novel and those who thought it socially compliant. Ward suggests that
French literary fiction, reflecting challenging French social and political
models, is a subconscious influence in *Jane Eyre*, underlying conscious
elements of the text that are much more conservative.

Ward is also one of the first critics to emphasise the fact that
Charlotte Brontë' is 'first and foremost *an Irishwoman* [...] her genius
is at bottom a Celtic genius'. The 1890s saw a great revival of interest
in the Celtic – the languages, literature, and culture of early European
peoples who had settled in Ireland, Scotland, Wales, Cornwall, and
Brittany. This revival was associated with nationalist movements,
particularly in Ireland, that turned away from English colonial culture to rediscover prior influences and folk sources for language,
music, and art. Ward reads the qualities of Jane Eyre – pride, shyness,
endurance, and passion – as Celtic attributes; 'Celtic dreaming' allied
with 'English realism and self-control' accounts for the nature of the
Brontë family's works.⁵⁷ This new interest in reading novel and author
in terms of racial and national characteristics is common in the late
nineteenth century: it makes Ward's criticism both refreshingly pan-
European in scope and troublingly preoccupied with physical and
cultural heredity.

Mary Ward, then, scanning the legacy of the preceding 50 years,
could place *Jane Eyre* in various traditions and identify in it broader
trends. The novel, in her view, is deeply influenced by early nineteenth-
century French literature, and belongs to the European, rather than
English, Romantic movement. It is also a pivotal work in the development of the Victorian novel that would influence literature to come: as

she asserts, *Jane Eyre* marks the transition 'from the old novel of plot and coincidence to the new novel of psychology and character'.[58]

Her analysis illustrates the critical assimilation of *Jane Eyre* that had taken place in the course of the nineteenth century. As we have seen, when it appeared in 1847, *Jane Eyre* divided critical opinion. A unique, striking novel – vigorous and direct to the point of coarseness – it was advertised in its authorial preface and perceived by its first audience as challenging conventionality. When the gender and origins of its author were not yet known, *Jane Eyre* was a source of intrigue. Its language and incident, its politics, its treatment of religion and model of romance stimulated heated debate. After Charlotte Brontë's death in 1857, public interest turned to the relationship between author and text: the story of *Jane Eyre* became inseparable from the story of its genesis and composition. By 1900, the story could look uneven and dated, but *Jane Eyre*'s continuing importance and interest to readers were assumed; it had become a 'classic' and been placed within a narrative of cultural development that related the achievement of the 'English novel' to national character and history. The following chapter looks at what happened to *Jane Eyre* in the twentieth century, a tale of critical reception that has its own Cinderella narrative of domestic neglect, rediscovery, and triumphant elevation in status to become what one academic has dubbed the 'book of books'[59] in Victorian studies.

CHAPTER TWO

Jane Eyre's 'I': From Humanism to Deconstruction

Unlike many Victorian novels, *Jane Eyre* remained a bestseller in the twentieth century. A divide emerged in the period between 1900 and 1950, however, between popular affection for *Jane Eyre* as a love story and academic disdain for *Jane Eyre* as a work of art. Lord David Cecil, a critic and biographer who would become Goldsmiths' Professor of English Literature at Oxford in 1949, described *Jane Eyre* in 1934 as 'a roaring melodrama' whose plot, like those of Charlotte Brontë's other novels, is 'conventional, confusing, and unlikely'.[1] He noted that among *Jane Eyre*'s other faults, it was formless, humourless, and exaggerated – saved from absurdity only by the power of Brontë's 'volcanic' imagination.[2] In a 1958 survey, *The English Novel,* the novelist and critic Walter Allen (1911–95) suggested that 'if it were not for the unity of tone, *Jane Eyre* would be incoherent, for as a construction it is artless'.[3] He added that Charlotte Brontë's novels need 'to be read in adolescence; come to them after that and a considerable act of imagination is called for before she can be read with sympathy'. F.R. Leavis (1895–1978), in his formidably selective account of the English novel, *The Great Tradition* (1948), deliberately relegated the Brontës to a footnote: 'Charlotte, though claiming no part in the great line of English fiction [...] has a permanent interest of a minor kind [...] The genius, of course, was Emily.'[4] Tom Winnifrith, even in 1977 felt the need to mount a critical defence of *Jane Eyre* as a great novel. As he explained, the Brontës' tragic lives and passionate prose had gained them a following of pilgrims, who were more inclined to visit the shrine of the Brontë Museum in Haworth than to subject the novels to measured appraisal : 'Such a cult has not found favour with the high priests of our more austere literary tradition, and just as there are some students of the Brontës who know nothing of any other major literary figure, so there are students of literature who profess to know almost nothing about the Brontës'.[5]

The schism between academic sceptics and amateur devotees over the merits of *Jane Eyre* narrowed around mid-century. Between the 1950s and the 1970s, *Jane Eyre*'s academic reputation rose, enhanced by formalist critical assessments that hailed it as a more innovative, well-crafted, and complex novel than many pre-war commentators would allow. Q.D. Leavis (1906–81), wife of F.R. Leavis, spoke for a younger critical generation when she protested in 1966 that *Jane Eyre* was not commonly thought of as a 'work of art', but rather as an 'artless concoction of uncontrolled daydreams'[6] and observed that: 'this reaction to *Jane Eyre* seems to me to show an inability to read, to see what is in fact staring one in the face, for the novel is strikingly coherent, schematic [...] and, with a few lapses, thoroughly controlled in the interest of the theme.' After 1970, there was an explosion of new academic work on *Jane Eyre*, much of it concerned with exploring the novel's 'themes' and establishing its social, political, and artistic importance. In subsequent chapters I discuss readings by some of the major critical movements to treat *Jane Eyre* in the late twentieth century: feminist, Marxist, and postcolonial criticism. This chapter traces a particular path through twentieth-century responses to *Jane Eyre*, exploring changing attitudes to Brontë's prose style and to a central critical challenge that this novel presents: the intense subjectivity of Jane's first-person narration.

From the first, critics have commented on the difficulty of objectively analysing a novel that so effectively sucks the reader into personal engagement with its narrative. As one early reader commented: 'we took up *Jane Eyre* one winter's evening somewhat piqued at the extravagant commendations we had heard, and sternly resolved to be [...] critical [...] But as we read on we forgot both commendations and criticism, identified ourselves with Jane in all her troubles, and finally married Mr. Rochester about four in the morning.'[7] You cannot get past Jane Eyre, if you want to read *Jane Eyre*. Her voice, her 'I', is the controlling medium through which the story is conjured. As Heather Glen puts it: 'hers is an extreme, absolutist version of that which is to some extent implicit in all first-person narrative: the power of the teller to shape the fictional world [...] The story that unfolds from Jane's perspective is one in which her view of the world is unequivocally confirmed, and she assumes a position of unassailable power.'[8] Or does she? Does the controlling voice of Jane Eyre engage our sympathy, submerging us in her consciousness, or does it alienate us from a narrator so self-involved? Does Charlotte Brontë speak through Jane, endorsing her point of view, or is the novel designed to let us see the difference between Jane's biased, subjective vision and that of others? Is Jane's voice transparent, unironised, establishing a coherent selfhood as its heroine's achievement in life and in art? Or might we read *Jane Eyre* as an oddly indeterminate, evasive text, in which 'Jane' remains a fragile fiction and, as Heather Glen concludes, her apparent 'egocentric triumph' is constantly shadowed by a different story, 'in which the protagonist is not all-powerful, but precarious, powerless, threatened: one that speaks not of self-confirming triumph, but of uncertainty and impotence'.[9] Underlying the many debates about the novel's themes and tendencies is the crucial and surprisingly thorny question of how we should read Jane Eyre's narrative.

In the early twentieth century, biographical readings draw heavily on the Brontës' lives to interpret their fiction: the explanation most often given for the intensity of the first-person narrative is that Jane's voice provides an expressive outlet for Charlotte Brontë's inner feelings. As David Cecil declared in 1934: 'Fundamentally, her principal characters are all the same person; and that is Charlotte Brontë.'[10] Critics portray this as both the source of *Jane Eyre*'s imaginative power and a mark of its intellectual limitation. Charlotte's life experience, they argue, was cramped, provincial, and isolated: *Jane Eyre* reflects this in its narrow scope and passionate egocentricity. Since, as readers, we see only through Jane's eyes – which are an extension of Charlotte's – we are prevented from seeing Jane, or other characters, 'in the round' and from calm examination of wide-ranging social issues, which matter in the narrative only in as far as they affect Jane's destiny. The critical tendency to see *Jane Eyre* as an inward novel, 'perfectly self-sufficient and perfectly self-centred' as Virginia Woolf put it, is so pervasive that even Kathleen Tillotson (1906–2001) in her groundbreaking comparative historical study *Novels of the Eighteen-Forties* (1954) refers to *Jane Eyre* as having, of the novels she includes 'the least relation to its time [...] it maps a private world'.[11]

By 1950 the trend in literary analysis had turned towards formalism. Formalism, as the name suggests, emphasises the form of the text: its appearance on the page, its structure, vocabulary, syntax, imagery. In its purest emanation, a formalist approach seeks to read the text free of biographical or other contextual data that might cloud judgement of the words as they stand before the reader. Although few readings of *Jane Eyre* wholly eschew biographical allusions, the influence of a new critical interest in form is evident in various seminal accounts of the novel from the 1950s to the 1970s, which dwell on the structure and symmetries of the text, running motifs in its imagery, and approach to genre, and the conscious art of its word choice and syntax. This kind of reading is one answer to the critical conundrum of how one might resist the overwhelming pull of Jane Eyre's narrative, to focus instead on the novel's architecture. Commentators on *Jane Eyre* in the mid-century also dwell on its formal art in order to defend it as a carefully composed technical achievement, worthy of serious and sustained study, against earlier claims that it was artless, formless, and preposterous.

From the 1970s, literary theorists increasingly reject the humanist belief that each of us is an 'individual' with a unique and coherent interior identity shaped by choice and agency, preferring instead to speak of the self as a 'construct' that is produced by the transpersonal forces of social and cultural systems within whose conventions the de-centred 'subject' is formed. This shift in thinking about selfhood accompanies a shift in thinking about writing. Structuralist criticism looks for the underlying codes and systems of signification that structure all communication, while poststructuralist criticism foregrounds the instability inherent in all texts, as words 'float' and 'slide', disconnected from any reality which would guarantee their meanings, and dependent always on prior ideas, conventions, and other texts. In this period, critics begin to reappraise *Jane Eyre*'s narrative strategy and, indeed, to question the coherence of 'Jane Eyre' as a narrator constructing her identity through fiction. Doreen Roberts in 'Jane Eyre and "The Warped System of Things"' (1980), analyses some of the peculiar rhetorical effects whereby *Jane Eyre* 'manages' the reader's responses and argues that Jane's voice is marked by distortion. In *The Cover of the Mask: The Autobiographers in Charlotte Brontë's Fiction* (1982), Annette Tromly (1982) suggests that Jane is an unintentionally unreliable narrator, comparing her with the troubling first-person narrators of Brontë's other novels; in *Charlotte Brontë and the Storyteller's Audience* (1992), Carol Bock emphasises the struggle between Jane and other characters for control of her tale; while, in 'Jane Eyre: "Hazarding Confidences"' (1999), Lisa Sternlieb regards Jane as a practised liar, whose treacherous seduction of the reader is a deliberate revenge for Rochester's similar behaviour to her. Late twentieth-century critics routinely unpick the apparently linear and unitary qualities of the novel, suggesting that Jane is a divided, duplicitous, evanescent, or perpetually threatened subject, everywhere and yet nowhere in the text, and that the dynamics of reading *Jane Eyre*, and of reading in *Jane Eyre*, are always less straightforward than they look.

'A NOVEL OF THE INNER LIFE': EARLY TWENTIETH-CENTURY CRITICISM

There is considerable evidence that the power of *Jane Eyre* to engage and move individual readers remained strong in the early years of the twentieth century and that its readership cut across gender and class lines. Alice Foley (1891–1974), a mill worker and later a suffragette, remembered in her autobiography that, aged thirteen, in 1904 she asked for *Jane Eyre* as a prize from her night-school class and was initiated into a 'new romantic world'.[12] Philip Inman (1892–1979), a working-class chemist who became a Labour MP, also recorded reading *Jane Eyre* with delight around 1912: he felt solidarity with Jane, he recalled, for her 'dogged determination and lack of frills', which she used as weapons against her haughty and wealthy rivals.[13] The novel also early became a subject for silent movies: at least thirteen *Jane Eyre*s were screened between 1900 and 1920.

Literary commentators in the early years of the twentieth century, however, tempered their praise for *Jane Eyre*'s imaginative grip on the reader with criticism of its limited scope and passionate subjectivity. These traits, argued the French priest and writer, Ernest Dimnet (1866–1954) in his biography *The Brontë Sisters* (1910), arise because while Charlotte Brontë is writing 'her regard is turned inward, not outward'. In his view, 'egoism' is 'the great defect of *Jane Eyre*':

■ the most patient man will be conscious of a nervous irritation on remarking the extent to which Charlotte identifies herself with her heroine, and the peaceful and profound pleasure she feels in following herself through six hundred pages. It is nothing that Jane Eyre should be unhappy and a governess, that a pompous erudition, with French phrases and poetical phrases abounding, should characterize her; but what seems intolerable is that Charlotte is so evidently pleased to be Jane Eyre, plain but mysteriously and irresistibly seductive, pure, strong, heroic, intelligent, a naïve child yet a perfect woman, modest yet alluring, fascinating and elusive.[14] □

Like Leslie Stephen, Mary Ward and other late Victorian critics, Dimnet ascribes the subjectivity of *Jane Eyre* to the biographical circumstances of the author. Egoism may be the great defect of the novel:

■ but one feels instantly that this defect is a fault of genius. All the time while she was writing this novel, on almost every page of which passion broods or breaks forth, Charlotte was in the Haworth parsonage, where it was very cold, where nobody was well, where the living corpse of Branwell added horror to day and night [...] This sickly little woman, occupied with the kitchen and linen closet, confined to the narrow ideas and conversation of provincials, had within herself a reserve of passion sufficient for ten lives and a library of novels.[15] □

In Dimnet's reading, Charlotte Brontë's selfless and repressed suffering is the necessary back-story explaining and excusing the self-centred and passionately expressive voice of her fantasy life in *Jane Eyre*.

A 'self-centred and self-limited' writer

Virginia Woolf's memorable essay on '*Jane Eyre* and *Wuthering Heights*' in *The Common Reader* (1925) similarly begins with biographical reflections. She comments on how strange it is to think that Charlotte Brontë might have lived a long life and been a familiar literary figure in

London until the end of the nineteenth century: if this had happened, many alive in 1925 would have had comparatively recent memories of her. Instead:

> ■ When we think of her we have to imagine some one who had no lot in our modern world; we have to cast our minds back to the 'fifties of the last century, to a remote parsonage upon the wild Yorkshire moors. In that parsonage, and on those moors, unhappy and lonely, in her poverty and her exultation, she remains for ever.[16] □

This historically questionable image of an impoverished and isolated Charlotte bears a striking resemblance to that of Jane Eyre, when she spends a night on the moors alone, destitute and desolate. Like Dimnet, Woolf emphasises the similarity between author and novel and argues for the passionate integrity, yet self-absorption of Brontë's situation as the key to her work. Reading *Jane Eyre*, says Woolf, is still a fresh and exciting experience. Exhilaration:

> ■ rushes us through the entire volume, without giving us time to think, without letting us lift our eyes from the page [...] The writer has us by the hand, forces us along her road, makes us see what she sees, never leaves us for a moment or allows us to forget her. At the end we are steeped through and through with the genius, the vehemence, the indignation of Charlotte Brontë. Remarkable faces, figures of strong outline and gnarled feature have flashed upon us in passing; but it is through her eyes that we have seen them [...] Think of Rochester and we have to think of Jane Eyre. Think of the moor, and again there is Jane Eyre.[17] □

Here, the writer Charlotte Brontë, who 'makes us see what she sees' and the heroine Jane Eyre, whose eye/'I' is the only medium for perception in the novel, coalesce and become identified as a single figure from whom the reader cannot escape. Charlotte's indignation and Jane's resentment are one. For Woolf, as for her father Leslie Stephen, whose analysis we encountered in the previous chapter, this concentrated subjectivity is poetic in its intensity but inherently limiting. Woolf compares Charlotte Brontë unfavourably with the English novelist Jane Austen (1775–1817) and the Russian writer Leo Tolstoy (1828–1910):

> ■ The characters of a Jane Austen or of a Tolstoi have a million facets compared with these. They live and are complex by means of their effect upon many different people who serve to mirror them in the round. They move hither and thither whether their creators watch them or not, and the world in which they live seems to us an independent world which we can visit, now that they have created it, by ourselves.[18] □

By contrast, Charlotte Brontë's first person narrative is not 'rounded'; the reader is not given an opportunity to see a variety of characters and issues from a range of possible perspectives. This means, in Woolf's view, that the secondary characters in *Jane Eyre* have no 'independent' life; they are not fully realised. The pace and dramatic narrative momentum of *Jane Eyre* also do not permit the reader 'to brood and ponder and drift away from the text', thinking of questions of which the characters themselves are unconscious. This is unimportant, however, Woolf argues, because Charlotte Brontë is not trying to raise social issues:

■ She does not attempt to solve the problems of human life; she is even unaware that such problems exist; all her force, and it is the more tremendous for being constricted, goes into the assertion, 'I love', 'I hate', 'I suffer'.[19] □

Woolf, in *A Room of One's Own* (1929), which I discuss in Chapter Three, would return to the subject of Charlotte Brontë, and consider her situation as a woman writer in a way that complicates the assertion here that Brontë's writing is unconscious of the problems of human life. Woolf's approach to *Jane Eyre* in *The Common Reader*, however, while appreciative, fits the broad critical pattern of response to *Jane Eyre* from 1900–45: it is biographical in thrust, and it emphasises that the intense first-person narrative of the novel and its limited intellectual and social scope are integrally related.

'all the same person; and that is Charlotte Brontë': Biographical Readings

Lord David Cecil in *Early Victorian Novelists: A Revaluation* (1934) comes to a more sweeping conclusion about the biographical basis of Charlotte Brontë's art when he remarks that:

■ Fundamentally, her principal characters are all the same person; and that is Charlotte Brontë. Her range is confined, not only to a direct expression of an individual's emotions and impressions, but to a direct expression of Charlotte Brontë's emotions and impressions [...] The world she creates is the world of her own inner life; she is her own subject.[20] □

Cecil's perception of a need to 'revalue' the early Victorian novelists says a great deal about the dip in critical reputation that Victorian literature in general had suffered in the early twentieth century, despite the continuing popularity with ordinary readers of individual works such as *Jane Eyre*. Victorian novels sit on the library shelf, says Cecil, but learned critics value them less than French or Russian works and the 'bright young things' of the literary world, 'if they mention them

at all, do so with boredom and contempt and disgust'.[21] Victorian
literature was not fashionable in the period between the First and
Second World Wars. It was associated with the ornate, the exces-
sive, and the sentimental. Even Cecil, who seeks to draw scholarly
attention back to Victorian literature, concludes that the Victorian
novel, whose business was to entertain the middle classes, was not
the central medium of serious thought in that age. Cecil points out
a varied range of defects in Charlotte Brontë's work: she is a naïve,
both childish and Puritanical, writer and 'her range is confined to the
inner life, the private passions'.[22] Her dialogue is 'often preposterous'[23]
and she 'fails often' in creating character.[24] However, *Jane Eyre*, like
her other novels, is saved from its 'formless, improbable, humourless,
exaggerated'[25] qualities by the passionate vitality of Brontë's 'volcanic'
imagination.[26] Cecil comments that it is the strange combination of
self-absorbed passion with a self-denying philosophical outlook that
sets Brontë apart; he compares and contrasts her with, on the one
hand, the Romantic poet Lord Byron (1788–1824) and, on the other,
the playwright George Bernard Shaw (1856–1950):

■ Childish naïveté, rigid Puritanism, fiery passion, these would seem
incongruous elements indeed; and it is their union which gives Charlotte
Brontë's personality its peculiar distinction. Other writers have been equally
passionate, Byron for instance; but their passion went with a reckless outlook. Other writers, like Mr. Bernard Shaw, have been puritanical; but their
Puritanism is the natural expression of a cool intellectualistic temperament.
It is the fact that Charlotte Brontë is both, that her passion is enrolled in
the service of a severe moral philosophy, that constitutes her individuality.
Jane Eyre astonished the public on the one hand because its heroine was
a plain governess; on the other because she was so frankly violent in her
love. And naturally: for it was in the combination of qualities which these
two facts implied, that Charlotte Brontë's originality lay.[27] □

Notice here that again the peculiar compound of qualities attributed
to Charlotte Brontë's personality, to Jane Eyre the character and to
Jane Eyre the book, are identical. Cecil's mixed estimate of Brontë as a
clumsy craftsman yet an imaginative genius causes him to observe that
her achievement is 'almost impossible finally to estimate [...] She is pre-
destined to hover restlessly and for ever, now at the head now at the foot
of the procession of letters, among the unplaceable anomalies'.[28] This
view, that Charlotte Brontë's work is set apart from that of other writers
by its idiosyncrasies, and by its irresolvable position as good (powerful,
imaginative) *and* bad (exaggerated, limited), literature was common in
the early twentieth century. The argument tends to fulfil its own cir-
cular logic: the books are written in circumstances of social isolation
and personal frustration; they are thus powerfully self-absorbing but of

limited range; they must thus be seen in literary isolation, as 'special cases' in the history of the novel.

An Anomalous Novel – and a Minor Author?

Treatment of the Brontës' works as anomalous and unique also led critics to downplay the importance of contemporary literary and social influences upon their writing. May Sinclair (Mary Amelia St Clair (1863–1946)) in her 1922 introduction to *Jane Eyre* asserts that it is:

> ■ a book that has had innumerable descendants, but no traceable descent. Charlotte Brontë was not shaped by any influence that we can discover among her predecessors and contemporaries. Out of her curious and varied reading she formed a style exclusively and inimitably her own.[29] □

Virginia Woolf contends in *The Common Reader* that 'Charlotte Brontë [...] owed nothing to the reading of many books'.[30] *Jane Eyre* thus stands alone, apparently without literary parentage. Standing beyond contemporary events and outside literary tradition, *Jane Eyre* the novel, like Jane Eyre the character, could be critically depicted as an orphan.

Some early twentieth-century literary critics were unwilling to concede that *Jane Eyre* fitted into the lineage of 'major' literary works at all. F.R. Leavis (1895–1978) in his influential study, *The Great Tradition* (1948) insists that 'Jane Austen, George Eliot, Henry James [1843–1916], [Joseph] Conrad [1857–1924], and D.H. Lawrence [1885–1930]: the great tradition of the English novel is *there*.'[31] In a deliberate snub, the Brontës are dispatched in a footnote, 'NOTE: 'THE BRONTËS', on the same page, which announces:

> ■ It is tempting to retort that there is only one Brontë. Actually, Charlotte, though claiming no part in the great line of English fiction [...] has a permanent interest of a minor kind. She had a remarkable talent that enabled her to do something firsthand and new in the rendering of personal experience, above all in *Villette*. The genius, of course, was Emily.[32] □

As was typical in the early twentieth century, F.R. Leavis rates Emily Brontë's work above Charlotte's and ignores Anne's altogether; moreover, he considers *Villette* (1853) Charlotte's most important novel, refusing to mention *Jane Eyre* at all. Leavis's 'great tradition' is a model based on inheritance, a family tree of influence and innovation that claims to trace the highest line of artistry in the English novel. *Jane Eyre*, seen as a self-limited and anomalous piece, is readily excluded from that perceived tradition, treated as a 'minor' novel that focuses on 'personal experience' rather than broader themes and is therefore inherently of lesser scope and significance than other contemporary works.

THE MOVE TOWARDS FORM 1950–1970

In the mid-twentieth century, purely biographical reading increasingly fell out of favour as a critical approach. Critics instead became interested *in Jane Eyre* as an example of a particular literary form – the early nineteenth-century novel – and began to reconsider its formal features: the relation of particular episodes, incidents, and figures to the work as a whole; the patterns of symbol and imagery in the text; and its distinctive vocabulary, syntax, and structure. Analysis of novels based on their patterns of formal devices and strategies was stimulated by the work of the American New Critics, such as Cleanth Brooks (1906–94), W.K. Wimsatt (1907–75) and Monroe Beardsley (1915–85), who advocated 'close reading': intensive technical analysis of the text as an object to be considered free of historical and biographical information. New Critics emphasised that the meaning of a literary work is independent of the author's intention and is not equivalent to its effects, especially its emotional impact on the reader. This preoccupation was shared by European formalists, who also stressed that literature is defined by its verbal art, rather than its relationship to 'reality'.

Key words of formalist approval were 'unity' and 'organic form' and critics after 1950 often apply these words to *Jane Eyre*, pointing to ways in which the novel's narrative structure, language, themes, and imagery are integrally related. David Cecil had accused *Jane Eyre* in 1934 of being 'formless' and ill crafted. Part of the quiet rehabilitation of *Jane Eyre* as a novel worthy of serious and detailed literary study was a demonstration of its formal coherence and meticulous design. F.R. Leavis had dismissed *Jane Eyre* as lying outside the English 'great tradition'. Attention to shared aspects of the novel's literary art (genre, tropes, and motifs) also served to 'place' it within a historical framework of collective importance.

Kathleen Tillotson's study *Novels of the Eighteen-Forties* (1954) was ground-breaking in treating *Jane Eyre* alongside other novels of the decade in which it was composed, looking at it as part of a shared social and literary phenomenon. At this moment in history, she contends, the novel was taking over the functions of drama and epic and was becoming increasingly outspoken and intellectually serious. It was thus turning away from frothy romances of fashionable society to previously ignored settings and aspects of inner life and displaying a new concern for the 'condition of the people', especially the separation between rich and poor, employer and employed. *Jane Eyre* should be seen in this context which, Tillotson argues, explains the house-party scenes with Blanche Ingram at Thornfield, which some critics have dismissed as weak: these satirical scenes deliberately mark Brontë's departure from the society novel of manners.

Tillotson considers the economic reasons why novels were published in three-volume editions in this period. (Novels, typically costing a guinea and a half, were very expensive for the average reader; circulating libraries, with subscriptions of a guinea a year, profited by being able to lend out each volume as a single unit.) In *Jane Eyre*, volume one ends with Jane rescuing Rochester from his burning bed. Brontë thus turns the suspense important to the three-volume format to good account.

Although Tillotson concedes that *Jane Eyre* is 'primarily a novel of the inner life' and 'such social commentary as it may offer is oblique, limited, incidental',[33] she emphasises the relation between *Jane Eyre* and its times, dismissing the idea that it is an eccentric or anomalous work. She notes, for example, that many of the themes in *Jane Eyre* had been treated individually by other contemporary writers: oppressed childhood in Dickens's *Oliver Twist* (1838), the child working out moral problems in *The Fairy Bower* (1841) by Harriet Mozley (1803–51), middlebrow provincial society in *Deerbrook* (1839) by Harriet Martineau (1802–76), the deliberate deflation of heroic convention in the early works of William Thackeray. *Jane Eyre*, then, was in tune with contemporary social and literary concerns:

■ The few attacks upon *Jane Eyre* are not directed against breaches of literary convention; indeed, they testify indirectly to its timeliness, hearing it as a voice from the dangerous north and the dangerous class of oppressed or 'outlawed' women; using it as a text on which to hang warnings about female emancipation and a rebellious and un-Christian spirit in society. The influence of *Jane Eyre*, both social and literary, also bespeaks its importance in its own time; on the lower level, it started a vogue for plain heroines and ugly masterful heroes; on the higher, it affected the autobiographic children in Dickens's later novels, and at least smoothed the path for Mrs. Gaskell, [Anthony] Trollope [1815-82], and George Eliot.[34] □

Tillotson is also at pains to point out that *Jane Eyre*, rather than 'the mysterious first-born offspring of adverse circumstances and untaught genius', is the 'culmination of years of writing by one of a family of five long-practised writers'. The novel is not a fluke, or a lucky hit. It reflects a long apprenticeship during her childhood and youth when Charlotte was writing stories with her brother Branwell about the fictional country of Angria, while her sisters Emily and Anne were working on stories about another fictional country, Gondal. The work of all four surviving Brontë siblings, Tillotson argues, should be seen as interdependent and cooperative and the influence of their father Patrick Brontë, a published writer, is also crucial. Although Tillotson's reading draws on biographical materials, it differs from that of earlier critics in two important respects. Firstly, it makes detailed scholarly use of the Brontë's early writings to show how *Jane Eyre* relates to Angrian plot materials and to the work of the other members of the Brontë family. Secondly, in doing so, it insists upon *Jane Eyre* as a book stemming from a web of relationships – involving family but also wider social and historical forces – dismissing romantic critical portraits of *Jane Eyre* as a novel born of existential isolation.

Charlotte Brontë's 'New' Gothic

The landmark essay by Robert Heilman (1906–2004), 'Charlotte Brontë's "New" Gothic' (1958), also contributed to the revaluation of *Jane Eyre* as a novel in creative dialogue with other contemporary work. Heilman argues that the Gothic genre served to breach the 'classical' and 'rational' order of life, breaking taboos and opening horizons 'beyond social patterns, rational decisions and institutionally approved emotions'.[35] A typical example of the late eighteenth-century Gothic novel would be *The Mysteries of Udolpho* (1794) by Ann Radcliffe (1764–1823) in which the orphan heroine is imprisoned by her wicked uncle in the castle of Udolpho, whose architecture conceals various terrible secrets, until she eventually escapes to financial independence and marriage. In Heilman's view, the first Gothic writers took an easy route, using 'the excitements of mysterious scene and happening', which he terms 'old Gothic'.[36] Charlotte Brontë in *Jane Eyre* takes a more subtle approach to the elements of Gothic style. On the one hand, she tends towards humorous modifications, a kind of anti-Gothic that gently critiques the genre. On the other, she indirectly incorporates and naturalises elements of the Gothic in a way that liberates her work from the limitations of the conventional, the rational, and the socially acceptable. This is her 'new Gothic'.

Where earlier critics often disparaged the Gothic influence in *Jane Eyre*, Heilman regards it as a key to the novel's strength: the transformed Gothic elements are not there simply to provide thrills and chills but offer a direct means of connection with our subconscious life, in its potentially violent, sexual, aggressive, and self-annihilating aspects. One of Heilman's examples of *Jane Eyre* undercutting Gothic conventions is the scene in which Rochester is nearly burned in his bed, only to find himself comically baptised in a pool of water when Jane puts out the flames. An example of the book integrating and modifying Gothic elements is the use of symbol: Bertha is not literally a vampire, but when she tears Jane's wedding veil in two, she embodies the dead hand that will reach out to destroy Rochester's planned bigamous marriage. Brontë thus 'finds new ways to achieve the ends served by old Gothic – the discovery and release of new patterns of feeling, the intensification of feeling'.[37]

■ Charlotte moves toward depth in various ways that have an immediate impact like that of Gothic. Jane's strange, fearful symbolic dreams are not mere thrillers but reflect the tensions of the engagement period, the stress of the wedding-day debate with Rochester, and the longing for Rochester after she has left him. The final Thornfield dream, with its vivid image of a hand coming through a cloud in place of the expected moon, is in the surrealistic vein that appears most sharply in the extraordinary pictures that Jane draws at Thornfield: here Charlotte is plumbing the psyche, not inventing a weird *décor*. Likewise in the telepathy scene, which Charlotte [...] does her utmost to actualize: 'The feeling was not like an electric shock; but it was quite as sharp, as strange, as startling [...]' In her flair for the surreal, in her plunging into feeling that is without status in the ordinary world of the novel, Charlotte discovers a new dimension of Gothic.[38] □

In Heilman's account, *Jane Eyre* is re-envisaged as a surprisingly and refreshingly modern text: the physicality of the passion evoked in the relationships reminds him of the much more sexually explicit work of D.H. Lawrence (1885–1930) in the early twentieth century; the dream imagery is 'surreal'. (Comparisons between *Jane Eyre* and the work of D.H. Lawrence occur also in other contemporary criticism.) Heilman approaches the novel through the medium of genre to hail it as a 'radical revision' of earlier modes of writing that deserves recognition for its innovative and extraordinary 'openness to feeling, this escape from the bondage of the trite'.[39]

'A Unique Organic Structure'

During the 1960s other critics, including Robert Martin (1918–99) in *The Accents of Persuasion: Charlotte Brontë Novels* (1966), Wendy Craik in *The Brontë Novels* (1968), and Earl Knies in *The Art of Charlotte Brontë* (1969), would re-examine *Jane Eyre* and find it a more impressive technical achievement than most commentators of the 1930s and 1940s had allowed. As Martin put it: 'In the past decade or so, there has been in the criticism of Charlotte Brontë, as in the criticism of other Victorian writers, an increased willingness to treat her novels as seriously conceived works of art, worthy of rigorous examination rather than rhapsodic appreciation, and deserving of a close scrutiny to determine [...] how her novels manage to reduce the untidy flow of experience to the proportions and the order of art.[40]

Q.D. Leavis wrote an introduction to *Jane Eyre* in 1966 in which she took issue with the tradition of regarding it as a formless outpouring of subjective emotion. Lord David Cecil in *Early Victorian Novelists* (1934) had claimed that Charlotte Brontë had 'no gift of form, no restraint [...] no power of analysis'. Q.D. Leavis strongly disagreed. On the contrary, she insisted, *Jane Eyre* was 'quite as deliberately composed as any novel in existence' but its 'unique organic structure' often escaped critics because it involved patterns of imagery and symbolism, which unite the different phases of Jane's progress into a coherent whole:

> ■ *Jane Eyre* moves from stage to stage of Jane's development, divided into four sharply distinct phases with their suggestive names: childhood at Gateshead; girlhood, which is schooling in both senses, at Lowood; adolescence at Thornfield; maturity at Marsh End, winding up with fulfilment in marriage at Ferndean. Each move leaves behind the phase and therefore the setting and characters which supplied that step in the demonstration [...] A good deal of the effect of the book depends on the reader's making out associations, and the parts are not mechanically linked by a plot as in most previous fictions but organically united (as in Shakespeare) by imagery and symbolism which pervade the novel and are as much a part of the narrative as the action.[41] □

Leavis, like Robert Martin, points to the allegorical significance of the different houses in which Jane resides as stages in a moral-psychological pilgrimage akin to that of the central figure in *The Pilgrim's Progress* (1678–1774), the religious allegory by John Bunyan (1628–88). As an example of the imagery that unites *Jane Eyre*, she cites Brontë's symbolic use of books in the novel. In the opening scene, Jane's mental state is conveyed through an icy landscape in *A History of British Birds* (2 vols, 1794, 1804) by Thomas Bewick (1753–1828). Images from *Gulliver's Travels* (1726) by Jonathan Swift (1667–1745), also part of Jane's childhood reading, echo her strangeness in the Reed household and her need to escape it, while *Rasselas* (1759) by Samuel Johnson (1709–84), a tale that debates the stoic philosophy of resignation, embodies the debate Jane has with Helen Burns at Lowood about the proper response to ill-treatment: Helen admires the book, while Jane rejects it. Leavis traces similar patterns of symbolic form in the names of people and places in *Jane Eyre*. 'Eyre', for example, is linked by association with 'air', 'Ariel', and 'eyrie': all words that suggest Jane's ethereal yet indomitable spirit. Likewise the chapter devoted to the period before Jane's ill-fated wedding is full of symbolic dreams and pregnant images (the wailing child, Thornfield in ruins, the lightning-struck tree) remarkable for their 'psychological truth'. Leavis compares this subtlety favourably with Dickens's early work, stressing that

■ the novel is strikingly coherent, schematic [...] and, with a few lapses, thoroughly controlled in the interest of the theme. The theme has, very properly, dictated the form, and the theme is an urgently felt personal one, an exploration of how a woman comes to maturity in the world of the writer's youth.[42] □

Jane Eyre is, then, a specifically female *Bildungsroman* – a novel about the education and growth of its central character – which successfully deploys satire (David Cecil had claimed that Brontë was 'no more a satirist [...] than a ballet dancer') but is unusually emancipated in avoiding moral preaching. The poetic prose that some earlier male critics had considered digressive is, Q.D. Leavis contends, integral to the novel's symbolic structure.

'A System of Objective Correlatives': Symbol and Image as Unifying Elements

In his essay 'Fire and Eyre: Charlotte Brontë's War of Earthly Elements', also published in 1966, David Lodge (born 1935) like Q.D. Leavis, defends the coherence and unity of *Jane Eyre* in terms of symbol and image. He notes, as many critics had done before, that *Jane Eyre* is a product of the Romantic Movement, influenced by Romantic landscapes such as that of the unfinished poem *Christabel* (1816) by Samuel Taylor Coleridge (1772–1834) and with a characteristically Romantic theme: the struggle of an individual consciousness towards self-fulfilment. However, Lodge argues, it is not a pure expression of Romanticism because 'the instinctive, passionate, non-ethical drive of Romanticism towards self-fulfilment at any cost, is held in check by an allegiance to the ethical precepts of the Christian code and an acknowledgement of the necessity of exercising reason in human affairs'.[43] The dominant energies of the book are on the side of passion, but these energies are in constant dialogue with the forces of reason, judgement, and conscience. The novel's resolution involves the domestication of the mythical Romantic landscape of feeling, as individual freedom and social order are finally brought into harmony.

The 'really interesting question', to Lodge, is how Brontë creates a literary structure in which the domestic and the mythical, the realistic presentation of social scenarios and the romantic presentation of intense inner feeling can co-exist. She achieves this, he argues, 'by employing a system of "objective correlatives"': objects that embody a particular emotion, which is evoked whenever they appear in the text.[44]

The four elements – earth, air, fire, and water – form the core of this system in *Jane Eyre*. References to the elements recur constantly in the novel and through them the struggle between passion and reason, self-fulfilment, and self-destruction is played out. The novel thus has a unified structure of imagery and vocabulary that can contain and resolve both the tensions in its world-view and the weaknesses in its plot and characterisation.

Lodge chiefly analyses the imagery of fire that pervades *Jane Eyre* and the way in which fiery images are routinely contrasted with images of snow, ice, and water. Jane is throughout the novel associated with fire in terms of her passionate nature. Her name can be pronounced the same as another free element 'air', but it can alternatively be pronounced 'ire' – a word that evokes burning rage. At the very beginning of the novel Jane is depicted reading Bewick's *History of British Birds*, studying a picture of a frozen landscape: equivalent to the harsh emotional climate in which she lives at the Reeds' house. By contrast, whenever she meets human comfort and love it is by the warmth of the domestic hearth. Rochester and Jane's passionate relationship is evoked through fire imagery. When their marriage is halted at the altar, Brontë uses imagery of fields and orchards damaged by sudden frost. Likewise, the thwarting energies of St John Rivers, incompatible with Jane's, are embodied in images of water (in his name) and ice. The fire at Thornfield figuratively embodies uncontrolled passion. When it is spent, however, Jane and Rochester can be united in front of the domestic fire at Ferndean, which is going out until Jane enters and rekindles it. Lodge demonstrates how Brontë can move seamlessly between literal images – of Jane's physical coldness when she realises that Rochester cannot marry her – and figurative images, such as the orchard destroyed by frost, which represents Jane's blighted prospects. Through this web of related, elemental images, the novel can bind domestic realism and visionary imagination, reason and passion, into a satisfying union akin to that between the protagonists.

Stylistic Analysis: *Jane Eyre*'s Radical Syntax

In the 1960s and 1970s, the analysis of the formal aspects of *Jane Eyre* became extremely detailed, with some scholars even enumerating Brontë's use of different parts of speech and kinds of sentence. Stylistic analysis reflected the legacy of the New Criticism, with its emphasis on close reading, but also the growing reputation of structuralism and semiotics, discussed more fully below. David Lodge had provided a count of the number of times that 'fire' or 'fires' occurred in the novel. Karl Kroeber in *Styles in Fictional Structure: the Art of Jane Austen, Charlotte Brontë, George Eliot* (1971) and Margot Peters in

Charlotte Brontë: Style in the Novel (1973) went further. Using multi-page samples, Kroeber analysed the ratio of verbs to adjectives and other aspects of lexical and syntactic choice in *Jane Eyre* compared with those in other mid-Victorian classics. Kroeber explained that he was looking for a method of approaching the novel that would be more 'systematic' and 'objective' than the 'arbitrary' preferences and prejudices of scholars such as F.R. Leavis.[45] He concluded that conflict was key to Charlotte Brontë's use of language: the 'rivalry between what an individual intrinsically is and what his social role presses him to become' was inscribed in the linguistic tensions of the prose.[46]

Margot Peters begins by looking at Charlotte Brontë's use of adverbs and finds that the number of adverbs in Brontë's writing is unusually high and the emphasis upon them is unusually intense. In a random 500-word sample, Charlotte Brontë's average was 40.5 adverbs compared with 27.5 for other Victorian novelists. The positioning of these adverbs, often before the verb rather than after it, as is more usual, also forces them on the reader's notice:

■ Taken together, adverbial frequency and stress shed some light on the psychology of the author who uses them so conspicuously. It seems evident that to Charlotte Brontë both the action and its object are eclipsed in importance by the way an act is performed – its duration, its intensity, its manner.[47] □

This technique, Peters argues, contributes to the intensity of the experience of reading *Jane Eyre*. Other authors wrench syntax (word order) out of its usual pattern only at extreme moments, whereas in Brontë this is 'not an occasional trick but a prevailing mode of expression'.

Peters goes on to demonstrate other ways in which Brontë disrupts conventional patterns of syntax, investing her prose with 'its prevailing effect of brevity, vigor, and swiftness'.[48] David Lodge had commented that Brontë often used the semi-colon or colon in place of a full stop, and that this habit of punctuation seemed to be modelled on the Old Testament in the King James (1611) Version of the Bible.[49] Peters shows that Brontë creates swift pace and the impression of short sentences by using multiple independent clauses (constructions that grammatically could stand alone) within sentences, separating them with a semi-colon or uniting them with a conjunction. This paratactic style, marked by the absence of complex sentences involving subordinate clauses, differs markedly from, for example, George Eliot's prose style, and is partly responsible for the effect observed by Virginia Woolf and others on reading *Jane Eyre* that the writing

'rushes us through the entire volume, without giving us time to think'.
Charlotte Brontë employs:

> ■ a prose of action, uncomplicated by speculation, ramification, qualifica-
> tion, or parenthesis. We are constantly confronted by subject and verb,
> and, significantly, by more verbs than subjects [...] It comes as a surprise
> to find that much of this action is internal, dealing with longing or wishing,
> or the state of being collected, careless, or embarrassed. But in Brontë's
> prose even thought is dramatized, concretized, and externalized, often lit-
> erally, by the device of personification.[50] □

Peters analyses the stylistic effects whereby Charlotte Brontë conveys
the feeling of action to the reader and indeed presents feeling and
thinking themselves as active, energetic, dramatic processes. She links
the unconventionality of Brontë's word-choice, syntax and punctuation, which had been criticised by some earlier critics as awkward and
quaint, to the ways in which Jane Eyre defies restraint and convention: the style thus becomes an appropriate vehicle for the heroine.
In this reading we again move away from an expressive view of *Jane
Eyre* as passionate personal outpouring, towards a view in which *Jane
Eyre* deliberately develops particular rhetorical tropes associated with
emotional engagement in order to create the effect/affect of heartfelt,
unrestrained communication. In the 1980s, various critics would look
more closely at the rhetorical strategies of *Jane Eyre* and how they solicit
and manage the reader's involvement.

A CONTESTED TEXT: ACTIVE READING AND
INTERPRETIVE STRUGGLE 1970–2000

Formalism, so crucial in shaping literary criticism in the early twentieth
century, generated a critical reaction in the late twentieth century that
challenged its tenets and approach. Formalists had insisted that the focus
of literary criticism should be on the text alone: the audience's percep-
tions (unreliable, various, and unknowable) lay outside the analytical
realm. *Reader response theory*, developed by Wolfgang Iser (1926–2007) in
the 1970s, argued that, on the contrary, readers take an active part in the
composition of the novel's meaning. Literary texts, in Iser's view, invite
an implied reader to interpret them. Reading is an active, creative process, in which audiences both react to guiding principles within the text
that invite particular questions or leave gaps to be filled, and bring their
own backgrounds and preferences, which affect how they read. Each
individual reading is thus the product of interaction and cooperation
between reader and text: each of us makes our own *Jane Eyre*. 'Reader
response' theory informs the essays by Doreen Roberts and Mark M.
Hennelly on *Jane Eyre* detailed below.

Another important influence on late twentieth-century critical reading is *structuralist* theory, which emerged from the linguistic studies of Ferdinand de Saussure (1857–1913) and the anthropological studies of Claude Lévi-Strauss (born 1908–). Saussure was fascinated by the underlying sign systems, codes, and conventions (semiotics) that allow language to function in society, structuring all our communications. You do not need to be told, for example, that *Jane Eyre* is a novel, that *Jane Eyre: An Essential Guide to Criticism* is a critical survey, and that you should therefore read these texts with different expectations. But why should the word 'novel' signify fiction and 'survey', fact? Saussure argued that the relationship between the signifier (word) and signified (concept) is arbitrary and that it is the particular cultural sign system within which we operate that determines our expectations as we read. Lévi-Strauss considered the phenomena documented by anthropologists, such as rituals and kinship systems, as further examples of cultural sign systems. Structuralism emphasises the importance of binary oppositions in the semiotic models that structure culture. You can see structuralist elements in David Lodge's 1966 essay (above) on 'fire' and 'ice' as the binary opposition that represents *Jane Eyre*'s internal conflicts and in other contemporary accounts that read the narrative in terms of its oppositional pairings (red and white; Helen and Bertha; Rochester and St John; Reed and Rivers families).[51] Structuralist theory also informs Peter Allan Dale's account (below) of how *Jane Eyre* seems to follow the pattern of two familiar story types, only to disrupt the expectations readers bring to those narrative models.

The ideas of Mikhail Bakhtin (1895–1975) also permeate many modern readings of *Jane Eyre* as a *dialogic* text. Bakhtin, like Saussure a writer whose work achieved posthumous prominence in the 1970s, argued that Saussure's theories were flawed because they assumed a unified shared system of language within which each speaker operated as an individual. On the contrary, Bakhtin asserted, living language is characterised by *heteroglossia* (a mixture of different tongues) formed through the interplay of dialects and jargons particular to different class, social, age, regional, and professional groups. Thus, even though discourse may apparently originate from a single person, it is inherently multi-voiced and dialogic: each use of language depends on prior and competing uses; each piece of writing is what the French feminist Julia Kristeva (born 1941) would later call an *intertext* – a mosaic of references to other texts. Although it may seem that Jane's is the single, governing voice of *Jane Eyre,* in fact, as critics including Jerome Beaty and Carolyn Williams argue, the novel is multi-voiced.

Where much formalist criticism of *Jane Eyre* stressed its unity and coherence as markers of value, much *poststructuralist* criticism points towards the text as a contested space that (productively) refuses to be 'resolved' by any single reading. Jacques Derrida (1930–2004) and Paul de Man (1919–83), exponents of *deconstruction*, promoted the idea that attempts at a determinate interpretation of a text are doomed to failure. Deconstructive literary analysis involves acknowledging the presence of different, incompatible readings of a text without choosing between them, instead looking to understand the tensions that its verbal web (a mesh of differing threads) articulates. The text is, in Paul de Man's terminology, naturally and inevitably 'undecidable'; efforts to make a particular critical reading of it are thus necessarily 'misreadings'. Jerome Beaty, in *Misreading Jane Eyre*, the final work discussed in this section, looks at the many different expectations of story type, structure, and genre that *Jane Eyre* calls up, each of which proves insufficient to comprehend a text that ultimately eludes critical capture.

These different approaches to textuality inevitably affect the ways in which late twentieth-century critics approach Jane's first-person narration. Some earlier critics, such as Wendy Craik, had already drawn attention to the fact that Jane's narrative voice is discontinuous, slipping between past and present tense, with the mature Jane Rochester alternately reflecting on her experience and speaking as her younger self, as if the events were happening right now. Most critics, however, had agreed with Craik that: 'the reader's emotional and moral sympathy with Jane Eyre is vital, and no one questions Charlotte Brontë's power of obtaining and keeping it'.[52] Later twentieth-century critics do question this. They ask how we view Jane and how the novel seeks to influence our view. Is she a coherent presence or an elusive absence? Is her account of events reliable? Are readers inevitably 'sucked in' to the first-person narrative, or do we maintain a certain distance from Jane's viewpoint? Or should we, rather, regard *Jane Eyre* as a space in which different types of plot and different sources of textual authority vie for dominance without ever resolving their differences?

How We Make Jane and She Makes Us: Reader Response in *Jane Eyre*

Doreen Roberts in '*Jane Eyre* and "The Warped System of Things"' (1980), like Margot Peters, uses elements of stylistic analysis, but she is particularly interested in how the unusual linguistic patterns of *Jane Eyre* affect readers' encounters with the novel and their experience of characters and moral issues within it. In this way, her argument is also indebted to Iser's 'reader response' theory. To Roberts, *Jane Eyre* offers 'a mixed and restless reading experience':

■ The power of [Charlotte Brontë's] work seems to depend on the way it bulldozes through our notions of decorum and stylistic restraint, our respect for balance and a sense of proportion and – at a quite radical level – our notions of fairness.[53] ☐

The narrative method and tone of *Jane Eyre* are thus especially important influences shaping the reader's response, which tends to be personal and often immoderate. Roberts argues that Brontë's style and her purpose, her 'medium and message', are inextricably connected:

> ■ The style itself enacts the struggle which is the theme of the plot: between Id and Superego, reaction and quiescence, private and public.[54] ☐

Roberts's terms 'Id' and 'Superego' come from the psychoanalytic work of Sigmund Freud (1856–1939); Freud posits that the self is in a state of perpetual conflict between the 'id', which represents our instinctive, subconscious desires and the 'superego', which restrains these desires, acting as the voice of cultural decorum and conscience. According to Roberts's detailed close reading of Brontë's style in *Jane Eyre*, this struggle becomes visible through various tensions and oddities in the novel's use of language. The style of *Jane Eyre*, she feels, is 'extremely un-colloquial and un-modern' when compared with the novels of, for example, Brontë's contemporary and friend Elizabeth Gaskell (1810–65).[55] Charlotte Brontë is borrowing rhetorically from the balanced, formal, stylised constructions characteristic of eighteenth-century prose: she likes to use balanced or antithetical clauses, harmonious word-runs of three adjectives such as 'waste, wild, and white' often reinforced by alliteration or assonance, and structures of echoing serial phrases or clauses, often arranged to produce a crescendo. Yet she constantly disrupts these harmonious and balanced lines with 'rhetorical questions, exclamations, exhortations, appended clauses and appositional phrases'.[56] These 'private' interventions break up the symmetries of the 'public' voice with staccato abruptness: an effect augmented by the heavy punctuation and short sense-units, noted by Margot Peters, within longer sentences. The effect is a style that, rather than flowing 'is more like a sustained series of small explosions'.[57]

Other verbal qualities of *Jane Eyre* that Roberts considers typical of the 'struggle' between 'the style of the Age of Reason' and the 'style of romance' include Brontë's unusual word order and her 'recurrent and weird use of passive constructions where one would have expected active ones',[58] for example in Jane's sentence 'these words went wandering up and down in my rayless mind, as something that should be whispered; but no energy was found to express them':

> ■ This is only one of many dissociation techniques in the style. It gives the effect of someone behaving compulsively, or being acted upon by external forces. That is, the self is presented as object, not subject.[59] ☐

One result of this projection of subject onto object is that inner and outer landscapes are blurred in *Jane Eyre* and there is little differentiation between local and cosmic scales of experience. This produces an impression of Jane's overwhelming egocentricity, which can alienate readers. Her honesty includes bigotry: she is 'a fiercely Protestant, chauvinistic, and self-righteous heroine'.[60] In Roberts's view 'persistent distortion [...] is the essence of the book's method'[61] as it moves in the course of the shift from Lowood to Thornfield increasingly close to expressionism. (Expressionism was an early twentieth-century movement in which artists sought to communicate inner emotional states through depicting subjective reactions to reality rather than directly observed objects, often using symbolic forms and deliberate distortion.) Roberts departs from Q.D. Leavis's influential reading of *Jane Eyre* as a *Bildungsroman* charting the heroine's growth to mature womanhood and self-realisation. In Roberts's view, Jane does not really change: the violence of her childhood rage persists into an adult vision in which all her experience, in particular her erotic drive, is charged with conflict.

Roberts uses her analysis of the extreme and absolutist qualities of the style in *Jane Eyre* to account for the 'all-or-nothing' feelings that the reader is encouraged to share with Jane, towards characters like Mrs Reed, Blanche Ingram, and St John Rivers. Jane habitually conflates other characters' temperamental characteristics with their moral qualities and readers absorb her equation of emotional reaction with moral judgement. Jane, as she admits herself, 'knows no medium'; all the events in her narrative, big and small, are presented with equal drama; 'attitudes throughout the novel are not balanced or compromised, but polarised'.[62] In turn, the reader's response to *Jane Eyre* will tend to be immoderate: we respond in kind to the novel's presentation of immediate and intuitive attraction or antipathy as the natural condition of human response.

How Reliable is Jane as a Narrator?

Annette Tromly in *The Cover of the Mask: The Autobiographers in Charlotte Brontë's Fiction* (1982), asserts that Jane's voice is quite distinct from Charlotte Brontë's and that 'the novels invite us to see the narrators quite differently from the way these narrators see themselves'.[63]

Tromly compares *Jane Eyre* with Charlotte Brontë's earlier novel *The Professor*, whose first-person narrator William Crimsworth is 'obviously troubling' with a 'tightly constricted self-image' and with *Villette*, Brontë's last novel, whose first-person narrator, Lucy Snowe, suffers from a psychological malaise that casts doubt over her version of events. Jane Eyre, Tromly argues, is an equally unreliable narrator, but in a different way. She does not purposely mislead us, but her tale is designed to show the inevitable distance between the self as it shapes and justifies its own existence and the perspective of the onlooker, who can perceive the 'personal mythology' that is being related to them:

■ Brontë's fictional autobiographies presage a number of modern attitudes toward self-presentation, among them that the psychological motivation behind writing a life of oneself is complicated, that autobiography distorts the truth (or creates its own), and that the faculty of memory is untrustworthy [...] Brontë's narrators create personal mythologies about themselves, mythologies which in their view endow their lives with heightened moral significance. In their accounts of their past – of the choices they made, the priorities they established, the wrongs they perceived – they often present to us, to use Charlotte's terms, 'pattern[s] of perfection', with all the blots veiled.[64] □

We as readers, then, can see that Jane is organising her experience in a way that presents it as a moral progress in which she stars as the heroine. This does not necessarily mean that she is a coercive or objectionable narrator, but that we should be constantly aware (and Charlotte Brontë means us to be aware) that Jane's view is restricted and biased. It also changes. Her perspective 'fluctuates as she relates her life to us'[65]: we experience both the thoughts of the happily married, mature Jane Rochester and the thoughts and experience of her earlier selves, sometimes related in the present tense. It may be appropriate, therefore, to speak as Lawrence Jay Dessner does, of 'a continuum of Jane Eyres'.[66]

What does Brontë achieve through allowing the reader to see Jane Eyre as autobiographer, crafting a picture of herself that others might dispute? Tromly argues that this narrative method draws attention to the process of art itself. Jane Eyre is an artist, who constantly paints portraits (visual and verbal), for example of Blanche Ingram and Rosamond Oliver; but these portraits are not objective representations – rather they embody the principle that art is made, invented. It necessarily contains elements of the inner, imaginative and outer, observable world and cannot be securely located in the realm of 'fantasy' or of 'truth':

■ Jane creates the portraits to contain and control feelings (her own and others') rather than to represent her subjects. As her imagination advances and retreats, creates and refines, we are forced to see characters, as well as their visual images, as somehow arbitrary, as made things. The inter-relation between visual and verbal representation dissolves the boundary between what is inside Jane's frames and what is outside. Both partake of the same substance; both emphasize the invented quality of the entire work. When Jane at the end of her autobiography, assumes the role of word-painter for the blind Rochester and shapes the entire image of his world, she is only devoting more time to an already well-practised skill. For Jane Eyre, then, the distinctions between art and life are never quite clear. Her ostensible transcript of experience is in fact a work of art. We read it as something that hovers precariously in a strange land – a land half way between what happened in the outer world of Jane's experience and in the inner world of her imagination.[67] In Tromly's view, then, we should read *Jane Eyre* self-consciously, aware that 'Jane' is a mask through which the artist-narrator plays out her highly subjective construction of events. □

Jane and Rochester as Competing Storytellers

Carol Bock explores the performative, self-inventing quality of Brontë's narrators from a different angle in *Charlotte Brontë and the Storyteller's Audience* (1992). Bock notes that when, aged thirteen, Charlotte Brontë gave the first written account of the literary productions that she and her brother and sisters had created as children at Haworth, she referred to them as 'our plays'. Charlotte's stories, from the first, involved performance, an active mode of storytelling that demands that the narrator is highly conscious of her audience and of the fact that the roles of narrator and listener are dynamic and involve shifts of power. Brontë, Bock maintains, learned further about the performative qualities of narration from her childhood reading of *Blackwood's Magazine* and the novels of Sir Walter Scott (1731–1832). She brings this understanding to *Jane Eyre*, where Jane must learn to tell her own tale, judiciously managing her audience, in order to assume power over her own life story.

> ■ The motif of reading and storytelling as it is used within Jane's narra-
> tive [...] implies that the interpretive and expressive faculties requisite to
> reading and storytelling are skills by which one creates and preserves
> one's self. These skills allow one to respond to experience in a way that
> constructively validates and actualizes the self. Furthermore, Jane's nar-
> rative presents this process of self-actualization through reading and
> storytelling as political in nature: nearly all of Jane's attempts to interpret
> her experience and tell her story involve a struggle for power to assert
> her own reading against those fictions that others would narrate about
> her.[68] □

Jane's progress, as many critics have noticed, involves various significant acts of reading. She is first introduced as a child, reading Thomas
Bewick's *History of British Birds*, which her cousin John claims as his
property, then throws at her. She is thus made aware, from an early age,
of the power of narrative to control as well as to console. In her time
at Lowood she learns both to read more fluently (language and character) and to become a better teller of her own tale. When explaining
her history to Miss Temple, she considers her audience and 'arranges'

her narrative to win her audience's trust. Thornfield presents a major challenge to Jane as reader and narrator. Rochester, who through concealment stymies attempts at reading his character, assumes the role of principal storyteller. Jane becomes his audience and the object of his scrutiny – a situation in which she has little power. This dynamic is uppermost in the gypsy scene, where Rochester conceals himself but demands to 'read' Jane's palm and face and to 'tell' her character and destiny.

Jane, however, escapes from Rochester's attempts to assume control over their tale. At Moor House, she tells a version of her story so well judged that it secures her both compassion and privacy. She must still evade the storytelling power of St John Rivers, who attempts to read her into his own preferred narrative of heroic self-sacrifice. But, having left him, she is free to return to Rochester, whose interpretive power is now limited by blindness. Her triumph is to become his Scheherezade (the character in *The Arabian Nights* who saves her own life and wins over the king by telling a succession of tales whose end is forever deferred). Jane wins the contest for narrative control and the novel is the story of her learning how to determine and to relate the story of *Jane Eyre*.

Secrets and Lies: *Jane Eyre* as a Revenge Novel

Some critics have gone further. Lisa Sternlieb in 'Jane Eyre: "Hazarding Confidences"' (1999) produces one of the most daring modern readings of Jane Eyre's narrative. Unlike Tromly and Bock, who see Jane's shaping voice as essentially benign, Sternlieb argues that Jane is a habitual liar, whose treacherous narrative seduction of the reader is the culminating triumph in a series of acts of revenge that characterise her biography. In Sternlieb's account, Jane's 'carefully constructed narrative strategy is developed specifically in response to Rochester, but it is in play from the first pages of the novel'.[69] Jane, Sternlieb proposes, artfully constructs the reader as confidante, just as she constructs herself as confidante to Rochester. Rochester remarks to Jane:

■ Know, that in the course of your future life you will often find yourself elected the involuntary confidant of your acquaintances' secrets: people will instinctively find out, as I have done, that it is not your forte to talk of yourself, but to listen while others talk of themselves; they will feel, too, that you listen with no malevolent scorn of their indiscretion, but with a kind of innate sympathy [...] therefore I proceed almost as freely as if I were writing my thoughts in a diary.'[70] □

However, Rochester is about to lie to Jane, involving her in an elaborate series of deceits. Jane, says Sternlieb, parries his trick with one of her own. She poses as silent and sympathetic confidante, but will prove in fact to be a spiteful and seductive tale-teller, who beats Rochester at his own confidence game, producing 'a revenge novel, one that exposes Rochester's cruelty to Bertha, to Adèle, and especially to herself.'[71]

Whenever Jane most intimately invokes the reader, Sternlieb suggests, she is 'most invested in concealing her position as narrator from Rochester'.[72] Jane's whole narrative is deliberately constructed to present herself as a trustworthy, modest, and moderate figure. Jane consciously presents Bertha as a foil, a figure through whom she 'demonstrates a kind of revenge that does not work. Her own revenge is successful because it is everything that Bertha's is not – controlled, sustained, articulate, and, above all, disguised'.[73] Generations of readers have 'abandoned themselves to the narrator's seduction', says Sternlieb – not realising that Jane has used them as a pawn in a game of secrets and lies that both replays Rochester's treachery towards her and serves him out for it.

A Structuralist Reading: Cinderella or Christiana?

Carol Bock depicts *Jane Eyre* as a struggle between characters for control of the narrative. Another way of looking at the tension between different possible narrative outcomes in *Jane Eyre* is to think of the novel as a text in which different archetypes of story – for example the Christian story involving a sinner's progress to redemption and the Cinderella rags-to-riches fairytale – jostle for dominance. Structuralist narratology offers a model for looking at texts in this way: it looks at the basic plot and character types that allow experienced readers to understand the kind of story they are reading and to anticipate its basic structure.

Peter Allan Dale in 'Charlotte Brontë's "Tale Half-Told": the Disruption of Narrative Structure in *Jane Eyre*' (1986) argues that Brontë is highly aware of 'the structures of expectation in our lives', whether these are the patterns of our own life story or the expectations about plot and convention that we bring to reading a novel. These structures have a reassuringly predictable shape but they also imply an undesirable conformity, a movement towards closure that is deadening. She therefore sets up structures of narrative expectation in *Jane Eyre* and then persistently disrupts them. The outcome is a 'tale that is never ended' or where the ending seems to point doubtfully in more than one direction.

Dale sees two fundamental narrative structures in *Jane Eyre* 'competing with one another for the reader's attention'. The first is a religious story and the second is a romantic one. In his view, to a Victorian audience the narrative expectations associated with a story of spiritual pilgrimage would have been uppermost:

■ The fundamental narrative type defining *Jane Eyre* is that which Robert Lee Wolff identifies as the most prevalent in early Victorian fiction: the spiritual pilgrimage. The 'inside' or 'home', which from the very beginning of the novel we are conditioned to expect for Jane, is the heavenly home of true faith.[74] □

Various critics have noted the resemblance between Jane's trials and the symbolic obstacles faced by Christian/Christiana in John Bunyan's story of spiritual pilgrimage, *The Pilgrim's Progress*. Dale, however, is unusual in seeing this story as the dominant narrative type structuring our expectations in *Jane Eyre*.

There are many clues in *Jane Eyre* that the heroine has not fully embraced the tenets of Christian belief. As a child she dislikes psalms and is in open rebellion against those who warn her about hellfire. At Thornfield, her love for Rochester is expressed in deliberately idolatrous terms: 'I could not, in those days, see God for his creature'. Her flight to Moor House seems to provide, Dale suggests, a ripe opportunity for a conversion experience: a moment in which Jane is illuminated by God's glory and embraces belief. The fact that this conversion never happens and that Jane goes back to Rochester, describing their reunion in terms 'really no less blasphemous than her earlier metaphorical association of their impending sexual union with the marriage of the Lamb', is significant:

■ It seems to me that the omission of the experience of conversion is quite purposeful, that it represents a deliberate withholding of an expected satisfaction from the reader.[75] □

As many readers forget, the novel does not end with Jane's declarations of happiness in marriage, but with St John's letter from India, anticipating his death. Instead of Jane's submission to God, we are presented with St John Rivers's declaration of self-abnegating faith. Dale suggests that here the words we might expect Jane to have spoken are displaced onto another character, about whose piety we had no doubt. Here the two plot types, religious and romantic, run parallel without either producing closure. The result is, however, empowering for the reader: we are left to decide for ourselves whether Jane achieves salvation or not:

■ This leaving of the ending to the reader may strike us as an especially modern gesture, a deconstructive challenge to the proposition that we

have any right to expect or intuit any 'foregone determination' of experience. But it is more interesting [...] to see it as the artist's recognition of a
problem with a particular historical structure of expectation. The inevitability of that structure has ceased to command implicit assent, but, at the
same time, it is too much part of the artist's consciousness to be transcended. It can, through the duplicitous effects of art, be suspended, but,
as we see, this aesthetic suspension is very unstable.[76] □

Brontë, in other words, feels the pressure to produce a pious ending and
resists it, but not enough to exclude it entirely: the religious and romantic plots remain hanging in unresolved tension with each other.

Poststructuralism and After: Where Is *Jane Eyre*?

Poststructuralist accounts of *Jane Eyre* go further in suggesting that *Jane
Eyre* as a whole is characterised by incompleteness and uncertainty.
Mark M. Hennelly in '*Jane Eyre*'s Reading Lesson' (1984) argues that:

■ The plot of Jane Eyre seems [...] to plot against the reader by its dogged
and mysterious indeterminacy.[77] □

Jane Eyre, Hennelly stresses, is a novel that foregrounds the process
of reading, from its opening pages, in which we are sympathetically
drawn to the isolated figure of Jane reading behind the curtains, to the
memorable scene, after Jane's wanderings on the moor, when she looks
through the window of Moor House to see Diana and Mary Rivers
reading *Die Räuber* (*The Robbers* (1781) by the German dramatist and
poet Friedrich Schiller (1759–1805)). As Hennelly remarks, Jane is
in that instance herself unknowingly being 'read' by St John Rivers,
while she 'reads' a scene of reading from which she is excluded, but
whose text relates closely to her own situation. The reader is constantly
reminded, through such scenes of reading in the novel, of his or her
own position as reader and of the ways in which the text anticipates
being read and manipulates its readers' responses through introducing
the bridging scenario of reading, the direct invocation of the reader
['Reader, I married him'] and the deceptive narrative structure of the
twice-told tale.

■ Jane Eyre is a twice-told tale in that the reader hears two narrative versions of much of the plot: an early version which, except for Mrs. Reed's
flashback, we live through with Jane until after the suspended marriage
ceremony, only to hear parts of its retold in a series of instalments by different narrators like Mrs. Reed, Rochester, Rivers, and the Rochester Arms
innkeeper.[78] □

As Hennelly points out, these 'retellings' of episodes that Jane has described earlier in the novel – such as Rochester's own, contradictory account of the early period of their courtship – are liable continuously to revise our judgement of what happened, making us aware that *Jane Eyre* is a palimpsest, a text where writing is overlayered with later writing, exposing each layer as a provisional, rather than final, version of events. Other clues also point to the teasing self-reflexiveness of the novel. When Jane tells us, at Lowood, that she was learning the first two tenses of the French verb 'être', we may notice that it is also figuratively true that she is able, at this juncture, to construe her past and present but not her future. Jane's initials 'J.E.' are both personal to her and represent 'je', the French word for 'I': her story demands that the reader, like St John Rivers questing after Jane's true identity, turns inwards to fill in the suggestive blank that links Jane's subjectivity to his or her own. Indeed, Hennelly asserts, the reader of *Jane Eyre* has to be attentive to Jane's silences as well as to her utterances and:

■ must learn to read between the narrative lines and be especially alert for lacunae [gaps] or blanks which signal Jane's crucial moments of self-suppression. The reader is then invited to fill in these blanks and creatively predict the nature, cause, and effects of the deletion.[79] □

This situation, says Hennelly, makes for a complex reading experience. We cannot simply dismiss Jane as an 'unreliable' narrator. Rather, we are continually made aware of the impossibility of a wholly candid narrative, of the spectrum of sincerity, deliberate untruth, and unconscious evasion that can characterise a single speaker, and of our own fickle and fictive role in desiring, anticipating, and attributing meaning. *Jane Eyre*, finally, does not answer our questions; it questions our answers.

Karen Chase in 'Where is Jane Eyre?' (1984) similarly finds that Jane Eyre, despite her controlling presence in her 'autobiography', is finally impossible to pin down:

■ The novel continually offers Jane versions of herself, which she continually disowns. But this leads to a striking peculiarity: the remoteness of that very 'I' which dominates the novel, which appears so often and so prominently.[80] □

Chase suggests that, as various critics have remarked, *Jane Eyre* is populated by characters who express an aspect of Jane that she needs to reject: the stoic Helen Burns, the violent Bertha Rochester, the coldly ambitious St John Rivers. The effect of constructing her story through these allegorical negatives, however, is that her own 'substantial self' remains illusory, a fact that Rochester understands when he persistently describes her as a sprite, something immaterial, evanescent. Since the inside of Jane's self stands outside of herself, 'embodied in characters, personified in faculties, embodied in conceits', Jane's world is an expression of her. This gives her story an extraordinary organic unity, yet it also means that her 'I' represents a 'vanishing point which can never be reduced to its various manifestations'.[81] Chase asks:

■ Who, then, is Jane Eyre? Indeed, where is Jane Eyre? If she is somehow distinct from her own reason, conscience, and feeling, if she flees from characters who embody her own impulses, if her narrating and narrated selves never quite converge – then her identity must remain a lambent, impalpable thing.[82] □

Heather Glen in *Charlotte Brontë: The Imagination in History* (2002) develops this sense of *Jane Eyre*'s undecidability, arguing that the novel exists simultaneously as two different stories:

■ *Jane Eyre* tells not a single, fictionally undermined story, but two opposing and incommensurate ones. The self at the centre of each appears in a radically different way: in one, as magically omnipotent, triumphing absolutely; in the other, as insubstantial, the constantly jeopardized object of forces beyond its control [...] Those opposing configurations of triumphant omnipotence and imminent annihilation which animate her narrative remain to the end unresolved [...][83] □

Must all Readings of *Jane Eyre* be Misreadings?

Like other critics influenced by poststructuralist theory, Jerome Beaty in *Misreading Jane Eyre: A Postformalist Paradigm* (1996) emphasises the multiplicity of different 'meanings' and interpretive pathways the novel can generate. He de-familiarises the text, relating it to various lesser-known types of Victorian novel, in order to demonstrate that no single reading of *Jane Eyre* can suffice. Charlotte Brontë herself, Beaty argues, misread *Jane Eyre*. She considered her heroine similar to the heroine of another contemporary novel, *The Neighbours* (1837; trans 1842) by the Swedish novelist and travel-writer Frederika Bremer (1801–65), whose protagonist and narrator, Francesca, is a mature married woman looking back at her 'unquiet and unreasonable' youth. Brontë, it seems, may have held in her mind a vision of the mature, domesticated Jane Rochester as the authoritative figure of *Jane Eyre*. Yet, Beaty suggests, for the majority of readers it is the wild, young, impious Jane Eyre who remains the driving force of the book. Our introduction to the happily married Jane Rochester is too brief and unsatisfying to erase the compelling voice of her more rebellious younger self. The novel thus hovers between the voices of young Jane and older Jane, between an understanding of the story that emphasises struggle and one that emphasises compromise:

> ■ *Jane Eyre* the novel [...] exists both as an experience of rebellion and as a meaningful statement of reconciliation to God and society. These two voices and ideologies are in dialogue: not in dialogue with a reconcilable thesis and antithesis [...] but interactively, as if the whole novel were a single utterance hybridized, 'a mixture of two social languages within the limits of a single utterance, an encounter, within the arena of an utterance, between two different linguistic consciousnesses.'[84] □

Beaty is drawing here on Mikhail Bakhtin's idea of the dialogic text, but also on Paul de Man's concept of undecidability. In *Jane Eyre*, he suggests, wild Jane and tamed Jane can coexist as narrative possibilities, in productive and perpetual conversation. Likewise, the novel as a whole can be seen as a space in which Brontë, like her contemporary Thackeray, employs elements of multiple existing types of story and plot in order to debate them:

> ■ Charlotte Brontë was involved in the same project as her revered Thackeray. He, by deliberate parody of contemporary conventional narrative types, was trying to forge a new novel for the new Victorian, bourgeois era; she was doing so by a different kind of parody, consciously, or not, incorporating the different generic ways of telling a story [...] holding up familiar, conventional 'plots' or novel species for examination and evaluation by putting them in an 'unfamiliar light' – an intertextual, mutually altering dialogue.[85] □

In Beaty's view, modern readers of *Jane Eyre* should also creatively hold up the text in an 'unfamiliar light': to produce accounts of it that reflect our own influences and contexts; we should endeavour to 'know the text as it cannot know itself'. Any attempt to reduce the novel to a single reading is a misreading; for the novel is naturally multi-voiced, an ongoing conversation rather than a statement, changing as its readers change.

CONCLUSION

This chapter has outlined the considerable difference between the approaches that critics took to *Jane Eyre* in the early, mid-, and late twentieth century. Where early twentieth-century critics were apt to stress the expressive relationship between Charlotte Brontë and her heroine, taking *Jane Eyre* as a personal outpouring of her frustrations and fantasies, mid-century critics turned away from biography to attend to the formal construction of the text, exploring its allegorical patterns of imagery and symbolism, and examining the links between its radical syntax and unconventional heroine. Where earlier critics had seen a remarkably unity in *Jane Eyre*, shaped by its first-person narration, late twentieth-century critics uncovered indeterminacy, dialogism, and dissonance. Jane's voice no longer appeared to be uncontested, candid, and transparent in the novel: instead, critics depicted a narrator who struggled for authority, whose voice might be seen as distorted, doubtful, or disturbed, or indeed who was elusive to the point of having no substantial existence.

However, despite the changes in critical language and ideas, certain issues recur. The idea that *Jane Eyre* is a conflicted text with a double identity seems to find a new mode of expression in every critical generation. You might, for example, compare David Cecil's account of the conflict between 'passion' and 'Puritanism' in *Jane Eyre*, David Lodge's description of the opposing imagery of 'fire' and 'ice', Doreen Roberts's stylistic arguments about the struggle of 'Id' and 'Ego', Jerome Beaty's analysis of 'two voices and ideologies [...] in dialogue', and Heather Glen's identification of 'two opposing and incommensurate stories' in the novel. It is tempting to depict critical history as an ongoing movement towards increased awareness and enhanced interpretive sophistication, but that progressive view of history, which privileges modern academic readings, is as partial as any other. Each critical approach to *Jane Eyre* reflects the specific historical circumstances in which it is produced and that, of course, includes our own. Jane Eyre's 'I' may be interpreted as reliable or unreliable, sympathetic or alienating, natural or distorted, emphatically present or troublingly absent: ultimately, perhaps, her 'I' reflects that of her beholder.

Importantly, as we have seen in this survey of changing twentieth-century attitudes to *Jane Eyre*'s narrative voice, there is a long-standing schism between popular and academic readings of this novel: the former tend to embrace the story as an affirming romance with a happy end, the latter to read it as a questioning narrative of unresolved struggle. That debate blossoms in feminist criticism of *Jane Eyre*, which is the subject of the following chapter.

CHAPTER THREE

An Iconic Text: Feminist and Psychoanalytic Criticism

Jane Eyre is the story of a woman's life. Since its publication it has been a novel enjoyed by female readers (although also by male ones), many of whom have felt convinced, as Harriet Martineau reported feeling, 'that it was by some friend of my own, who had portions of my childish experience in his or her mind'.[1] Is *Jane Eyre*, then, in some important respects, the story of *every* woman's life, its trials emblematic of the difficulties that face women everywhere in their quest for self-determination and self-fulfilment? This is the assertion of many feminist critics for whom *Jane Eyre* is an iconic text expressive both of the obstacles and injustices under which women labour and the power of the female protagonist and the female author to resist, reform, and flourish in a male–dominated world.

The history of feminist readings of *Jane Eyre*, however, is not one of untroubled unanimity. One of the first critics to read *Jane Eyre* as a manifesto for a new mode of conducting male and female relationships was Margaret Oliphant (1828–97), who wrote in 1855:

■ Nobody perceived that it was the new generation nailing its colours to the mast. No one would understand that this furious love-making was but a wild declaration of the 'Rights of Woman' in a new aspect.[2] □

Oliphant rejected the 'revolution' that she saw *Jane Eyre* as inciting. The traditional narrative depiction of polite wooing and romantic concord, she insisted, had become in *Jane Eyre* and its successors a battle of the sexes, women and men jousting for dominance in relationships characterised by violence and sensation. Young women reading novels of this kind would enter courtship and marriage with unrealistic and unhealthy models of gender relations before them. Some later Victorian critics, on the contrary, felt that *Jane Eyre* was insufficiently radical in its depiction of equality between the sexes. Peter Bayne in *Two Great Englishwomen: Mrs Browning and Charlotte Brontë* (1881), considered that 'in these days of vociferous debate concerning the place of women in the social system, when perfect equality between men and women is indignantly claimed as a right, or asserted as a fact, by a thousand voices', Jane accepted various unpleasant aspects of Rochester's treatment far too meekly: 'No man could have a right to bait and badger a woman like that; and if Jane had been a little more strong and a little more proud, she would never have favoured him with another look of her face.'[3] Later critics have continued to debate whether *Jane Eyre* strikes a blow for the 'Rights of Women' or whether the story fights shy of a truly emancipatory conclusion, as Jane returns to embrace her 'master' in marriage at Ferndean. *Jane Eyre* may be a novel that speaks particularly to women and about the experience of womanhood, but is it right to call it a 'feminist' novel and, if so, in what sense?

As we saw in chapter one, arguments about *Jane Eyre* and gender expectations are present even in the earliest reviews, when Brontë's identity and sex were not yet known. Some reviewers argued that the style of the novel proved it had been written by a man. Others maintained that it was a woman's work but decidedly unfeminine. This chapter, however, begins the story of feminist criticism of *Jane Eyre* in the twentieth century, with Virginia Woolf's formative work, *A Room of One's Own* (1929) and then fast-forwards to the 1960s and 1970s, when a new generation of feminist critics, most working within academia, began to write about *Jane Eyre* as a book that, in the words of the American poet Adrienne Rich (born 1929), 'has for us now a special force'.

AN EARLY FEMINIST READING

Virginia Woolf's multifaceted exploration of the subject of 'women' and 'fiction' *A Room of One's Own*, a founding document of twentieth-century feminism, considers Charlotte Brontë among the many female authors who have helped forge a path making it possible for modern women to write. Woolf's book, first developed through lectures to students of Newnham and Girton colleges, women-only colleges at Cambridge University, asserts that women 'look back through their mothers': a feminist literature requires a feminist history. Woolf thus traces a tradition of female writers in English from the sixteenth century to the Victorian period; she is, however, at pains to show the dangers and difficulties that beset women who attempted authorship before the twentieth century. Charlotte Brontë's achievement is considerable but, in Woolf's view, it is warped by the harsh circumstances in which she lived and wrote: Brontë's personal anger distorts her authorial voice.

Reading *Jane Eyre*, Woolf is struck by a passage that has preoccupied subsequent feminist critics of the novel: it seems the most overt general statement in the novel about women's situation. Since this passage comes up repeatedly in discussion, it seems appropriate to reproduce it here. In it, Jane recalls how she used to go up on the roof of Thornfield while the housekeeper was busy in the kitchen; there she looked out at the landscape, longing 'for a power of vision which might overpass that limit; which might reach the busy world, towns, regions full of life I had heard of but never seen [...] I desired more of practical experience than I possessed; more of intercourse with my kind, of acquaintance with variety of character, than was here within my reach'. Jane then addresses the reader:

> ■ Who blames me? Many, no doubt; and I shall be called discontented. I could not help it: the restlessness was in my nature; it agitated me to pain sometimes [...] It is in vain to say human beings ought to be satisfied with tranquillity: they must have action; and they will make it if they cannot find it. Millions are condemned to a stiller doom than mine, and millions are in silent revolt against their lot. Nobody knows how many rebellions besides political rebellions ferment in the masses of life which people earth. Women are supposed to be very calm generally: but women feel just as men feel; they need exercise for their faculties, and a field for their efforts as much as their brothers do; they suffer from too rigid a restraint, too absolute a stagnation, precisely as men would suffer; and it is narrow-minded in their more privileged fellow-creatures to say that they ought to confine themselves to making puddings and knitting stockings, to playing on the piano and embroidering bags. It is thoughtless to condemn them, or laugh at them, if they seek to do more or learn more than custom has pronounced necessary for their sex. When thus alone, I not unfrequently heard Grace Poole's laugh[4] □

Woolf is disturbed by Jane's defensive address to the reader ('who blames me?') and the awkwardness of Grace Poole's laugh at this juncture. She sees it as a break in continuity that is typical of the way in which Brontë's work is marred by the intrusion of her personal resentment into her art. For Woolf, *Jane Eyre* is 'deformed' by the constraints of the social system that prevents Brontë from full and free exercise of her powers:

> ■ The woman who wrote those pages had more genius in her than Jane Austen; but if one reads them over and marks that jerk in them, that indignation, one sees that she will never get her genius expressed whole and entire. Her books will be deformed and twisted. She will write in a rage where she should write calmly. She will write foolishly where she should write wisely. She will write of herself where she should write of her characters. She is at war with her lot. How could she help but die young, cramped and thwarted?[5] □

Woolf's criticism of Brontë's apparent failure to separate self and character reflects the literary taste of the 1920s, when the 'intrusive' narrator and the confessional novelist were deeply unfashionable. Her characterisation of Charlotte Brontë, however, as a thwarted woman writer whose cramped and angry life under a repressive patriarchy led to 'twisted' fiction, struck a new and influential note. Later twentieth-century feminists from Adrienne Rich to Patricia Yaeger would argue with Woolf's analysis while building on the tradition of feminist criticism of *Jane Eyre* that Woolf established.

JANE EYRE AS A FEMINIST TEXT IN THE 1960S

By 1966, Robert Martin in *The Accents of Persuasion: Charlotte Brontë's Novels* could claim that *Jane Eyre* 'is frequently cited as the earliest major feminist novel'. The rest of his sentence, however, reveals his own sense that it is *not* a feminist work and that its attitude towards the social role of women has been misconstrued:

■ The novel is frequently cited as the earliest major feminist novel, although there is not a hint in the book of any desire for political, legal, educational, or even intellectual equality between the sexes. Miss Brontë asks only for the simple – or is it the most complex? – recognition that the same heart and the same spirit animate both men and women, and that love is the pairing of equals in these spheres.[6] □

In Martin's view, *Jane Eyre* is 'at bottom [...] largely a religious novel, concerned with the meaning of religion to man and its relevance to his behaviour'.[7] Jane Eyre's famous plea that women ought not to be confined to making pudding and knitting stockings:

■ is not propaganda for equal employment but for a recognition of woman's emotional nature. The condemnation of women to a place apart results in the creation of empty, capricious women like Blanche Ingram, who tyrannize over men whenever possible [...] and can communicate only in the Byronic language of outdated romantic fiction.[8] □

Other critics published in the same year took a more positive, but still cautious, approach to the notion that *Jane Eyre* is a feminist novel. Q.D. Leavis, in her Penguin introduction to *Jane Eyre,* defined the novel's theme as 'how a woman comes to maturity in the world of the writer's youth'[9] and asserted that 'part of the undertaking involved examining the assumptions that the age made with regard to women, to the relations between the sexes and between the young and those in authority'. Inga-Stina Ewbank (1932–2004) in *Their Proper Sphere: A Study of the Brontë Sisters as Early Victorian Female Novelists* carefully pointed out in its introduction that:

■ This is not a book about feminism, in the commonly accepted sense of the word. None of the Brontë sisters has left a mark on the history of female emancipation, in the same ways that such of their contemporaries as Harriet Martineau and Frances Power Cobbe [1822–1904] did. The movement for Women's Rights was slowly beginning to gather force in the 1840s, but it received little support from the Haworth parsonage. And yet the art of the Brontës was in the deepest sense feminist. In his *Victorian England* [1936] G.M. Young [1882–1959] maintains that the fundamental issue of feminism, though 'often obscured by agitation for subordinate ends – the right to vote, to graduate, to dispose of her own property after marriage', was the entry of woman 'into the sexless sphere of disinterested intelligence, and ... of autonomous personality'. In this sense each of the Brontës is a feminist rejecting a collective classification as a 'female novelist', claiming an autonomous personality as a writer.[10] □

Ewbank notes Charlotte Brontë's interest in contemporary articles about 'the woman question' and the fact that in a letter of May 1848 Charlotte writes 'I often wish to say something about the "condition of women"'.[11] She also notes, however, that Brontë seemed chiefly interested in the professional opportunities available to unmarried women (she assumed married women were fully occupied) and that her ultimate position in the letter is resigned: the oversupply of men seeking professions leaves no opening for women to enter them. Brontë, then, was not a campaigner for women's rights. She does, however, in Ewbank's opinion, use her art to explore the 'emotional and intellectual needs of a woman', and 'independence [...] is a keynote in her thinking about her own life and the life of all unmarried women. It is also a central theme of all her novels'. Jane Eyre, unlike the female characters in Charlotte's Angrian tales, is 'an *individual* whose key-line is: "I care for myself"'.[12]

In the dialogue between Rochester and Jane Eyre, Ewbank argues, Brontë achieves something new both for her own writing and the English novel. Their agonistic yet mutually attractive banter explores the 'love-and-power game' in heterosexual relations. Jane likes to call Rochester 'master', but he also admits, 'you please me, and you master me'. In their struggle towards union, the idea of equality links and resolves various aspects of the plot:

■ In *Jane Eyre* [...] the love story, the woman question and the governess (social) problem coalesce. Jane initially wins the love of Rochester through her own fearless sense of equality [...] Her spirited assertion of equality is an essential step in the great love-scene in Chapter XXIII – 'You glowed in the cool moonlight last night, when you mutinied against fate, and claimed your rank as my equal', Rochester says.[13] □

The reciprocal teaching situation, where the man is master/teacher, but the woman he loves is also mistress/teacher, is, says Ewbank, one of Brontë's favourite devices, appearing in *Jane Eyre* as in her other novels.

This situation both 'obliterates conventional social superiority' and is 'an image of the ideal man-woman relationship'.[14]

Ultimately, however, for Ewbank it is the fact of Charlotte's self-appointed writing career and the nature of her attitude to authorship, rather than the narratives themselves, which constitutes her main feminist contribution. As an author, she is neither male nor female: as Charlotte responds to critics who judge her work appropriate if written by a man, but not if written by a woman: 'to you I am neither Man nor Woman – I come before you as an Author only – it is the sole standard by which you have a right to judge me – the sole ground on which I accept your judgement.'[15] This boldly asserted freedom, in writing, from the constraints and assumptions surrounding gender is the true form of Brontë's emancipation.

'IT HAS FOR US NOW A SPECIAL FORCE': *JANE EYRE* AND 1970S FEMINISM

Feminist literary criticism blossomed in the 1970s, in the wake of 'second-wave' feminism, a term given to the emergence of women's rights movements in the United States and Europe during the Civil Rights campaigns of the 1960s. Feminist writers of this period not only voiced demands for equal rights but also undertook a wide-ranging examination of patriarchal power structures dominating all areas of life, including religious narratives, sexual mores, political and corporate structures, academia, and the literary canon. Within universities, many feminists pressed for the recognition of a female counter-tradition in the novel that had been obscured by masculine emphasis on a 'Great Tradition' of male authorship. *Jane Eyre* became an iconic text for the new wave of feminist criticism. In particular, Sandra Gilbert and Susan Gubar's famous identification of Bertha Mason as Jane Eyre's angry double gave the title to their influential book, *The Madwoman in the Attic: The Woman Writer and the Nineteenth-Century Literary Imagination* (1979). Their reading of the conflict between 'good' Jane and 'bad' Bertha as symptomatic of the psychic split Victorian women writers use to dramatise the conflict between their socialised and rebellious selves put *Jane Eyre* at the forefront of feminist critical discussion.

One of the first books to express the new tone of urgency and outrage at the systemic abuse of power that perpetuated women's denigration was *Sexual Politics* (1969) by Kate Millett (born 1934), which anchored reflections on literature in hard-hitting analysis of the historical, social, and economic contexts of patriarchy. Millett complained that:

■ Literary criticism of the Brontës has been a long game of masculine prejudice wherein the player either proves they can't write and are hopeless

> primitives, whereupon the critic sets himself up like a schoolmaster to edit their stuff and point out where they went wrong, or converts them into case histories from the wilds, occasionally prefacing his moves with a few pseudo-sympathetic remarks about the windy house on the moors, or old maidhood, following with an attack on every truth the novels contain, waged by anxious pedants who fear Charlotte might 'castrate' them or Emily 'unman' them with her passion.[16] □

Charlotte Brontë, Millett argues, responds 'deviously' to the public and private censorship exerted by male-dominated society, pretending to compromise and appeasing convention by concluding her novels with marriages. But her critique of the typologies (beautiful/plain; virgin/whore) through which men seek to depict and construct women is apparent in her novels. She responds to 'division in the culture' by 'splitting her people in half'.[17] Millett is mainly talking here about the divided personality of Lucy Snowe, heroine of *Villette*, but her remarks are also pertinent to *Jane Eyre*, in which, later feminist critics would suggest, Jane and Bertha represent different but linked aspects of the female psyche.

Millett's book both inspired and irritated other feminist literary critics. Patricia Meyer Spacks (born 1929) in *The Female Imagination: A Literary and Psychological Investigation of Women's Writing* (1972) took issue with what she saw as Millett's overwhelmingly negative account of the lot of Victorian women writers: 'the Victorian woman, it is now fashionable to assume, inhabited a dungeon of hypocrisy and repression'.[18] Spacks suggests that Brontë, like other female novelists of her period assumed an essential difference between masculine and feminine nature and complained more about what women were prevented from doing than what they were prevented from being. Jane Eyre manifests strength in 'displaying her weakness' and can manipulate Rochester without losing 'her sense of her own deep submissiveness and dependency'.[19] Future feminists would continue to argue about whether *Jane Eyre* subverted or supported conventional gender typology. The mood of feminist criticism, however, swung away from Millett's emphasis on patriarchal abuses towards a re-appreciation of the achievements of Brontë and other pioneer women writers.

A Nourishing Tale: *Jane Eyre*'s Multiple Mothers

Adrienne Rich in 'Jane Eyre: The Temptations of a Motherless Woman' (1973) set the tone for a new celebration of *Jane Eyre* as a touchstone of women's literature when she contrasted it with other nineteenth-century novels which had often been ranked above it: Jane Austen's *Persuasion* (1818), George Eliot's *Middlemarch* (1871–72), *Jude the Obscure*

(1895) by Thomas Hardy (1840–1928), *Madame Bovary* (1857) by Gustave Flaubert (1821–80), Leo Tolstoy's *Anna Karenina* (1873–77) and Henry James's *The Portrait of a Lady* (1881):

> ■ Like Thackeray's daughters, I read *Jane Eyre* in childhood, carried away 'as by a whirlwind'. Returning to Charlotte Brontë's most famous novel, as I did over and over in adolescence, in my twenties, thirties, now in my forties, I have never lost the sense that it contains, through and beyond the force of its creator's imagination, some nourishment I needed then and still need today. Other novels often ranked greater, such as *Persuasion, Middlemarch, Jude the Obscure, Madame Bovary, Anna Karenina, The Portrait of a Lady*—all offered their contradictory and compelling versions of what it meant to be born a woman. But *Jane Eyre* has for us now a special force and survival value.[20] □

The reason that *Jane Eyre* has a 'force' more powerful than the technical accomplishments of other Victorian novels, is that it is not a novel like those of Leo Tolstoy or Thomas Hardy: it is a 'tale'. A tale, says Rich, is not primarily concerned with the workings of society or the workings of the psyche. It operates in a field 'between the realm of the given, that which is changeable by human activity, and the realm of the fated, that which lies outside human control'.[21] When a novelist writes a tale, she is moved by 'that vibration of experience which underlies the social and political, though it constantly feeds into both of these'. Virginia Woolf, then, was wrong to see *Jane Eyre* as deformed by the limitations of its first-person consciousness. And Q.D. Leavis was wrong to see Jane Eyre as a female *Bildungsroman* – a novel about the evolution of the individual through education. Rather, it is a novel that speaks to women at the deepest level about a woman who, through numerous trials, remains 'unalterably herself'. Importantly, those who sustain her are other women. One of the book's gifts is its presentation of women not merely as rivals but in 'real and supportive relationship' to one another:

> ■ Jane Eyre, motherless and economically powerless, undergoes certain traditional female temptations, and finds that each temptation presents itself along with an alternative—the image of a nurturing or principled or spirited woman on whom she can model herself, or to whom she can look for support.[22] □

All women are 'motherless children' in a patriarchal society, Rich posits, since they are kept in a dependent position, denied the inheritance of power and unable to pass on wealth, except to men. Jane's temptations are thus emblematic of those faced by women under patriarchy. Jane faces her first ordeal in the house of her Aunt Reed, where both psychic and physical violence are used to punish her spirited individuality. Her temptation is to respond by becoming a passive victim or a self-destructive runaway: in this crisis, the counsel of Bessie the servant that she shouldn't 'act afraid' helps her to maintain her courage. At Lowood, Jane voices her desperate need for love in terms of self-harm: to gain affection from someone she loves, Jane declares, she would submit to have a bone broken or let a horse dash its hoof at her chest. However, through Helen Burns and her teacher, Maria Temple, who give her a sense of ethical choice and of her own worth, she learns to reject this second female temptation of masochism. At Thornfield, Jane faces 'the central temptation of the female condition—the temptation of romantic love and surrender', but here again women help her: Mrs Fairfax the housekeeper, but, Rich suggests, also Bertha Rochester, who 'comes between Jane and a marriage that was not yet ripe', warning her by tearing her wedding veil, but, significantly, not harming her. To this point, Jane has relied on individual women for help. After the interrupted wedding, Jane calls on the 'Great Mother of the night sky' – the archetypal female goddess – and is told to 'flee temptation'. She does and is led to the house of Diana and Mary Rivers, whom, Rich points out, respectively bear the names of the pagan and Christian Great Goddess: Diana the virgin huntress and Mary the virgin mother. There Jane enjoys the intellectual and loving companionship of other women. She passes through a final trial, rejecting a loveless marriage presented as a duty by St John: a representative of the patriarchal 'high master spirit'. Instead she is called back to Rochester and to marriage, but 'marriage radically understood for its period, in no sense merely a solution or a goal'.[23]

Critics such as Richard Chase in 'The Brontës; or Myth Domesticated' (1948) had been apt to read Rochester's blinding as a symbolic form of castration that allows Jane to gain mastery over him.[24] Rich rejects this interpretation: for her St John is the emotional eunuch. Rather, in Rich's view, Jane and Rochester's marriage is an equal union in which Jane Eyre, finally, can participate without losing anything of her self, so fiercely guarded and maintained in the face of all temptations:

■ The wind that blows through this novel is the wind of sexual equality—spiritual and practical [...] Coming to her husband in economic independence and by her free choice, Jane can become a wife without sacrificing a grain of her Jane Eyre-ity. Charlotte Brontë sets up the possibility of this relationship in the early passages of the Thornfield episode: the verbal sparring of this couple who refuse to act out the paradigms of romantic, Gothic fiction. We believe in the erotic and intellectual sympathy of this marriage because it has been prepared by the woman's refusal to accept it under circumstances which were mythic, romantic, or sexually oppressive.[25] □

Jane's Marriage: A Mutilated Union?

Helene Moglen in *Charlotte Brontë: The Self Conceived* (1976) also lays emphasis on the importance of Jane's 'self', which is constantly under threat from social and psychic pressures. Moglen, however, presents Jane's progress somewhat differently. In her reading, at each stage of her journey towards integrated selfhood, Jane must learn to separate herself from another individual. Each time this happens, it seems at first as if the separation represents a loss and Jane's self is wounded, but in each case her self, apparently divided, has become stronger than before. Thus Bessie, Helen Burns, and Maria Temple, in Moglen's reading are not surrogate mothers but models of womanhood that Jane must absorb and then reject in order for her own selfhood to emerge strong and whole. The last of the figures from whom she must separate herself are Rochester and St John; leaving the latter 'marks the ultimate resolution of her spiritual and sexual being'.

Moglen calls her chapter on *Jane Eyre* 'Jane Eyre: The Creation of a Feminist Myth' and she sees the marriage of Jane and Rochester as a 'naïve resolution', an idealised dream of equality in marriage that did not exist in Brontë's world and barely exists in the 1970s. Its precondition is Rochester's mutilation, which is 'in terms of this nascent feminist myth, the necessary counterpart of Jane's independence: the terrible condition of a relationship of equality'. Moglen continues:

■ But what, in fact, is the nature of this 'equality?' Jane's flight from the orgasmic knowledge of St. John's sexual power and Rochester's last catastrophic struggle with his vampire-bride [Bertha] are not the bases of a mature sexuality which is an extension of social liberation. They are rather preludes to the desexualization which is the unhappy compromise necessary when psychosexual need is unsupported by social reality or political self-consciousness [...] Jane's sense of Rochester, as she looks at him on the morning after her return, is crucial [...] He is devitalized; the fire of his passion burnt to ash; the quick of his nature paralyzed. He is not the bereaved lover, expectantly awaiting his mistress's return. His is a comatose soul, unable to cry out for rebirth. It is not a lover he requires, but a mother who can offer him again the gift of life. And it is this function which Jane will gratefully assume.[26] □

Maurianne Adams in '*Jane Eyre*: Women's Estate' (1977) is also unconvinced that Jane's marriage to Rochester is a triumph: to her it looks more like a compromise. Adams points out the 'forested-in, stagnant, and physically oppressive atmosphere at Ferndean' (which Rochester deemed too unhealthy a residence for Bertha). Its darkened and confined setting, she argues, 'indicates the price exacted by domestic romance, the impossibility of reconciling Jane's desperate need to be loved, to be useful, with her less urgent venturesomeness and independent curiosity'.[27] In Adams's account of *Jane Eyre*, Jane's story explores the competing and perhaps irreconcilable needs, emblematic of those of all women, for perpetual autonomy ('to be somebody in her own right, a woman of achievement and integrity, with an outlet in the world for her passions and her energies') and perpetual love.

Like Rich and Moglen, Adams is attentive to the symbolic and allegorical aspects of *Jane Eyre*. She discusses the way in which interiors and exteriors in the novel image Jane's psychic life. When Jane is oppressed by the social and domestic conditions that affirm her dependence, she withdraws into psychic concealment and estrangement. However, when she is outside, her spirit roams freely and she is able to express her independence. It is significant, Adams suggests, that Jane meets both Helen Burns and Rochester outdoors, in an environment that expresses her spiritual and intellectual freedom. Interestingly, Adams also considers the supernatural imagery associated with Jane and Rochester's courtship (she identifies him with the Gytrash, he calls her his 'fairy', 'elf', and 'sprite') a way of expressing their spiritual equality. Outside the house they relate to one another in spirit, as spirit beings; inside the house, they are bound by the physical confinements of class difference. This combination of fairytale motifs and domestic realism is, says Adams, typical of 'the "both/and" manner Jane's narrative has of pursuing a personal and economic dilemma simultaneously, using the psychic mode of fantasy interchangeably with the social mode of realism'.[28]

Helene Moglen traces, in *Jane Eyre*, Charlotte Brontë's 'coming of age' as a writer and as a feminist; for Adrienne Rich, Jane's speech about women feeling just as men feel is a 'feminist manifesto'. Maurianne Adams is more sceptical, finding 'Jane's feminism [...] ambivalent at best'.[29] In Adams' view, Rochester's entrance just after Jane's 'women feel just as men feel' speech answers Jane's voiced desire for wider horizons 'in terms of offering a domestic and romantic rather than autonomous and independent field for activity':

■ What seems to me most significant about her extended psychic explosion on Thornfield's battlements is not so much the fact of its existence within a novel that takes autonomy and action in the real world as at least one of its themes, but rather the various subterfuges by which it is quickly undermined.[30] □

Like Virginia Woolf, Adams is disturbed by the recurrent apologies that attend Jane's feminist outburst. Bertha's laughter at this juncture, in her view, also undercuts 'feminist outrage' as she 'characterizes the dangers of ungovernable passion and rage [...] She is like Jane in the Red Room, a hidden and ostracized figure, locked into solitary confinement and thereby presenting a monstrous equivalent to Jane's "deep ire and desperate revolt"'.[31]

Bertha as Jane's Alter Ego

Adrienne Rich, Helene Moglen and Maurianne Adams all identify Bertha as in some sense Jane's 'alter ego' – her 'other self' or textual double. As we have seen, Rich characterizes her as one of many mother figures who help Jane avoid temptations that would destroy her emergent selfhood, Moglen regards her as expressing a repressed, negative component of Jane's attitude towards her own sexuality, Adams takes her as a warning against the dangers of uncontrolled female passion and anger. The two most famous feminist readings of Bertha as part of Jane, however, are those of Elaine Showalter (born 1941) in *A Literature of their Own: British Women Novelists from Brontë to Lessing* (1978) and Sandra Gilbert and Susan Gubar in *The Madwoman in the Attic: The Woman Writer and the Nineteenth-Century Literary Imagination* (1979). Both of these landmark feminist studies develop ideas that relate Charlotte Brontë's work to that of other nineteenth-century woman writers and identify trends in the way that those writers deal with patriarchal pressures.

Elaine Showalter argues that there are three evolutionary stages in the development of a female literary tradition in the English novel from the Brontës to the present: the *Feminine* phase from the 'appearance of the male pseudonym in the 1840s to the death of George Eliot in 1880'; the *Feminist* phase from 1880 to 1920, or women winning the vote; and the *Female* phase from 1920 onwards, but entering a new stage of self-awareness around 1960.[32] As women move towards greater socio-political freedom, they are increasingly able to express themselves openly; in the earlier phases, self-assertion and rebellion must often be presented through encrypting devices such as symbol and metaphor. Charlotte Brontë, then, like George Eliot is a 'Feminine' novelist: a pioneer professional authoress who negotiates repression by finding covert ways to dramatize the inner life:

■ In *Jane Eyre*, Brontë attempts to depict a complete female identity, and she expresses her heroine's consciousness through an extraordinary range of narrative devices. Psychological development and the dramas of the inner life are represented in dreams, hallucinations, visions, surrealistic paintings, and masquerades; the sexual experiences of the female body are expressed spatially through elaborate and rhythmically recurring images of rooms and houses. Jane's growth is further structured through a pattern of literary, biblical, and mythological allusion. Brontë's most profound innovation, however, is the division of the Victorian female psyche into its extreme components of mind and body, which she externalizes as two characters, Helen Burns and Bertha Mason.[33] ☐

Helen and Bertha both function at a realist level in the story and are archetypes, respectively representing mind and body, expressing the dualism at the heart of the Victorian woman's experience of selfhood. Both Helen, the 'angel' of spirituality, and Bertha, the 'devil' of fleshliness, must be destroyed before Jane can emerge as an integrated individual.

Showalter associates Jane's experience in the Red Room, 'a paradigm of female inner space', with the onset of puberty and the menarche – the first occurrence of menstruation. Although she is only ten when it occurs, Jane's 'emotional menarche' is an experience of rebellion depicted in 'a strain of intense female sexual fantasy and eroticism'[34] that runs through the first four chapters of *Jane Eyre*, which, in Showalter's reading, recalls Victorian pornographic fantasies of restraint and flagellation. Jane is thus symbolically being punished for the crime of growing up and beginning to assume adult sexual desires. Her unruly flesh is subdued at Lowood, which 'represents sexual diminishment and repression'.[35] The 'animal' aspects of female sexuality, so sternly repressed at Lowood, however, reassert themselves at Thornfield in the person of Bertha Mason, who 'is the incarnation of female sexuality in its most irredeemably bestial and terrifying form'.[36] Bertha is a 'vampyre' and a 'hag': both mythical creatures associated with sucking the vital juices from men against their will. She suffers from 'moral insanity', a condition in Victorian psychology associated less with deranged reason than with perverse appetite. The periodicity of Bertha's attacks is similar to that of the menstrual cycle, widely considered at the time an index of women's sexual urges. Physically, she is large, florid, and violent. Bertha, then, embodies intemperate female sexual passion, an aspect of Jane's psyche that must be exorcised before she can become her 'own mistress' and achieve a safe union with Rochester. Like Moglen and Adams, Showalter deems the marriage between Jane and Rochester a compromise dependent on sacrifice:

■ Jane's marriage to Rochester is essentially a union of equals, but in feminine fiction men and women become equals by submitting to mutual limitation, not by allowing each other mutual growth.[37] ☐

But she sees in Brontë's dramatisation of the conflict between passion and repression a powerful symbolic language of female sexuality that has its parallel in George Eliot's *The Mill on the Floss* (1860), where the heroine, Maggie Tulliver, meets Philip Wakem in the 'Red Deeps', a space in which dread and desire mingle.

Sandra Gilbert and Susan Gubar in *The Madwoman in the Attic: The Woman Writer and the Nineteenth-Century Literary Imagination* (1979) also consider Bertha to represent one side of a Victorian female psyche, split by social demands and taboos that produce a 'double self'. In their interpretation, however, Bertha is the essence of female anger and rebellion, a *political* rather than a carnal figure, repressed in all nineteenth-century women writers, who can only let her loose on the textual margins, voicing their unspeakable rage against patriarchal oppression. As they argue:

■ [*Jane Eyre*] providing a pattern for countless others, is [...] a story of enclosure and escape, a distinctively female *Bildungsroman* in which the problems encountered by the protagonist as she struggles from the imprisonment of her childhood towards an almost unthinkable goal of mature freedom are symptomatic of difficulties Everywoman in a patriarchal society must meet and overcome: oppression (at Gateshead), starvation (at Lowood), madness (at Thornfield), and coldness (at Marsh End). Most important, her confrontation, not with Rochester but with Rochester's mad wife Bertha, is the book's central confrontation, an encounter [...] not with her own sexuality but with her own imprisoned 'hunger, rebellion, and rage', a secret dialogue of self and soul on whose outcome [...] the novel's plot, Rochester's fate, and Jane's coming-of-age all depend.[38] □

For Gilbert and Gubar, Jane's incarceration in the Red Room and the 'fit' she has there in which she is 'out of herself' constitute a 'paradigm [model] of the larger drama that occupies the entire book'.[39] Jane's anomalous position outwith social norms, her forced enclosure, and her escape through flight, starvation, and 'madness', are recalled at various crucial moments in the plot: when Mr Brocklehurst torments her at Lowood and, after her abortive wedding, when she resolves to flee Rochester. When Jane encounters 'Grace Poole's' laugh at Thornfield, we should thus be attuned to the fact that the dangerous hysteria of the madwoman in the attic is an aspect of Jane's own psychic life.

Signs of the links between Jane and Bertha appear in the words that are used to describe them both: when she is a rebellious, angry, and violent child Jane is a 'bad animal', a 'fiend' – words later used for Bertha. Jane is otherworldly, an 'elf' and 'sprite'; Bertha too is associated with the supernatural, the goblin and vampire, with her spectral appearance and uncanny laughter. Like many psychological manifestations of self, Bertha appears in Jane's sleep. She sets fire to Rochester's bedclothes: an ambiguous act that suggests both sexual desire and anger against male sexuality. Similarly, when Bertha appears in the mirror dressed in Jane's bridal veil on the night before her wedding and rends the veil in two, she embodies Jane's anxieties about losing her self in marriage and marriage's propensity to turn into the prison for women – Bridewell – that is imaged in an earlier game of charades. The many games and tricks that Rochester plays with Jane, Gilbert and Gubar argue, highlight his possession of the ultimate secret: of male sexual knowledge and woman's unequal power.

Gilbert and Gubar also investigate the space within the house – often in Freudian analysis a symbol for the body – that Jane and Bertha share. Thornfield's third storey, in their view, becomes the focal point where Jane and Bertha coalesce. This is, of course, the location in the novel of Jane's famous declaration to the reader of her desire for action and her 'women feel just as men feel' speech, which is followed by mocking laughter. Virgina Woolf regarded this sudden laughter as an unfortunate interruption. Gilbert and Gubar contend that it is an essential clue to the identity between Jane and Bertha: the laugh is the voice of Jane's submerged angry self, which lurks behind the bars of social restraint, seeking escape, revenge, and destruction. Indeed, Gilbert and Gubar suggest, many women writers create a monstrous figure such as Bertha, who can express their own sense of self-division under an oppressive patriarchy:

> ■ By projecting their rebellious impulses not into their heroines but into mad or monstrous women [...] female authors dramatize their own self-division, their desire both to accept the strictures of patriarchal society and to reject them [...] the madwoman in literature by women is not merely, as she might be in male literature, an antagonist or foil to the heroine. Rather, she is usually in some sense the *author's* double, an image of her own anxiety and rage. Indeed, much of the poetry and fiction written by women conjures up this mad creature so that female authors can come to terms with their own uniquely female feelings of fragmentation, their own keen sense of the discrepancies between what they are and what they are supposed to be.[40] □

Unlike Showalter, Gilbert and Gubar see Helen Burns as another figure of repressed female rage: a passion evident in her name and in her defiantly disorderly personal effects. Unable to find an outlet for her inner fire, she dies a victim of 'consumption'. The fate of the Victorian woman who, like Helen, cannot express her anger or, like Bertha, cannot contain it, is erasure from the text.

In all the above readings, Bertha Mason Rochester is a sympathetic figure. Feminist accounts often view the real obstacle to Jane's initial union with Rochester as an imbalance of power between them, which Jane rightly perceives as threatening her identity. Bertha is a symbol or a symptom of the repressed violence that haunts relations between men and women rather than herself an agent of terror. Feminist critics of the

1970s comment on the ways in which later women novelists re-imagine the figure of Bertha in a more positive light. Jean Rhys (1894–1979) in *Wide Sargasso Sea* (1966) makes Antoinette (renamed Bertha by her husband) the heroine of a Caribbean prequel to *Jane Eyre*, presented from Bertha's point of view, in which it is evident that her 'madness' is brought on by the abuses she suffers. Doris Lessing (born 1919) in *The Four-Gated City* (1969) tells the story of a housekeeper who falls in love with her employer, who has a mad wife in the basement: at the end, the heroine liberates the wife and the two women leave and take an apartment together. Such feminist re-writings of *Jane Eyre* express the sense that Bertha deserves rescue: she is not Jane's rival, but her suppressed shadow self.

MIRRORS AND DREAMS: FEMINISM AND PSYCHOANALYTIC CRITICISM OF *JANE EYRE*

Jane Eyre is a richly symbolic text, full of images, buildings, landscapes, characters, and events that can be interpreted as outward manifestations of the mind's inner life. All of the feminist readings from the 1970s that we have so far considered are attuned to this quality of the novel. Indeed, critics such as Adrienne Rich and Angela Carter locate the power of the book at a level of 'allegory' or 'tale' that is not confined by the narrow dictates of realism, but speaks to deeper, unconscious needs in its audience. As Carter remarks in her Introduction to the Virago edition, *Jane Eyre*:

■ fuses elements of two ancient fairy tales, *Bluebeard*, specifically referred to in the text when Thornfield Hall is compared to Bluebeard's castle, and *Beauty and the Beast*, plus a titillating hint of *Cinderella*. The archaic sub-literary forms of romance and fairy tale are so close to dreaming they lend themselves readily to psychoanalytic interpretation. Episodes such as that in which Rochester's mad wife rips apart the veil he has bought Jane to wear at his second, bigamous wedding have the delirium of Freudian dream language. As a result, *Jane Eyre* is a peculiarly unsettling blend of penetrating psychological realism, of violent and intuitive feminism, of a surprisingly firm sociological grasp, and of the utterly non-realistic apparatus of psycho-sexual fantasy — irresistible passion, madness, violent death, dream, telepathic communication.[41] □

Since the techniques of psychoanalysis involve deciphering repressed unconscious wishes, typically through reading a person's fantasies, processes of association, and dreams, they have been useful to various critics of *Jane Eyre*, who uncover in the text 'repressed' ideas, associations, and wishes that find an outlet through symbol, archetypal figure (such as 'the witch' and 'the virgin'), and story. There is a strong relationship between psychoanalytic and feminist readings of this text.

Gilbert and Gubar, among others, use Freudian theory to discuss symbol and dream in *Jane Eyre*. They comment, for example, on the phallic imagery of pillars that Brontë uses to describe the Reverend Brocklehurst, director of Lowood School, and St John Rivers, who are both associated with the 'superego': that part of the self, in Freudian terminology, that polices and inhibits our desires, imposing moral restrictions and insisting we strive toward perfection.[42] Such imagery symbolically unites in the novel the threat of overbearing masculinity and of psychic control. Gilbert and Gubar analyse Jane's dreams, in one of which she imagines walking among the ruins of Thornfield, carrying an 'unknown little child', who haunts her sleep. The child, they theorise, represents Jane's self, which is threatened with dissolution in the run-up to her abortive wedding. The fact that Jane dreams of Thornfield in ruins is both prophetic and may, in some sense, be an expression of her subconscious wish: a wish that Bertha, her repressed double, enacts.

Later feminist critics make more extensive use of the ideas of Jacques Lacan (1901–81), Hélène Cixous (born 1937), Luce Irigaray (born 1932), and Julia Kristeva (born 1941), French theorists who in different ways challenge Freud's views, while expanding the horizons of psychoanalytic theory as applied to literature. Lacan is interested in the 'pre-oedipal' period of a child's infancy, when it does not yet distinguish its own body and self from those of its mother or have any concept of sexual difference. In Kristeva's view, this pre-oedipal period of 'presymbolic' communication before the child enters the 'symbolic' order of language is the source of the primal 'music' in poetry and prose. The presymbolic is connected to the female body and to a form of communication in which there is no distinction between 'subject' and 'object', no male-centred hierarchy in which woman is objectified. Language, by contrast, is a dangerous space for women: entry into its symbolic order involves writing and speaking oneself within a patriarchal system in which woman is defined in male terms. In the patriarchal order, woman is associated with the body, the literal, that which receives, while man is associated with the mind, the figurative, that which creates. The two accounts of *Jane Eyre* addressed below examine Charlotte Brontë's resistance to the 'symbolic order' of patriarchal language.

Margaret Homans in *Bearing the Word: Language and Female Experience in Nineteenth-Century Women's Writing* (1986) argues that Charlotte Brontë, like her sister Emily, is attracted to presymbolic communication, of the kind that Catherine Earnshaw in *Wuthering Heights*, perpetually childlike, has with the moorland that mothers her, and that Jane Eyre has with the Great Mother, on whose 'breast' (the moorland) she rests when fleeing Thornfield. Charlotte, Homans suggests, is however highly aware of the ambivalent gesture involved in identifying 'Mother' with 'Nature': in a sense this plays into the patriarchal symbolic scheme in which woman is associated with the 'literal', and the body. Thus, her use of images of Mother Nature and childbearing generally in *Jane Eyre* is fraught with tension. Jane's night in the embrace of Mother Nature nearly kills her. And Jane's recurrent dreams of children express a fear that runs throughout the novel, of women becoming literalised into objects:

> ■ *Jane Eyre* presents the fear of the objectification of the self in a variety of ways that make particularly explicit the connection between femininity and objectification. Jane fears that Rochester objectifies her when he wants to dress her in jewels and silks that correspond, not to her individual character, but to his abstract idea of Mrs. Edward Fairfax Rochester. Like Cathy shocked by the alienness of her mirror image, Jane is shocked twice by what she sees in the mirror, in the red room when 'the strange little figure there gazing at [her] had the effect of a real spirit,' and again on the morning of her wedding, when the mirror's 'robed and veiled figure, so unlike [her] usual self that it seemed almost the image of a stranger' represents both the appeal and the threat of having her subjectivity replaced by a beautiful object.[43] □

It is only reasonable, Homans argues, that in the nineteenth century women should perceive marriage and childbirth as threatening: many women died in giving birth and female identity was challenged by the change of name and loss of property rights that attended marriage, the erasure of legal right to inheritance that accompanied the birth of a male heir. But in *Jane Eyre*, the dream of children, which Bessie the servant has warned Jane betokens 'trouble', is also a figure for the loss of female subjectivity, as the self fractures and becomes an object beyond the woman's control: 'childbirth enters the figurative structure of the novel as a way of describing the danger that the self will become something other than itself'.[44] It is significant that these dreams of children surround Jane's love affair and engagement at Thornfield: when Jane fears that Rochester will marry Blanche Ingram, she strangles 'a new-born agony – a deformed thing I could not persuade myself to own and rear'; when she returns to Mrs Reed's deathbed, she finds that her aunt has been dreaming of her as a 'sickly, whining, pining' baby; when she surveys her trunks before the wedding, Jane refuses to put the name 'Mrs Rochester' on them because 'she would not be born till to-morrow [...] and I would wait to be assured she had come into the world alive'. These dreams directly precede Jane's ultimate struggle with the force of objectification, her exposure on the moor, during which she is tempted to 'decay quietly' into the 'fatally

literal' object world. She survives, however, by retaining her capacity
for subjective figuration: she sees a light and interprets it multiply as
an 'ignis fatuus' (will o' the wisp), a distant bonfire, or a candle in a
window. Pursuing the light and reading it as her 'guiding star', she
asserts her subjective agency and ensures her continued existence as a
subject. In Homans's view, this ending is a revisionist commentary on
Emily's ending to *Wuthering Heights*, where Catherine Earnshaw dies
in childbirth. In Charlotte Brontë's novel, both author and heroine
choose to work within the patriarchal symbolic order, but both do so
self-consciously and sceptically.

Patricia Yaeger, in *Honey-Mad Women: Emancipatory Strategies in
Women's Writing* (1988) focuses on Charlotte Brontë's use of French
in *Jane Eyre* as, for both author and heroine, a way of challenging the
boundaries of the patriarchal symbolic order, reclaiming and reinvent-
ing the capacity for language to be empowering to women rather than
defining them and keeping them in their place. Brontë's bilingual heroines are, says Yaeger:

> ■ women who consume, to an excess, the languages designed to
> consume them. Mad for the honey of speech, Brontë's heroines not only
> challenge the communal norms of their society but are of special inter-
> est to the feminist critic because, in their multi-voicedness, they refuse to
> comply with critical ordinances which limit our understanding of women's
> relation to speech.[45] □

Yaeger discusses the scene at Lowood school where Jane Eyre removes
the piece of pasteboard with the word 'slattern' that has been bound
around Helen Burns's forehead. This word, 'slattern', is exclusively used
to describe women; it is an example of the patriarchal order that is
bound into language. It implies that women are prone to a kind of
disorderliness, a slackness that is not present or at least not punishable
in men. When Jane intervenes to remove this word, she is thus inter-
rupting the symbolic order and dispelling the power of the myth system
it perpetuates. Jane escapes punishment for this act and within a few
weeks is learning French and drawing her first cottage. In embarking
on the first two tenses of the French verb être ('to be'), Jane embarks,
Yaeger suggests, on a second method of subverting patriarchal order:
the multi-voiced heroine is able to find a new tongue for aspects of
her life that are repressed in the language into which she was born.
Jane Eyre, after beginning French and drawing lessons, stops dreaming hungrily of food each night and begins to dream more healthily of
attainable goals: improving her ability to decipher French and to depict
the world through art. French has liberated her into a new sense of her
own agency. As Yaeger comments, the similarity between the word

'être' and the word 'Eyre' underlines the connection between learning 'to be' in French and learning to be herself:

■ The second language serves an emancipatory function in Brontë's texts, enacting a moment in which the novel's primary language is put into process, a moment of possible transformation when the writer forces her speech to break out of old representations of the feminine and to posit something new.[46] □

Although not all psychoanalytic readings of *Jane Eyre* are feminist readings, and vice versa, there has been a rich dialogue between these approaches. Homans and Yaeger see *Jane Eyre* as critiquing patriarchal structures at a pre-conscious level, using language and symbol to express the threat posed to women by the male symbolic order and their need to escape or subvert it.

Intertextuality as a Strategy of Contradiction and Resistance to Patriarchal Authority

Carolyn Williams, in 'Closing the Book: The Intertextual End of *Jane Eyre*'(1989), also considers the way in which *Jane Eyre* uses language to signal a challenge to the patriarchal order. Williams, however, focuses on the idea that the novel is an 'intertext', a word coined by the French feminist Julia Kristeva to describe the way in which each piece of writing is constantly in debate with pre-existing writing, implicitly and explicitly deploying echoes, references, and responses, often subverting the sources of textual authority it incorporates. Williams shows that *Jane Eyre* frequently deploys the Bible, the ultimate patriarchal source of textual authority, and John Bunyan's *The Pilgrim's Progress* in ways that emphasise the heroine's resistance to a patrilineal narrative of authority and control.

Williams focuses on the final pages of *Jane Eyre*, which many readers find strange and unexpected. The novel closes not with Jane's words but with those of St John Rivers, which Jane quotes from what she predicts will be his last letter from India. Williams points out that the last words of *Jane Eyre* are also the last words of the Revelation of St John the Divine, which are the last words of the Bible:

■ For Jane to end her story by quoting these last words of the book about last things, which is itself the last book of the Book of Books – this is having the last word, with a vengeance. And yet it seems as if it is not Jane herself who has this last word, even in her own story. 'I Jane' seems to have disappeared into 'I John'.[47] □

On the face of it, it might seem odd that these last words of Jane's 'autobiography' are not strictly her own: Jane quotes St John's letter, which in turn is echoing the Bible, which represents the word of God mediated through the apostles. Williams, however, argues that Jane's 'double-edged' deployment of St John's letter and the Revelation of St John is the culmination of many acts in which she defines herself by contradiction: by engaging with sources of authority, struggling with them, and defining herself through difference.

Williams sees Jane's struggle to define herself, in Freudian terms, as an oedipal[48] struggle against both female (mother) and male (father) figures of authority. Having come through her struggle for survival against the hard maternal force of Nature in her wanderings on the heath, Jane, at Moor House, confronts the full force of patriarchal authority in St John Rivers and his chilling certainty that he is a medium for God's word and God's will. St John's proposal that Jane should marry him in order to accompany him to India as a missionary is framed in the language of scriptural certainty. When she hesitates, he reads to her (and his sisters) from the twenty-first chapter of Revelation in which the fearful and unbelieving are condemned to second death in a lake of fire and brimstone. At this important juncture, Jane tells St John that she would go with him 'if I were but certain [...] that it is God's will'. St John, who is certain that his will and God's correspond identically, exclaims 'My prayers are heard!' Jane, however, now, as Williams puts it 'makes a prayer of her own, which is answered instead – and answered in such a way that her deepest wishes, not St. John's, are expressed as correspondent with God's voice'.[49] Jane asks to be 'shown the path' and the voice that she hears is Rochester's, crying 'Jane! Jane! Jane !' She responds 'I am coming! [...] Oh I will come!' This episode, argues Williams, with its similar reference to the Book of Revelations, is a precursor to the intertext presented by the final pages of *Jane Eyre* and is very clearly an occasion on which Jane defines herself through opposition. Jane resists St John's attempt to assert that he is the conduit of God's word; instead, Jane becomes the figured medium, in a radically secularised image of divine calling as psychic communion with a lover who is her second self.

Williams reads the final pages of *Jane Eyre* similarly, as an intertextual web that 'forms a covert protest' against St John's assumption of the role of mediator, relaying God's word and representing the male tradition of literary authority. This protest is registered in subtle ways. Jane calls St John 'Greatheart' – a back-handed compliment, since Greatheart appears only in the second part of Bunyan's *The Pilgrim's Progress*, as a guide for Christiana, the wife of Bunyan's pilgrim. Jane chooses not to be led by such a guide, nor to occupy the secondary role of Christiana, but to generate her own calling and define her own progress. Moreover, St John's use of the Bible in his letter is both arrogant and self-cancelling: he refuses to speak for himself, failing to acknowledge the necessary distinction between his voice and the

Lord's. Jane's reintroduction of St John in the last moments of her story may offer a 'sincere' tribute, but is 'a culminating act of self-definition' by contradiction, in which we are reminded 'of her refusal to follow him (or Him)'. St John's vision of apocalyptic marriage in death is counterpointed by Jane's blissful vision of domestic marriage and childbearing and we are left in no doubt about which source of textual authority is left out in the cold: 'She turns the tables on the patrilineal principle of voice by pushing the insider outside, memorializing him at the edges of the text, anticipating his death, soon and far away. This is poetic justice, after all'.[50] Invoking the male-dominated language of the Bible and of Bunyan, then, is a strategy in *Jane Eyre*: the narrator's claim to speak for herself is threatened by these sources of traditional authority but she generates her own voice within and against these verbal power structures, borrowing and transforming male power in the process.

Speaking with Two Voices: *Jane Eyre* as Oedipal Wish-fulfilment

Jean Wyatt's *Reconstructing Desire: The Role of the Unconscious in Women's Reading and Writing* (1990) is also influenced by the work of French feminists on language as a repressive patriarchal order to which women's writing often responds through 'presymbolic' communication and by appealing to readers' unconscious fantasy structures. *Jane Eyre* is a typical 'women's text' in this respect. Clearly, Wyatt argues, *Jane Eyre* satisfies certain powerful female psychic desires. But is its fulfilment of these desires entirely healthy? Wyatt proposes that it is not. To Wyatt, the romance between Jane Eyre and Rochester is essentially an oedipal fantasy: Rochester occupies the position of father, while Jane occupies the position of a daughter who is, problematically, also a lover:

■ Rochester offers Jane the excitement combined with frustration and enigma that characterize father-daughter interactions in a traditionally structured nuclear family. Against the pull of its oedipal love fantasy, *Jane Eyre* presents an equally passionate protest against patriarchal authority. The contradiction, I claim, mirrors a female reader's ambivalence toward her father. Part of *Jane Eyre*'s appeal lies in the way it allows female readers to work out fantasies of desire for the father and rage against him, fantasies that stem from the power and inaccessibility of a father in a traditional nuclear family structure and his ambiguous position with regard to his daughter's sexuality.[51] □

Rochester, suggests Wyatt, is like a father in being twice Jane's age. His much-anticipated returns to the household, which waits expectantly to do his bidding, echo those of a father entering the domestic sphere after work. Moreover, his 'bizarre' behaviour towards Jane, 'compounded of ambiguity, disguise, and deception', is characteristic of the contradictory impulses of a father who, in psychoanalytic theory, both appropriately directs his daughter's erotic impulses into heterosexual avenues and must resist consummating their relationship because incest is taboo. It is appropriate, then, that it is Bertha, the legitimate wife, who intervenes to prevent the father-daughter union.

If *Jane Eyre* is essentially an oedipal fantasy in which the daughter succeeds in marrying her father, why then should it strike so many women as instead a rebellious novel that challenges patriarchal authority? Wyatt argues that this is because the text inscribes different messages to the reader's conscious and unconscious mind. At a conscious level, this *is* a story of female growth and change that overturns social barriers. Bertha, expressing the rage and desire for revenge that also exist in the female subconscious, may offer the reader a vehicle through which infantile anger can be re-experienced in a more mature and liberating form. On the whole, however, Wyatt suspects that *Jane Eyre* remains so compelling to female readers because it layers an apparently feminist crust of rhetoric over a volcano of regressive oedipal desire that is unhelpful to modern women as it prevents change:

> ■ many readers, including feminists like myself, are attached to *Jane Eyre* because it reflects so vividly our own ambivalence. On the level of lucid and compelling rhetoric, Brontë advocates feminist ideals, arguing against patriarchal institutions that confine and warp women's energies and for an open field for women's ambitions; yet underneath flows unchecked a passionate desire for that most restrictive of all female spaces, the bubble of bliss promised by romantic love. Intellectual conviction is notoriously ineffectual in changing what is deeply felt – not only in Brontë but in her readers as well. A text whose conscious ideals of female autonomy and sexual equality are sabotaged by images of symbiosis with a strong oak of a man probably reflects the contradictions of women who, like Brontë, have grown up in a family structure dominated by a strong father but wish to construct their lives differently. If the text mirrors readers' conflicts between high ideals and unregenerate unconscious desire, however, it does nothing to move readers beyond that impasse, toward change. Instead the ideologically correct structure of an egalitarian marriage enables readers to enjoy without guilt the old fantasy of having one's patriarch all to oneself.[52] □

Opinion is divided, then, in psychoanalytic as in other feminist readings, between those, such as Patricia Yaeger, who emphasise the vital emancipatory strategies for the female author, heroine, and reader that *Jane Eyre* develops, and those, like Jean Wyatt, who counter that *Jane Eyre* equally inscribes traditional and reactionary messages to women about the patterns available to them.

Later Feminisms: Race, Class, and Ideology

In the 1980s and afterwards, earlier feminist readings of *Jane Eyre* faced challenges from various quarters. Postcolonial critics such as Gayatri Spivak (born 1942) pointed out that the narrative result that white feminists celebrated, the triumph of Jane as an autonomous individual, was achieved through the oppression and death of the racially 'inferior' colonial subject (Bertha). The notion of Jane as a poster heroine for female self-determination was thus fatally compromised: her success and accession to the Eyre inheritance were not hard-won triumphs over the patriarchal order so much as developments wholly in keeping with a colonial order of exploitation and racism on which Jane's fortune is founded. Marxist critics, too, noted that early feminist accounts of the novel were often blind to questions of social class. Jane may be liberated, but what about the servants, Bessie and Hannah? If Jane is really committed to the feminist cause, why doesn't she remain in the rural school at Morton, giving working-class girls an education? Later feminist approaches to *Jane Eyre* have had to absorb these criticisms and produce accounts of the ideology of gender in the novel that are responsive to the ideologies of class, race, and nation also present in the text.

Mary Poovey in *Uneven Developments: The Ideological Work of Gender in Mid-Victorian England* (1989) combines methodologies drawn from Marxist, psychoanalytic, and poststructuralist criticism to examine Victorian ideological constructions of gender. She places *Jane Eyre* in the context of contemporary controversy surrounding the position of the governess in society. As the governess occupied a peculiar position in the upper middle-class household, Poovey argues, being a paid employee but not a servant, an educated 'lady' of sorts but not eligible to join the family, a woman who cared for children but not a mother, the problem of defining her proper social status and role was ideologically troubling:

■ Because the governess was like the middle class mother in the work she performed, but like both a working-class woman and man in the wages she received, the very figure who theoretically should have defended the naturalness of separate spheres threatened to collapse the difference between them. Moreover, that discussions of the governesses' plight had dove-tailed, by the mid-1850s, with feminist campaigns to improve both employment opportunities for women and women's education reveals the critical role representations of the governess played, not, as conservatives desired, defending the domestic ideal, but in capitalising on the contradiction[s] it contained.[53] □

Governesses were expected, suggests Poovey, to uphold and police various important boundaries in Victorian society. They were supposed to encourage sexually and socially appropriate behaviour in the children they supervised, while being themselves sexually neutral and socially unambitious. Contemporary commentators, however, worried about their vulnerability to sexual temptation. They were expected to uphold a boundary between the working and middle-class woman, while their position showed that this boundary was permeable. They maintained an ideology of 'separate spheres' between male and female activity, while operating on the margin between male professional work and female domestic labour. These contradictions made the governess a focus for a variety of anxieties in this period surrounding women's economic, sexual, and social situations. Governesses, like other workers, suffered from the economic downturn of the 1840s, raising the uncomfortable spectre that woman's labour – not distinctively domestic and moral – was also market-determined and might produce unrest. Moreover, the fact that, as contemporary statistics showed, governesses accounted for a high proportion of institutionalised female lunatics raised the uncomfortable possibility that the categories of governess, madwoman, and fallen woman were not discrete. The language in which Jane refuses Rochester's proposal that she become his mistress, where she says she is not 'mad' and is 'worth' more than the pleasure such a scheme would yield, vividly dramatises, argues Poovey, the potential for a governess to become a Bertha Mason or a Céline Varens, though Jane chooses neither role.

Jane Eyre, on the one hand, seems to support a conservative view of governesses. Jane resists inappropriate sexual advances and in marrying legitimately after a rise in station leaves class boundaries untroubled. On the other hand, the very improbability of the stroke of fortune that relieves her and Diana and Mary Rivers from the burden of being governesses points to the unhappy dependency of the governess as typical of the unhappy dependency of the female condition. In making her heroine a governess, then, Charlotte Brontë played upon a tender spot in which contemporary ideologies of gender, labour, and social class were fused: her intervention is provocative. In Jane's dreams of children, Poovey theorises, we see the repressed anger of an unwilling dependence that is highly visible in the role of the governess, but in fact 'marks every middle-class woman's life'.[54]

Arguments such as Poovey's serve to narrow the gap between feminist and Marxist accounts of *Jane Eyre*, drawing attention to shared ground between the Victorian labour movement and the Victorian women's movement and the subordinate position women shared with the working class.

Both Cora Kaplan in *Sea Changes: Culture and Feminism* (1986) and Susan Fraiman in *Unbecoming Women: British Women Writers and the*

Novel of Development (1993), whose ideas are examined more fully in chapter four, critique earlier feminist writing for being insufficiently alert to 'the way issues of gender in *Jane Eyre* are crucially bound up with those of class'[55] and to the fact that 'Brontë deliberately and defiantly associates political and sexual rebellion'.[56] Both these writers draw connections between *Jane Eyre*'s feminist rhetoric and its interrogation of the structures of class.

Critics such as Mary Ellis Gibson in 'The Seraglio or Suttee: Charlotte Brontë's Jane Eyre' (1987) and Laura Donaldson in *Decolonizing Feminisms: Race, Gender and Empire-Building* (1993) effect a similar rapprochement between feminism and postcolonial criticism, arguing that the subordinate position of Victorian women and of 'subject peoples' in colonised countries had much in common, and that *Jane Eyre* dwells on this similarity. Rather than an unthinkingly imperialist text, *Jane Eyre* is, they suggest, a novel in which discourses of race and gender intertwine. Gibson proposes that Brontë consciously deploys images of slavery, the harem, and the ritual sacrifice of Hindu widows for feminist ends. During the period of their first engagement, when he is trying to load her with silks and jewellery, Jane compares Rochester to a sultan, in an extended dialogue that explores the power imbalance and commodification of the female body that such patronage entails. In refusing to be his 'slave', Jane links herself with the colonial subject; her suspicions of his 'sultan's gaze' are realised by the fact that he is in fact attempting, like a sultan, to have more than one wife. The subject of race helps the novel to point to the linked subject of gender inequality: both forms of subjection are critiqued. Laura Donaldson similarly proposes a 'womanist' reading of *Jane Eyre* that can reconcile feminist and postcolonial insights, arguing 'for Jane and Bertha as oppressed rather than opposed sisters'.[57]

Not all feminist critics are persuaded that *Jane Eyre* respects this sisterhood. In 'The Sultan and the Slave: Feminist Orientalism and the Structure of Jane Eyre' (1993) Joyce Zonana argues that Brontë is embedded in a long tradition of 'feminist orientalist' discourse that seeks to obtain emancipation for Western women by prejudicially representing Eastern practices (the harem, the sacrifice of widows) and Eastern societies as alien and barbarous. Nonetheless, appreciating the interplay of gender and race issues in the novel, in her view, can point the way towards a more fruitful dialogue between Western feminist criticism and readings emergent from other traditions and world views. This and other readings of race and nation in *Jane Eyre* are treated more fully in chapter five of this Guide.

Feminist criticism today often prefers to describe itself as exploring 'feminisms', acknowledging the diversity of persons and approaches involved and the modern perception that the categories of 'gender' and 'sexuality', whose boundaries were once commonly portrayed as fixed, may be experienced by individuals as loose, shifting, constructed, and performed rather than essential and instinctive. Critics such as Carla Kaplan have drawn attention to the way in which Rochester 'transgenders' himself, when he dons his gypsy disguise and pretends to talk to the women at his house party as if he were another woman. Perhaps Rochester's masculinity and patriarchal power are not as fixed and secure as they seem? If becoming a woman is, as Susan Fraiman suggests, 'an incessant project, a daily act of reconstruction and interpretation', becoming a man may also involve ongoing negotiations with social expectations of gender roles.

The question of whether *Jane Eyre* is a feminist text resists a categorical answer. The question will mean different things to different people. Modern feminist critics continue to debate the models of womanhood, the plot, the voice(s), and the reading experience that *Jane Eyre* offers. Most identify a tension in the novel between an aspiration towards greater freedom and opportunity for women and an acknowledgement of the limitations within which women actually conduct their lives. Penny Boumelha in *Charlotte Brontë* (1990) connects this tension with the mixture of genres that *Jane Eyre* incorporates, concluding that the unresolved debate regarding female power is played out via competing narrative modes:

■ This story of passion, ambition and power continually restates and challenges that contradiction between feminine and heroic character ideals, self-abnegation and self-assertion, so common in Victorian novels centring upon a growing woman. There is, unquestionably, a heroic narrative of consciousness in *Jane Eyre* in which self-assertion threatens an expansion that will absorb the whole world, but this fantasied female power is continually tethered and troubled by the realist narrative of social determination and patriarchal imbrication. It is the tension between the two – sometimes seen as an opposition between Gothic and realist elements, or Romantic and realist, or fairy-tale and novel – that gives the novel its peculiar intensity and force, acting out as it does at the very level of form the mutual dependencies and incompatibilities of desire and restraint.[58] □

Is Jane, in Elaine Showalter's phrase, a 'heroine of fulfillment'? It is important to acknowledge the personal testimony of many women that *Jane Eyre* has helped them in some way: to express their anger, their desire, to feel that they are not alone, to rejoice in the possibility of a woman demanding more from society and getting it, despite all the odds. Jane Lazarre, a feminist novelist, speaks for many when she says:

■ Like Jane, I was a rebel, a chronic bad girl by social definition, and Jane exploded my life into reality [...] I was a non-being in a way; I had looked into the mirror of fiction for so long and seen at best distorted reflections, at worst emptiness [...] I was looking for connection, the opposite of escape [...] I was looking for company in the real world, validation of what I sensed to be true. When I first read *Jane Eyre*, it was as if I had found a sister, or more precisely an aunt, who, however dead she might be to others, assumed flesh for me. I knew she was alive because I clearly heard her voice [...] She shouted and fought for her rights.[59] □

Yet others, such as Carla Kaplan in *The Erotics of Talk: Women's Writing and Feminist Paradigms* (1996), remain doubtful about the nature of the 'fulfilment' that *Jane Eyre* offers women. She suggests that the novel consoles feminist readers, who have a 'romance' with the book, because of the way it talks to us. Intimate, self-revealing, impassioned, chatty: Jane Eyre knows all the secrets of 'girl-talk'. Indeed the novel as a whole speaks about the erotic pleasures of talk: the repartee between Jane and Rochester expertly conveys the delight of conversation. The married Jane reports that she and her husband 'talk all day long'. Why, then, does she feel the need to tell *the reader* her story? If the wished-for dialogue between men and women were real, the narrative would not exist. Unsatisfied female needs lurk at the heart of *Jane Eyre*'s story, needs that must be articulated because they cannot be fulfilled. Like Boumelha, then, Kaplan portrays *Jane Eyre* as a novel 'torn' between asserting female desire for change and acknowledging the difficulty of imagining or realising that change:

■ Jane is never unsure of what she wants or why she wants it. Her desires – for intimacy, recognition, sisterhood, a change in her gender and class position and in the meanings attached to such categories – resonate with every important theme in the history of feminist struggle. Our romance with this text, in that sense, is hardly unfounded. But if Jane knows just what she wants, the novel – quite rationally in my view – does not know how to give it to her. Even as it creates a paradigm of transcendence and romance, *Jane Eyre* also resists the articulation of easy or utopian solutions. It remains unsure about how hierarchical Victorian conventions of gender, class, sexuality, and status might be overturned, ambivalent about the limits of both constructionism and essentialism, uneasy about the promises of romance and idealism, torn between identification and desire.[60] □

This mixed conclusion, where critics alternately identify the spirit of feminist reform in *Jane Eyre* and an attachment to more traditional and conservative values, is echoed in the chapter that follows on social class and political ideology in the novel.

CHAPTER FOUR

CASTE TYPING: MARXIST AND MATERIALIST CRITICISM

Most readers forget the names of the servants in *Jane Eyre*. There are, after all, a lot of them: Bessie and Abbot at Gateshead, Sophie, Leah, John, and Grace Poole at Thornfield, Hannah at Moor House, John and Mary at Ferndean – we do not know the full names of most of the servants and there are others whose names we do not learn at all. Indeed it is very easy, when reading a novel, to ignore the economic and class structures that support the plot. Whose work was necessary to make the money that Jane Eyre inherits from her uncle in Madeira? Where does Rochester's money come from? And why, exactly, is it that gentlemen in Mr Rochester's social station are 'not accustomed to marry their governesses'? As we involve ourselves in Jane's story, it is also easy to forget that the book we are holding is an industrial product, involving multiple hands, from paper-makers and binders to printers and distributors: the novel exists within a particular social and economic system in which it accomplishes and demands certain kinds of work. This chapter deals with criticism of *Jane Eyre* that deliberately chooses to focus on economic and class structures within and around the novel.

Marxist theory, which stems from the insights of the German economist and philosopher Karl Marx (1818–83), argues that the socio-economic elements of society form its 'base' or foundation. The cultural aspects of society – including politics, law, and religion as well as art and literature – form a 'superstructure'. These cultural spheres circulate 'ideology', the ideas, beliefs, and values of the ruling class, which masks the realities of socio-economic life for the working class. It is in the interests of the ruling class to conceal from itself the foundation of exploitation upon which it depends, so it secures its position through 'hegemony', ideological domination of all classes through institutions including the education system, the media, and the arts. From a Marxist viewpoint, literature cannot be 'innocent' entertainment: writers depend upon the social structures in which they live and are involved, whether they recognise it or not, in transmitting ideology, thus maintaining the social order that supports their existence. Writers may of course, however, critique aspects of their society and the ideological tendencies of their works may thus be complex and even contradictory. Although not all of the critics discussed in this chapter would describe themselves as Marxist, all of the works discussed below are informed by Marxist theory and are interested in the ideological tendencies and politics of *Jane Eyre*.

From its publication in 1847, *Jane Eyre* was the subject of political readings that related its narrative to contemporary debate about social structures and government. As we saw in chapter one, Elizabeth Rigby's 1848 critique in the *Quarterly Review* connected *Jane Eyre* to the political protest movements which had that year produced revolution in Europe and Chartist agitation for democratic reforms in Britain:

> ■ there is a proud and perpetual assertion of the rights of man, for which we find no authority either in God's word or in God's providence – there is that pervading tone of ungodly discontent which is at once the most prominent and the most subtle evil which the law and the pulpit, which all civilised society in fact has at the present day to contend with. We do not hesitate to say that the tone of mind and thought which has overthrown authority and violated every code human and divine abroad, and fostered Chartism and rebellion at home, is the same which has also written Jane Eyre.[1] □

The biographer, critic and novelist John Gibson Lockhart (1794–1854) reported to Rigby that it was 'common rumour' that the authors of *Jane Eyre* were 'brothers of the weaving order in some Lancashire town': just the kinds of worker who might be expected to combine in revolutionary protest.[2] Yet, to Eugène Forçade (1820–69), writing in France just after the revolution of 1848, *Jane Eyre* seemed on the contrary to be an admirably anti-revolutionary text, a novel that refuted the ideals of utopian socialism, substituting for them the middle-class libertarian values of individual freedom, effort and responsibility. He had heard a suggestion that the author was Sir Robert Peel (1788–1850), the moderate Conservative who had lately served as Prime Minister. Is *Jane Eyre*, then, a novel whose radical sympathies are with the oppressed worker and political rebel or is it at heart a conservative novel that ultimately endorses the ruling class and the existing social system? The critics who follow formulate and answer this political question in different ways.

THE MOVING EARTH: *JANE EYRE*'S RADICAL SYMPATHIES

Raymond Williams (1921–88), a Cambridge professor with a working-class background and socialist political views, was influential in establishing Marxist thought within British literary criticism. In *The English Novel*

From Dickens to Lawrence (1970) he argues that the industrial revolution is the key context for the Victorian novel which, at its best, is an instrument of social criticism that responds to the human crisis of an early nineteenth century scarred by the social cost of industrialisation: displacement, alienation, class conflict, inequity, and, for many, material hardship. Although *Shirley* does deal directly with industrial unrest, the Brontës' novels are not, as a whole, so obviously engaged with such problems as those of Elizabeth Gaskell (1810–65) and Charles Dickens (1812–70). For example, both Gaskell's *Mary Barton* (1848) and Dickens's *Hard Times* (1854) feature an industrial strike. Nonetheless, Williams argues, *Jane Eyre* is part of the same positive trend in the novel toward 'clashing' with the 'emergent system'. It might not be a politically radical novel in an obvious way, but *Jane Eyre*'s commitment to passion expresses a revolutionary sympathy:

■ It is some indication of the originality of those twenty months in 1847 and 1848 that two novels should come out as different from Dickens and from each other as *Jane Eyre* and *Wuthering Heights*. Since Charlotte and Emily were sisters the novels have always been linked in a general way, and there is something else, more specific, that links them: an emphasis on intense feeling, a commitment to what we must directly call passion, that is itself very new in the English novel [...] And this belongs, I think, in the moving earth, the unprecedented disturbance of those English years [...] an intensity of desire is as much a response, a deciding response, to the human crisis of that time as the more obviously recognisable political radicalism. Indeed, to give that kind of value to human longing and need, to that absolute emphasis on commitment to another, the absolute love of the being of another, is to clash as sharply with the emerging system, the emerging priorities, as in any assault on material poverty.[3] □

Williams considers that the central loss inflicted by nineteenth-century industrial capitalism is a loss of humanity and community. As people are treated like objects in a cycle of profit-led exchange, communities fracture into atomised industrial societies. The novel is a meaningful intervention against this process because it insists upon the value of human needs and desires as they struggle with social constraints and because it emphasises love for another as the central force of human experience. The bearing of the novel is towards community: 'what community is, what it has been, what it might be'.[4] The Brontës, moreover, as women denied equal education and pushed into one of the few available jobs open to them (Charlotte, Emily, and Anne all worked for a time as governesses or tutors), were in a position to know from the perspective of the subordinate worker what it was like to be oppressed:

■ the Brontë sisters knew directly a whole structure of repression in their time; knew it and in their own ways broke it with a strength and courage that puts us all in their debt.[5] □

Williams, then, reads *Jane Eyre* as a text with radical sympathies – part of a literary reform movement that broke with convention, voiced the hunger, rebellion, and rage of the oppressed, and forged emotional bonds between readers and characters that produced a new sense of community at a time of alienation.

HAVING IT ALL WAYS: *JANE EYRE*'S BOURGEOIS GENTILITY

Terry Eagleton (born 1943) in his influential book *Myths of Power: A Marxist Study of the Brontës* (1975) takes a completely different line from Raymond Williams on the ideological tendencies of *Jane Eyre*. In his view the 'deep structure' of all Charlotte's novels involves a 'struggle between two ambiguous, internally divided sets of values'. This structure of conflict and compromise reflects the 'tensions and alliances between the two social classes which dominated the Brontës' world: the industrial bourgeoisie [business owners], and the landed gentry or aristocracy':

> ■ On the one hand are ranged the values of rationality, coolness, shrewd self-seeking, energetic individualism, radical protest and rebellion; on the other hand lie the habits of piety, submission, culture, tradition, conservatism. I call these patterns of value 'ambiguous' because the elements of one may be displaced or 'inverted' into the other; and this, indeed, is precisely the point [...] I read Charlotte's novels as 'myths' which work towards a balance or fusion of blunt bourgeois rationality and flamboyant Romanticism, brash initiative and genteel cultivation, passionate rebellion and cautious conformity; and those interchanges embody a complex structure of convergence and antagonism between the landed and industrial sectors of the contemporary ruling class.[6] □

The Brontë family's own ambiguous social standing, Eagleton suggests, underlies the conflict in their work between the bourgeoisie and the gentry. Charlotte's father, Patrick Brontë (1777–1861), came from a relatively poor family of Irish farmers but managed to win a place to study at Cambridge University and became an Anglican minister. His life was marked by dramatic self-invention and awareness of poverty and exploitation by the ruling class, but also by 'piety, submission and conservatism' appropriate to his new position as a cleric in the Established Church. The Brontës' was a Tory (politically conservative) household, but one built on slim financial foundations by an entrepreneurial social climber.

The story of Jane Eyre, says Eagleton, similarly combines a bourgeois ethic of self-making and progress through the class structure with an aristocratic ethic of inheritance, entitlement, and continuity. Jane, as an orphan, has no social identity and like a good bourgeois entrepreneur, she independently works her way up in the world until she legitimately achieves status and power. But, Eagleton also reminds us, Jane's destiny is actually also a *retrieval* of a social status as a member of the gentry that, like her inheritance, is her temporarily lost birthright. The Eyres and the Rivers are 'old families'; Jane, the servant Bessie comments when she leaves Lowood, is certainly a 'lady'. When Jane is at her lowest, asking food and shelter from the Rivers, she still rebukes the servant, Hannah, for assuming that her social status is that of a beggar – as Eagleton says 'even in beggary, class counts'. So, Jane's progress in class terms could be seen not as scaling an unfamiliar ladder but as a long march home. Thornfield is, in fact, the only residence she feels to be 'home' in the book. The instinctive kinship and 'equality of souls' that Jane feels for Rochester is not such a radical sympathy after all if it is premised on an equally instinctive distance from the lower orders. Eagleton claims that central to all of Charlotte Brontë's novels:

> ■ is a figure who either lacks or deliberately cuts the bonds of kinship. This leaves the self a free, blank, 'pre-social' atom: free to be injured and exploited, but free also to progress, move through the class-structure, choose and forge relationships, strenuously utilise its talents in scorn of autocracy or paternalism. The novels are deeply informed by this bourgeois ethic, but there is more to be said than that. For the social status finally achieved by the déraciné [uprooted] self is at once meritoriously won and inherently proper.[7] □

Jane Eyre, then, in terms of social class and power, has it all ways. She achieves the intellectual self-determination of the professional petit-bourgeois, inherits a commercial legacy that renders her economically independent, then marries into the gentry and produces an heir. Eagleton judges that this compass of different positions, all of which Jane occupies, reflects an ambiguous attitude to power that permeates Charlotte Brontë's fiction, emerging in the sexual as well as the political sphere. Indeed, Eagleton hints, *Jane Eyre*, like Charlotte's other novels, has a sadomasochistic undercurrent: 'submission is good, but only up to a point, and it is that point which Charlotte Brontë's novels explore'[8]:

> ■ Charlotte's protagonists want independence, but they also desire to dominate; and their desire to dominate is matched only by their impulse to submit to a superior sexual will. The primary form assumed by this ambiguity is a sexual one: the need to venerate and revere, but also to exercise power, enacts itself both in a curious rhythm of sexual attraction and antagonism, and in a series of reversals of sexual roles [...] This simultaneity of attraction and antagonism, reverence and dominance, is relevant

to a more general ambiguity about power which pervades Charlotte's fiction. It parallels and embodies the conflicting desires of the oppressed outcast for independence, for passive conformity to a secure social order, and for avenging self-destruction over that order.[9] □

Jane's final triumph in marrying Rochester deftly unites bourgeois and aristocratic values, a desire for social change and social continuity, enacting, in Eagleton's reading, the negotiation that was in fact occurring in the early nineteenth century between industrial capitalists and landed gentry to consolidate a new ruling class. Although it articulates competing values that include rebelliousness and conformity, the ideology of the novel works ultimately to cement existing power structures rather than to unsettle them.

Eagleton's Marxist reading of Charlotte Brontë's novels won admirers but also many critics. In particular, feminists objected that his analysis took little account of the oppression Brontë experienced as a woman, which complicates her social position and that of her heroines, and that Eagleton's determination to read all the novels as 'mutations' of the same structure ignores their individual character. Eagleton was accused of a chauvinistic and unsympathetic approach, which critics such as Carol Ohmann and Susan Fraiman (below) challenge.

AN UNDERLYING CRITIQUE OF BOURGEOIS AUTHORITY

Nancy Pell, in 'Resistance, Rebellion, and Marriage: The Economics of *Jane Eyre*' (1977), argues that, despite the fact that Charlotte Brontë 'thought of herself as the meekest of Christian Tories', *Jane Eyre* contains an underlying critique of the Victorian social system in terms of class and gender and the effects of power:

■ Charlotte Brontë never fully recognized the extent to which her first published novel calls basic institutions into question in ways more concrete than the 'murmuring' or 'pervading tone of mind' that so offended Elizabeth Rigby. In *Jane Eyre* Charlotte Brontë's romantic individualism and rebellion of feeling are controlled and structured by an underlying social and economic critique of bourgeois patriarchal authority. Although this does not describe the entire scope of the novel, which includes countercurrents and qualifications as well, the formal and dramatic elements of a social critique are manifest in Jane's resistance to the illegitimate power of John Reed, Mr. Brocklehurst, and St. John Rivers; allusions to actual historical incidents involving regicide [the killing of a king] and rebellion; and, finally, the dynamics of Rochester's two marriages – both his marriage to Jane and his earlier marriage to Bertha Mason.[10] □

Pell follows Raymond Williams in deeming *Jane Eyre* a book 'rooted in economic realities and social relationships'. She identifies, however, specific ways in which *Jane Eyre*'s critique of existing economic and social structures is located just below the surface of the narrative, requiring readers to make connections and analyse the source of various systems of oppression. In the first part of the novel, John Reed, Jane's spoiled and insolent cousin, becomes the emblem of unjust authority, the vicious 'emperor' who tyrannises unfairly over Jane, the 'slave', merely because she is a financial dependant in a house that, through patriarchal systems of inheritance, ultimately belongs to him. Readers are invited to sympathise with the child who has, as she is well aware, 'less right to be here than a servant' and who is condemned to 'a life of ceaseless reprimand and thankless fagging'. We are subtly, through the adult narrator's analysis of her childhood sufferings, led to take the side of the young Jane, who resists and rebels against the power structures that oppress her. These include the clerical authority of the Reverend Brocklehurst, which is exposed as equally tyrannical and unjust, and later that of St John Rivers, whom Pell compares with John Reed as a self-destructive figure of violent patriarchal power.

Pell points out that 'two allusions to actual rebellions in English history suggest Charlotte Brontë's awareness that Jane's struggle for a wider life has significant historical implications'.[11] The first occurs at Lowood, where after a lesson on tonnage and poundage in the early reign of King Charles I (1600–49; reigned 1625–49), Helen Burns confesses her liking and pity for Charles, who was accused of tyranny and executed in 1649 during the English Civil Wars (1642–51), after which the country briefly became a Commonwealth under Oliver Cromwell (1599–1658; Lord Protector of England, 1653–58). Jane criticises Helen for her royalist sympathies and for her doctrine of passivity in the face of tyranny: 'if people were always kind and obedient to those who are cruel and unjust', Jane asserts, 'the wicked people would have it all their own way: they would never feel afraid, and so they would never alter, but would grow worse and worse'. Pell suggests that Jane's 'resistance to the abuse of power' here clearly puts her on the side of the regicides, those who wish to replace a decadent monarch with a democratic state.[12] 'Tonnage and poundage' alludes to the unfair taxes on shipping that Charles I levied on the realm so, says Pell, this dialogue between Helen and Jane is crucially concerned with the just limits of authority. Helen's submissiveness does her no good: in the end she submits to death. Although Jane learns a measure of useful self-restraint at Lowood, the implication is that her political refusal to submit to unjust authority is the attitude that enables her to survive and prosper. Pell also notices that Jane Eyre is twice associated with Guy Fawkes, the rebel who plotted to blow up the Houses of Parliament on 5 November 1605. Mrs Reed's maid, Abbot, suspects that the young Jane 'is a sort of infantine Guy Fawkes'. Then much later in the novel, St John Rivers visits Jane at Morton on 5 November, a holiday from her work, on which he makes the momentous discovery of her true name, which will enable her to claim her uncle's inheritance. That date, Pell notes, is also the anniversary of the 'Glorious Revolution' of 1688, when Protestantism was restored to England with the arrival of King William III ('William of Orange' (1650–1702; reigned 1689–1702)) and Queen Mary II (1662–94; reigned 1689–94): 'Thus both violent and bloodless rebellions are juxtaposed on the occasion of Jane's passing from the dispossessed to the possessing class'.[13]

Lastly, Pell claims, *Jane Eyre* critiques existing structures of authority through its depiction of the relationship between Jane and Rochester in which Jane 'rejects being hired as a mistress or bought as a slave' and finally redefines the term 'independent woman', choosing to split her legacy and to enter marriage on equal terms. Rochester was, Pell suggests, just as much a 'social victim' as Jane: he was traded by his family in marriage for wealth to maintain their social position and Bertha is the 'psychological symbol' of his 'repressed awareness of his true social situation'. Jane's rebellion may seem at a first a private struggle, but it ripples outward to connect with the millions of 'rebellions beside political rebellions' that, as she asserts in her reverie on Thornfield's battlements, 'ferment in the masses of life which people earth'. *Jane Eyre*, says Pell, anticipates Charlotte Brontë's more overt engagement with social and economic problems in *Shirley*: it is a practical effort to imagine how the 'state in which things are' might be altered for the better.

RADICALISM IN TENSION WITH CONSERVATISM

Similarly, Carol Ohmann in 'Historical Reality and "Divine Appointment" in Charlotte Brontë's Fiction' (1977) agrees that Charlotte Brontë in the course of her novel-writing career 'moved toward a radical critique of the English society she knew', but concludes that:

■ Her radicalism was always in tension with conservative tendencies, and she was better, even in *Jane Eyre* and *Shirley*, at posing social problems than at sighting ways to solve them.[14] □

Ohmann sees a progressive movement in Charlotte's novels between her first work *The Professor* (published posthumously in 1857), where subversive elements are present only on the fringe of the narrative, *Jane Eyre*, where revolt and resistance 'move to centre stage', and *Shirley* (1849), whose 'aesthetic difficulties' are a product of mounting conflict between Brontë's radical and conservative ideas. The signs of this conflict between radicalism and conservatism in *Jane Eyre* are that the novel leaves behind unresolved problems. The first problem is that of Rochester's conversion from despot to egalitarian husband. Brontë struggles, Ohmann suggests, to conceive of manliness apart from mastery, to preserve Rochester's potency while reducing his power. His lost hand and eye are an awkward narrative solution to this political conundrum. The second problem is that, although Brontë provides fulfilment for Jane, she cannot thereafter relate her to the society from which she has come. Jane's achievement of escape from financial hardship, subservience, and marginalised status convey 'a moral imperative with broadly social implications [...] which might be read to say that not only Jane but everyone like her has a right to what she claims and receives'. But Jane Eyre does not reach out to those countless other millions who suffer a similar fate; once the heroine is happy she is preserved in splendid social isolation:

■ Logically there is no reason to stop with Jane, as Elizabeth Rigby saw, reading the novel with alarm and damning its writer in the *Quarterly Review*. If governesses are admitted to be as good as their masters, then there is no telling where the demand for equality might take us next. This *is* the very 'tone of mind' that overthrows authority and reconstitutes society. Brontë does not go so far in *Jane Eyre*. The moral imperative is there in the story she tells of how one man and one woman come to make an unconventional marriage. But the novel itself does not follow out the implications of this event, nor does it in any way suggest how they might be followed out. Jane, for example, is well dowered after all, but how? By a lucky inheritance from an uncle dead in Madeira. Conceiving as best she can her ideal marriage, Brontë is concerned to make her heroine economically independent. But there is no democratic imperative in Jane's inheritance, no potentiality for significant social change, nothing that matters to anyone else born poor. The life Jane and Rochester live together fails similarly to make connection with the social fabric and resonate there. They are no longer sovereign and slave, master and servant; they are citizens, but citizens of a state whose population numbers only two. Brontë brings Jane and Rochester through vicissitudes to a marriage of equals, but once she has them there she cannot relate them again to the society from which they've come. On their two inherited incomes, they live islanded in a country retreat, companioned by books and nature.[15] □

Igor Webb in *From Custom to Capital: The English Novel and the Industrial Revolution* (1981) similarly reflects that

■ The novel endows Jane with a necessary social stature and asserts the practical and thus essential need for a developed social base for marriage. Yet the novel hesitates to believe the fulfillment of self which it has traced, the fulfillment of a poor, plain woman, can actually find social expression [...] the transformations of self once achieved, the full transformation of society seems daunting, and the novel retreats into its overgrown paradise.

This paradise serves at once as a criticism of that other, public world and as an announcement of a deep, dispiriting gulf between active self-fulfillment and social possibility.[16] □

CONSOLIDATING CLASS POSITIONS: AN ANTI-FRENCH NOVEL

Jina Politi's well-known essay 'Jane Eyre Class-ified' (1982) goes further in critiquing the ideological 'contradictions' of *Jane Eyre*. The novel, she argues, begins with the apparent agenda of depicting and vindicating the struggle of a socially underprivileged woman against patriarchal oppression. Charlotte Brontë's 'preface' and certain other passages where she consciously voices her ideology, aim to liberate female representation from the constraints of convention. But *Jane Eyre* sells out – by the end, the heroine has become complicit with and inseparable from the society that, at first, she seemed to reject:

■ *Jane Eyre* comes to celebrate the very *ethos* upon which bourgeois capitalism and its patriarchal ideology rest. What the novel originally sets out to de-mask, it then artfully conceals. Although the plot explicitly refuses at first to organise its future on the comic convention of 'foundling reinstated' it forgets its promises and reconstitutes Jane as a subject of Comedy. In suppressing social causation and in admitting the workings of Providence, it also denies authorship by making God complicit in the writing of the novel. In the world of *Jane Eyre* 'improper' discourse has no place. Revolution, sexuality, insanity, belong 'abroad'. These Mr Rochester locks in the attic, and places Grace Poole, the working-class woman, to guard them! Drink, which like books offers the possibility of liberation, allows the spectre to emerge to burn down mansions and to tear the hypocritical marriage veils. But the novel's movement is not towards liberation. It is towards a tidying, a consolidating of class positions.[17] □

The ending of *Jane Eyre*, Politi claims, reverts to the literary conventions of comedy, in that Jane's lowly social station proves to have been merely a temporary reverse of fortune, a mistake, which is mended by her happy reinstatement to the ruling class through inheritance and marriage. Since the later part of the novel also much more explicitly invokes God's providence – as the famished Jane stumbles upon her cousins' house and Rochester, having done penance for his sins, prays to God and is rewarded by Jane's return – Politi deems that Brontë has abandoned a narrative model that emphasises social responsibility for events, substituting a model that bows to divine authority. This, too, represents a step back from the social critique *Jane Eyre*'s opening seemed to launch.

In Politi's analysis the young Jane is marginalised in class terms, rejected both from above and from below. She is neither master nor servant and recognises that she would not be willing to join the working poor even in order to escape the miseries of her Aunt Reed's household: 'I was not heroic enough to purchase liberty at the price of caste'. Realising through her confrontation with John Reed, who insists she call him 'Master', that it is the upper class that dictates the limits imposed on speech, Jane rebels. But that rebellion marks the end of Jane's anti-authoritarian voice. The narrative enacts a process in which the youthful Jane, heard in the first five chapters, is progressively silenced by the mature Jane Eyre, a governess who censors both herself and her pupils. 'Master' changes its register in the course of the book until it applies to Rochester in tones of 'feminine sweetness and submissiveness'. The political ideology behind this shift is that 'races, nations, classes' are happy in inequality so long as they can choose their masters and so long as exploitation is masked under the cover of mutual love and duty. Politi argues that just as the two distinct discourses of young Jane and mature Jane blend seamlessly into one, suppressing the ideological tensions between them, so there is a concealed rift in the narrative structure of *Jane Eyre* between the realist mode, which is associated with rebellion, and the mode of 'erotic fable', which dominates the later part of the novel and is associated with submission to patriarchal ideology. Politi identifies the scene in the Red Room where Jane sees herself in the mirror and perceives a split between her self and visual image as the crucial point at which Jane disconnects from the 'rebel girl' and becomes an 'eery' version of herself (a revised kind of Eyre): her physical body translated into the realm of the supernatural and otherworldly. Henceforth, her sexually desirous and politically unruly body will be alienated from her speaking self.

Jane Eyre, says Politi, persistently locates revolution and the other forms of troubling excess in the novel in the realm of the foreign. English values are identified as those of order, restraint, and self-discipline. The fact that madness and rebellion are non-English and not to be condoned is signalled by Jane's description of her childhood fit when she is arrested and imprisoned in the Red Room, as a moment when she was beside herself 'or rather *out* of myself, as the French would say':

■ It is important that the word 'French' appears at this point in the narrative and in connexion with the state of being *out* of one's self. Charlotte Brontë italicises the foreign *out*. Here, the text is not simply signifying Mrs Rochester's linguistic achievements and her progress from being 'a mad cat', 'a noxious thing' as a child to being an accomplished, refined lady-writer of her memoirs. It is primarily signifying nineteenth-century English beliefs concerning the state of revolution. Revolution was that aberrant state in which an individual, a class or a nation went 'beside' itself – *hors de soi même* – a condition indelibly linked in the English mind with the frenzy and irrationality of the French Revolution. It is from this moment onwards that the narrative will begin to construct its ideological, national-istic discourse on the opposition French/English, an opposition which in turn will subsume contradictory representations of femininity symbolising a natural and un-natural political behaviour which at a deeper level signifies the native hostility and fear of anything *foreign*.[18] □

Politi suggests that Bertha, Rochester's Creole wife, embodies the promiscuous sexuality and consequent physical and mental insanity asso-ciated in *Jane Eyre* with foreign lands. Céline Varens, Rochester's French mistress, likewise exhibits all the vices of France: whoredom, deception, fickleness, and theatricality. Her daughter, Adèle, shows all the femi-nine symptoms of being equally frivolous, vain, and worldly until, Jane informs us, 'her French defects' are corrected by 'a sound English educa-tion' at a school from which she emerges 'docile, good-tempered, and well-principled'. Rebelliousness, which is ideologically equated with unabashed female sexuality, is alienated through its association with degenerate foreign countries. Like Terry Eagleton, then, but with much greater emphasis on the roles of sexual ideology and nationalism in the novel, Politi argues that *Jane Eyre* is at heart a conservative text. 'Contrary to conscious intentions' the journey of the narrative, like that of its hero-ine, is one 'from revolted marginality to quiescent socialization'.[19]

WORKING WOMEN: GRACE POOLE AS JANE'S DOMESTIC DOUBLE

Later feminist critics such as Susan Fraiman, while admitting that Brontë's class politics are 'incoherent', have stressed the relationship between the plight of women and the plight of workers in *Jane Eyre*, arguing that the novel draws important connections between these two groups: connections that were strong and apparent in early nineteenth-century politics between the Chartists and other groups pressing for labour rights and the emergent women's suffrage movement. Fraiman in *Unbecoming Women: British Women Writers and the Novel of Development* (1993) announces that:

■ My project [...] is to stress the 'Chartism' of *Jane Eyre* – the way it inter-rogates (though it may not finally threaten) the structures of class, the way it is part of a moment when coherence about class was failing – and to see this as inseparable from its feminism. What is at issue for me in this text, what is rattling in its attic and recurrently at large, is a woman who is also a worker.[20] □

Fraiman, like Eagleton and Politi, draws attention to Jane's uncertain, marginal class position, but rather than regarding Jane as a hybrid of the industrial bourgeoisie and the gentry, she sees Jane as straddling the border between haves and have-nots, owners and workers: 'Jane's socially ambiguous position corresponds to a different tension, less readily resolved and potentially more disruptive to existing class arrangements: between the propertied classes (Reeds and Rochesters) and the working poor'.[21] As Fraiman points out, Jane's 'nonbourgeois status becomes increasingly clear'. She tidies the nursery like a sort of 'under-nursery maid', preparing herself for a life of work as service. The maid, Bessie, is much more of surrogate mother or sister to her than Mrs Reed and her cousins: a fact underlined when Bessie rewards Jane for declaring that she does not love her aunt and that her cousins are not 'worthy to associate' with her, by singing her sweetest songs and telling her most enchanting stories. Fraiman argues that, although Jane does not join Bessie's class, she claims and re-imagines Bessie's place – the place of the working woman – 'as a "heroic", morally righteous, and potentially revolutionary one'. By contrast, the parasitic life of the middle-class woman who does not work is presented as morally inferior. Eliza Reed's mercenary hoarding and Georgiana Reed's passive indulgence as conspicuous consumer are alike dismissed as worthless and reprehensible. Jane's solidarity is with female workers, from the 'slave' she identifies herself with when bullied by John Reed to the maid, Mary, whose place she takes in bringing Rochester a glass of water in their reunion scene.

■ the formation of Mrs. Rochester [...] is continually interrupted and essentially destabilized by a second, subversive narrative, one that [...] involves the heroine's identification with other working women. Though written over by subsequent chapters, this radical narrative originates in the very first, Gateshead section of *Jane Eyre* [...] and persists, submerged and contested, throughout the novel.[22] □

Fraiman comments that previous feminist writers such as Showalter, Gilbert and Gubar have sometimes, in 'reading for gender', ignored the issue of class in *Jane Eyre*. They thus tend to treat Rochester's bigamy as a purely symbolic matter, presenting the real obstacle to Jane's union with him as her own instinctive dread of an unequal marriage. Yet this ignores the class reality that working women were everywhere vulnerable to the predatory sexual behaviour of male employers: that Jane's potential fate as mistress is both more typical and more degrading than that as unequal wife. In conceiving this threat, Brontë emphasizes Jane's affinity with Céline, Rochester's discarded mistress, who works as an opera-dancer, and with Adèle, whose stigmatised origins and uncertain prospects echo Jane's own.

Brontë then, in Fraiman's view, deliberately shows readers the ways in which Jane's trials as a woman are linked to her trials as a worker. This connection is particularly explicit in Jane's outburst on the battlements at Thornfield where she protests the confinement of her life and female employment in the context of a much wider unrest:

■ It is in vain to say human beings ought to be satisfied with tranquillity: they must have action; and they will make it if they cannot find it. Millions are condemned to a stiller doom than mine, and millions are in silent revolt against their lot. Nobody knows how many rebellions besides political rebellions ferment in the masses of life which people earth.[23] □

Cora Kaplan in *Sea Changes: Culture and Feminism* (1986), identifies this as 'a significant moment of incoherence' in *Jane Eyre*, 'where the congruence between the subordination of women and the radical view of class oppression becomes, for a few sentences, irresistible'. The laughter, which notoriously interrupts Jane's rooftop reverie, is, Kaplan decides, a narrative reaction to this moment of defiance, warning the reader 'quite literally that the association of femininity and class struggle leads to madness'.[24] Fraiman, on the contrary, finds in 'Grace Poole', whom Jane still at this point thinks is behind the laughter that 'thrills' her, a strong figure in whom the energies of the exploited worker and the repressed, sexually powerful woman coalesce:

■ I would offer, then, the madwoman 'Grace Poole' as a figure capable of gathering into her all the unseen or scarcely seen lower-class women in this book and acting out their collective revenge. In her role as nurse she refers to Bessie; in her hypothetical past as Rochester's mistress she refers to Céline; and in her riotous outbreaks she refers to the young, disinherited Jane. I want [...] by emphasizing Grace over Bertha to link her incendiary recurrence not only back to Bessie but also out to contemporary mass movements on behalf of women and of workers – to see her eruption into the text as the reemergence with a vengeance of that alternative formation introduced by the novel's first scene.[25] □

The invisible woman whose eerie laughter disturbs Jane can, in this reading, be a composite character containing both Bertha and Grace, representing both female and working-class anger. Although Jane at various stages in her progress tries on the trappings of bourgeois womanhood, 'rising' at Lowood to become the 'first girl of the first class' and accepting Rochester's marriage proposal, the novel, Fraiman insists, continually finds ways to return her to consciousness of the plight of the lowly female worker. Jane is unfairly obliged to nurse the wounded Richard Mason through the night. After her flight from Thornfield, she becomes a beggar-woman: facing starvation and seeking any employment, she is told that there is little possibility of finding work because Mr Oliver employs no women in his needle factory. At Morton, although conscious of the fact that becoming a village schoolmistress constitutes a fall in the social scale, she is at pains to stress that serving the working community is a valid and satisfying activity and that 'these coarsely-clad little peasants are of flesh and blood as good as the scions [descendants] of gentlest genealogy'. Finally, Jane arrives at Ferndean and is reunited with Rochester but, Fraiman suggests, her romantic triumph is undercut by her continued life of service as his nurse:

> ■ if *Jane Eyre* [...] is split between rival narratives – between the two class positions evoked by the miscegenated[26] child and ambiguous governess – then these result, by the final scene, in two opposing images of the mature heroine: the happy, rich, and conventionally respectable lady *and* the over-worked, always potentially irate nurse. While the story of gentrification and heterosexual romance ostensibly prevails, it is interrogated to the end by the subtler, homosocial story of Jane's continuing service, binding her to those she earlier calls the 'millions [...] in silent revolt against their lot'.[27] □

Jane's life of service continues to ally her with less fortunate working women throughout her autobiography, disrupting the notion that she has transcended the class struggle embodied in her revolt against John Reed at Gateshead.

Several other feminist critics share Fraiman's perception that Brontë, in exposing Jane Eyre's marginal class status and vulnerability to exploitation as a working woman, is commenting more broadly on the socio-economic situation of uneasy dependence faced by the majority of women. Mary Poovey in *Uneven Developments: The Unequal Work of Gender in Mid-Victorian England* (1989), whose ideas were explored in chapter three, examines the situation of the governess as embody-ing anxieties in this era regarding the permeability of lower-class and middle-class female work and the difficulty of maintaining bounda-ries between the moral and domestic sphere of the wife and mother and the ambiguous, sexually vulnerable and potentially unruly role of the female employee within the home. Sally Shuttleworth in *Charlotte Brontë and Victorian Psychology* (1996) also finds that in *Jane Eyre* 'the realm of psychic struggle is clearly associated [in Brontë's mind] with the dynamics of social struggle and insurrection'.[28] Shuttleworth draws attention to Brontë's preface to the second edition of *Jane Eyre* in which, Shuttleworth argues, she 'warns that her work will constitute a radical, political act of unveiling'[29] and praises William Thackeray as 'the first social regenerator of the day' – a strong hint that her own novel also critiques society and aims to amend it.

Shuttleworth reads the letters of 1847 and 1848, in which Brontë expresses scepticism about the results of the recent French Revolution but supports the Germans' 'rational and justifiable efforts for liberty', as explorations in which Brontë negotiates her ambivalence about the political rebellions that preoccupied Europe at the time. The letters seem to favour the German 'rational' model of pursuing social change, which Brontë links to Thackeray's highly controlled satire. But a postscript to one letter recommending 'self-control' for governesses overturns the doctrine of patience it seems to advocate:

> ■ I conceive that when Patience has done its utmost and Industry its best, whether in the case of Women or Operatives, and when both are baffled, and Pain and Want triumphant – the Sufferer is free – is entitled – at last to send up to Heaven any piercing cry for relief – if by that cry he can hope to obtain succour.[30] □

Jane Eyre, says Shuttleworth, is full of the same imagery of volcanoes and uprising that permeates contemporary political discourse about the likelihood of revolution in Britain. It debates the proper relationship between restraint and the full expression of latent energies in terms that cut across the psychological, socio-economic, and political arenas. All of these critics suggest that while Brontë's class politics may be ambivalent, *Jane Eyre* 'strains against' dominant ideologies even as it reproduces them.

JANE EYRE IN THE MARKETPLACE

As a woman who has to make her own way in life, how does Jane Eyre negotiate the nineteenth-century economy? Sharon Marcus in 'The Profession of the Author: Abstraction, Advertising, and Jane Eyre' (1995) combines Lacanian and Marxist theory to consider both Jane Eyre and Charlotte Brontë as operators in the Victorian marketplace. Since the novel's publication, Marcus notes, it has been celebrated and criticised as a tale in which a 'willful female subject claims her own identity'. However, Marcus contends, critics have failed to recognise that 'the most basic and encompassing marker of that identity, her name, tends to emerge when her will is most in abeyance'. The most striking example of this is when Jane doodles her real name in a 'moment of abstraction' in the margin of a portrait-cover – a lapse that enables the keen-sighted St John Rivers to penetrate her pseudonym, Jane Elliott, and thus unite her with her uncle's money. It also occurs, however, at Lowood when she advertises for a position as a governess. Jane recounts this episode in terms of an inner dialogue between a person who knows nothing about how to seek work and one who says 'you must advertise': a 'kind fairy' seems to drop the suggestion on her pillow while her conscious mind is absent. Marcus suggests that this process of self-division and alienation in order to participate in the marketplace is typical of an era in which capitalism required the worker to abstract themselves to an increasing degree:

> ■ The importance of abstraction in *Jane Eyre* is due in part to the text's contemporaneity with the height of British capitalism and imperialism, historical phenomena that moved spatial and human relations in the direction of greater and greater abstraction through developments in areas such as statistics, cartography, a bureaucratic civil service, and a manufacturing system that increasingly organized workers' space and time [...] The capitalist ideology of political economy defined human relations and economic value in terms of abstractions – money, markets, and generalized exchange.[31] □

In Marxist thought 'alienation' can have both a negative and a positive meaning. It can refer, negatively, to capitalists' exclusive appropriation of wealth and the pain this inflicts on workers through reducing human relations to commodities and exchange value. It can also refer, more positively, to human labour as a process in which individuals learn to conceive of material products abstractly and to view themselves in a world they have created. Marcus suggests that Jane Eyre's 'alienation into abstraction' when she becomes in her advertisement 'a young lady accustomed to tuition [...] desirous of meeting with a situation' involves her in both 'the gains and losses attendant on subjection to political economy'. Where critics such as Terry Eagleton have seen Jane's rise to power as triumphantly uniting the capitalist activities of landowning and entrepreneurial commerce and feminist critics have often seen Jane's journey as a progression toward identity as a unified subject, Marcus sees Jane Eyre as a figure of internal divisions and contradictions who is both made and unmade by capitalism:

> ■ Jane Eyre's transformation of her self into an other suggests that the split subject and the imperialist-capitalist subject may be equivalent [...] Jane becomes an economic actor and the apparent author of her fate only when she alienates herself into writing, into advertisements, and into an abstract professional body.[32] □

In this respect, Marcus suggests, Jane has much in common with Charlotte Brontë, who shares a similar process of abstraction in becoming the author, 'Currer Bell': an act that both effaces and promotes her identity.[33] Where earlier criticism debates Jane's social alignment (as dominant mistress or harassed employee of Thornfield), Marcus prefers to situate Jane Eyre as a woman alienated into a capitalist marketplace where self-assertion paradoxically entails self-erasure and the profit for the individual subject is inseparable from the cost of self-division.

NO FIXED IDEOLOGY: *JANE EYRE*'S MULTIPLE CLASS IDENTITIES

Perhaps, after all, the critical effort to establish Jane Eyre's class identity has been misguided. Chris Vanden Bossche in 'What did Jane Eyre do? Ideology, agency, class and the novel' (2005) suggests that earlier readings have been limited by their assumption that the novel embodies 'a fixed ideology represented in the subjectivity of its heroine' and that ideology is itself a 'fixed field of discourse' that masks social reality, which literature reproduces. These unfortunate premises tend to lead critics to the commonplace conclusion that *Jane Eyre*, like many other Victorian texts, either subverts ideology (the heroine rebels) or supports it (she joins the existing social order), or a bit of both. Instead, Vanden Bossche maintains, it is more helpful to think of *Jane Eyre*, rather than reproducing a fixed ideology, as continuously engaged in ideological debate that sets different constructions of social reality against one another, and of Brontë's heroine mobilising multiple class identities and discourses at different times in the novel:

■ The question is not whether the novel supports or subverts class ideology, but rather how it deploys the languages of class in order to confront a series of social situations, each of which threatens to delimit Jane Eyre's social agency. Jane Eyre repeatedly shifts positions within class discourse, not in order to move towards a final class identity but in response to economic dependence, social exclusion, personal isolation, and other circumstances. It is not that she abandons the one achievement – the economic autonomy of the school teacher – in order to obtain the other – the social relationship of marriage – but rather that she shifts to one or another position depending on the needs of the particular social situation. In order to do so, she employs two distinct strands of class discourse. First, she draws on the triadic model of class in which the aristocracy and middle class each represent themselves as better able than the other to govern, and protect the interests of, the working class. However, rather than identifying exclusively with one or the other of these potential ruling classes, Jane strategically alternates between them, and, moreover, critiques both by setting them against one another. Second, she draws on a dichotomous model in which the lower classes demand the right of social inclusion from the upper classes that exclude them from access to power. Insofar as she seeks entry into the ruling classes in the terms of the triadic model, her desire for inclusion, as some critics have suggested, involves the exclusion of others, but insofar as her desire is expressed in terms of the dichotomous model, it does not involve exclusion but rather inclusion as one of the 'people'.[34] □

Vanden Bossche argues that whereas earlier critics (such as Eagleton) have assumed that the author 'belongs to' and the text 'serves' a particular class interest, this is not the case. Authors also 'constitute themselves across a range of markers of identity' and the language of class is only 'one means through which they attempt to come to terms with the social'. The text, moreover, is replete with meanings that are not determined or limited by the author's intended class affiliation(s).

Jane Eyre, in this reading, strategically deploys plural class identities. In some situations she mobilises genteel and middle-class identities; in certain contexts she mobilises a radical identity. This protean self-fashioning, in turn, allows readers to cast themselves in multiple roles in relation to the narrative:

■ The popularity of *Jane Eyre* may just as well result from the ways in which it offers up possibilities of self-constitution – enabling readers to produce alternate selves – as from the ways in which it reinforces an existing identity.[35] □

In Vanden Bossche's analysis, the political tendency of *Jane Eyre* is neither intrinsically radical nor conservative and it cannot be accused of merely reproducing bourgeois ideology to bourgeois consumers. Rather, it 'creates a space' that readers can appropriate in multiple ways as they, like Jane, produce identities 'through which to confront their own particular historical situations'. These identities are not shaped by class alone, but by social markers including gender, race, and nationality. The following chapter examines *Jane Eyre*'s use of discourses surrounding race, nation, and empire: a factor in the novel that many early critics ignored but which, since the 1980s, has magnetised and polarised critical opinion.

CHAPTER FIVE

Bertha's Savage Face:
Postcolonial Concerns

The British Empire is at both the geographical margin and the ideological centre of *Jane Eyre*. This is the view of many late twentieth and early twenty-first century critics, who draw attention to the various ways in which the novel's 'plot', in the twin sense of its outcomes and the space in which it locates its action, depends upon the far reaches of an empire that is outside the pale of the central romance between Jane and Rochester yet funds, defines, and threatens to undermine their union. Rochester's Creole wife, Bertha, comes from the West Indies, where Rochester was sent by his family to marry money. That money and perhaps the blood of his wife, who turns into a creature with a 'savage', 'blackened' face and swollen, dark lips, is infused by the legacy of African slaves, who were sold in the West Indies in a triangular trade involving commodities such as sugar and rum, which were then shipped to Europe. Jane's uncle in Madeira, another point on this trading route, is connected to the West Indies and her inheritance is thus also linked to imperial traffic that has slavery at its roots. India and the East also feature strongly in *Jane Eyre*'s plot. Most obviously, Jane considers going to India as a missionary with her cousin St John Rivers and the novel ends with a letter from St John in Calcutta [Kolkata] where, Jane remarks, he 'labours for his race' and is likely soon to die. More subtly, the imagery of the harem and of 'sati' – the practice in which Hindu widows sacrificed themselves on a pyre to burn alongside their dead husbands – recurs in Jane's conversations with Rochester about the boundaries of their relationship. The nature and meanings of *Jane Eyre*'s deployment of discourses of empire, race, and cultural difference have become among the most hotly debated topics of modern Brontë studies.

Postcolonial criticism stems from the period following the Second World War when most of the colonies held by European powers gained political independence. Such independence, however, served to highlight the lingering effects of colonialism on language, education, and the literature read, taught, and written in these states.[1] Postcolonial studies interrogate the relationship between culture and society with particular regard to the power relations and cultural assumptions woven into cultural exchange between former colonising and colonised countries and the role that culture plays in furthering imperialist ends. One of the first overtly postcolonial responses to *Jane Eyre* was *Wide Sargasso Sea* (1966), a novel by Jean Rhys (1890–1979), born on the Caribbean island of Dominica. Rhys's novel is an imaginative prequel to *Jane Eyre* that takes Bertha Mason as its central character and sympathetically depicts her tragic life before and after her marriage to Rochester. The novel is an important critical engagement with *Jane Eyre* that addresses, albeit through fiction, Brontë's depiction of the West Indies and Rochester's first wife, challenging the assumptions implicit in *Jane Eyre* and of readers for whom the focus and outcome of Brontë's classic text seem desirable and inevitable. In *Wide Sargasso Sea*, it is Jane who is a subsidiary figure, an unnamed girl in a white dress whom Bertha glimpses in a corridor. By choosing to make the experience of the colonial/colonised subject[2] central rather than marginal, Rhys suggests the exclusion practised upon Bertha's story and subjectivity in Brontë's text. Indeed, in *Wide Sargasso Sea*, Bertha's first name is Antoinette: she is called Bertha only by her husband, who fears the foreignness of her ancestry, her language, and the 'madness' that he has been told characterises her family history. In *Wide Sargasso Sea*, we see that Bertha's eventual psychological breakdown is caused by the violence, exclusion, and multiple displacements visited upon her as a consequence of her gender and ethnicity. What is construed from outside as 'mad' and inspires disgust in the colonist is, arguably, the colony itself and the anger, violence, and lawlessness of colonisation that it reflects back upon its occupiers. Rhys reappropriates elements present in *Jane Eyre*, such as the imagery of mirrors and supernatural motifs, but uses them to question the novel's unwritten code of self-identification and estrangement. Where Jane Eyre dubs Bertha a 'Vampyre', Rhys has Bertha face the taunt that she is a 'zombie', 'a dead person who seems to be alive or a living person who is dead [that] can also be the spirit of a place'; but Rhys shows both that this description might equally apply to Rochester and that, as a term of abuse, it has complex roots in interracial tension and unsympathetic cultural reading.[3] *Wide Sargasso Sea* comments on the various ways in which *Jane Eyre* uses the imagery of 'otherness' to legitimise and naturalise the progress of its white hero and heroine to affluence and dominance at the expense of the colonised.

'THE IMPERIALIST PROJECT DISPLACED AND DISPERSED': JANE'S JOURNEY TO POWER

The seminal academic postcolonial reading of *Jane Eyre* was Gayatri Spivak's 'Three Women's Texts and A Critique of Imperialism' (1985), which draws on *Wide Sargasso Sea*, although it is also critical of Rhys's novel. Spivak emphasises that her 'stance need not be an accusing one' and that her reading does not aim 'to undermine the excellence of the individual artist'. Rather, she seeks to examine the '"worlding' of what is today "the Third World"' by Western culture and to expose the ways in which an individualist feminism, based in Europe and Anglo-America, has unthinkingly reproduced the 'axioms of imperialism' in *Jane Eyre*. The process of 'worlding' is one in which cultural representations reinforce the imperialist map; other cultures appear distant, exotic, and in need of recovery and interpretation by the coloniser. Spivak argues that: 'It should not be possible to read nineteenth-century British literature without remembering that imperialism, understood as England's social mission, was a crucial part of the representation of England to the English'.[4]

Spivak notes the way in which 'the marginalization and privatization of the protagonist' is achieved in the very first scene of *Jane Eyre*, where Jane has slipped into the breakfast room and is 'shrined in a double retirement' in the window seat. Jane is an individualist and the reader is made complicit in her assertion of 'self-marginalized uniqueness'. We are to understand that she deserves to determine her own space and to read according to her own rules. In Spivak's analysis it is the active ideology of imperialism that provides the discursive field, enabling Jane to progress from the counter-family (the Reeds, where she does not belong) to the legal family (marriage to Rochester). Bertha, the Jamaican Creole, must be disinherited and then destroyed to make way for the superior Jane. Brontë makes this acceptable through blurring the human/animal frontier in her depiction of Bertha:

> ■ In the deep shade, at the further end of the room, a figure ran backwards and forwards. What it was, whether beast or human being, one could not, at first sight, tell: it grovelled, seemingly, on all fours; it snatched and growled like some strange wild animal: but it was covered with clothing, and a quantity of dark, grizzled hair, wild as a mane, hid its head and face.[5] □

The situation, Spivak argues, implicitly asserts an imperative above and beyond the letter of the law. Rochester is legally bound to Bertha but, in terms of the novel's narrative energy, cannot be expected to feel anything but pity and disgust for a creature that bears no visible social relation to him. The imperial axiomatic is again reproduced in Rochester's speech about Jamaica in which he compares the 'fiery West-Indian night', pierced by Bertha's screams, to Hell:

> ■ "'This life,' said I at last, 'is hell! this is the air – those are the sounds of the bottomless pit! I have a right to deliver myself from it if I can [...] let me break away, and go home to God!' [...]

"A wind fresh from Europe blew over the ocean and rushed through the open casement: the storm broke, streamed, thundered, blazed, and the air grew pure [...] it was true Wisdom that consoled me in that hour, and showed me the right path to follow.
"The sweet wind from Europe was still whispering in the refreshed leaves, and the Atlantic was thundering in glorious liberty [...]
"'Go,' said Hope, 'and live again in Europe [...] you have done all that God and humanity require of you.'[6] □

These passages validate the view of the coloniser, of Europe as the seat of wisdom, liberty, and purity and the 'Other' as a region of moral darkness. Rochester's right is asserted as divinely authorised while, as a creature on the boundary between human and animal, his wife's entitlement is deliberately weakened.

It is crucial, Spivak asserts, that we move our analysis beyond the 'minimal diagnosis of racism' to understand the imperialist project in which *Jane Eyre*, like other nineteenth-century novels, is involved. We need to reflect on our own critical mission. Marxist critics like Terry Eagleton, Spivak says, see Jane's transition from counter-family to family 'only in terms of the ambiguous class position of the governess', while feminist critics such as Sandra Gilbert and Susan Gubar 'have seen Bertha Mason only in psychological terms, as Jane's dark double'.[7] Attending to the absence of race and Empire from earlier readings of *Jane Eyre* involves acknowledging the tacit complicity of the (typically white) European or Anglo-American academic in reading and transmitting a story of nineteenth-century cultural achievement that obliterates the experience of the colonised subject. Feminists have celebrated *Jane Eyre* as the story of a woman's self-fulfilment and her achievement of companionate love and childbearing: but the ambition of nineteenth-century feminist individualism, Spivak suggests, is greater than this. It is also engaged in a project of 'soul making', which, in philosophical terms, justifies imperialism through the assumption that 'heathens' need to be 'humanised' so that they, too, can be treated as individual ends in themselves. In *Jane Eyre* this aspect of imperialism is presented through the narrative of St John Rivers, who is 'granted the important task of concluding the text'.[8] His mission to 'labour for his race' in India is given a privileged allegorical dimension through references to *The Pilgrim's Progress*; he is placed amongst the 'called, and chosen, and faithful' in language that is couched in the 'unquestioned idiom of imperialist presuppositions'.

Spivak's brief and provocative reading stimulated a series of responses exploring in greater detail the postcolonial mode of approaching *Jane Eyre* that she had outlined. Among these is Firdous Azim's *The Colonial Rise of the Novel* (1993), which sees *Jane Eyre* as following a pattern established by much earlier, prototypical novels including *Oroonoko* (1688) by Aphra Behn (1640–89) and *Roxana* (1724) by Daniel Defoe (1660–1731) in which the Enlightenment fantasy of the consistent, unified, speaking subject (the narrator) depends upon 'the effacement of *Other* subjects', usually differentiated by class, gender, and race. Possessing many of the attributes commonly associated in the European mind with native peoples (sexual promiscuity, abnormal physiology, violence, irrationality), Bertha is 'the site for the colonial encounter in the text'.[9] She is Jane's 'Other': a distorted mirror-image that enables Jane to define herself through difference. However, Azim disagrees with Spivak's analysis that Jane concludes the novel as a homogeneous, integrated subject in contradistinction to Bertha, who is smashed into pieces. Confrontation with the 'Other', in Azim's reading, serves as much to undermine Jane's identity as to reinforce it:

■ Savagery, madness, and sexuality, defined as Other, merge in the figure of Bertha Mason. Jane Eyre in confrontation with Bertha Mason faces, in a mirror, the 'dark' Other side of her own psyche. A mimetic relationship is set up between the two women. This process of mimesis is as much doubling as opposition and serves to destabilise, as well as to secure, Jane's identity. If Bertha Mason is Jane's antithesis, the distinction between them can only be secured by a type of initiation or rite of passage in which, momentarily, they are the *same*.[10] □

Twentieth-century feminists, Azim contends, have celebrated *Jane Eyre* as a female *Bildungsroman* in which 'the female author, the female protagonist and the female reader are joined together in sisterly harmony and recognition', but this is a misreading. In fact, Jane Eyre is a much less coherent figure than feminists wish her to be: she remains inevitably linked to and threatened by the 'Other', upon whose repression the novel as a form is founded, and who must be denied in order for the fragile fiction of her autonomous selfhood to stand.[11]

SLAVERY, THE SERAGLIO AND SATI: SYMPATHY WITH THE COLONISED?

Other critics have taken different slants from Spivak on the relationship between feminism and imperialism in *Jane Eyre* and in modern critical practice. In 'The Seraglio or Suttee: Charlotte Brontë's *Jane Eyre*' (1987) Mary Ellis Gibson argues that the imagery of empire in the novel is predominantly critical: 'the metaphors associated with empire in *Jane Eyre* create a subversive, if covert and ambiguous, criticism of domination in domestic relationships, a criticism that extends to British imperialist impulses themselves'.[12]

In Gibson's view, Brontë in *Jane Eyre*:

■ systematically develops the language of master and slave, of tyranny and submission; she draws analogies between Jane's position and that of subjects in various empires – the Roman empire, the Ottoman empire, the British empire in the West Indies and India, and even the Israel of the patriarchs [...] Brontë's allusions to empire allow her to make the curious move of criticizing domestic arrangements and British Christianity from the point of view of the 'pagan' woman.[13] □

Jane's repeated confrontation with male despotism, whether in the person of John Reed, Mr Brocklehurst, Rochester, or St John Rivers, Gibson argues, aligns her with the colonised female. The language of *Jane Eyre* is highly sceptical of the imperial mission, sympathising instead with those who suffer under its regime. Jane critically compares John Reed with the Roman emperors, 'Nero, Caligula, etc', and her own situation with that of an oppressed slave. In Brocklehurst's eyes, Jane, whom he accuses of being a liar, is 'evidently an interloper and an alien', 'worse than many a little heathen who says its prayers to Brahma and kneels before Juggernaut'. Jane rejects Brocklehurst's doctrine, which he describes as his Christian 'mission' to 'subdue nature' and teach the girls of Lowood 'to clothe themselves with shamefacedness and sobriety'. Gibson suggests: 'Metaphorically, then, Jane is on the side of heathen women – Hindu and Muslim – inciting them to mutiny she takes the part of the heathen against both oriental despotism and the Christian God as Master'.[14]

Again, when Jane confronts Rochester's overweening power in their relationship, the language Brontë employs is imperial. Rochester refers to Bertha as 'Messalina', implicitly identifying himself as Claudius, emperor of many wives.[15] When Rochester plays charades, he appears as an 'Israelitish' figure 'from patriarchal days'. During their engagement, Rochester behaves like a 'sultan'; he tells Jane that he would not exchange her for 'the Grand Turk's whole seraglio [harem]'. She responds with spirit that he is welcome to go out to Stamboul [Istanbul] and buy female slaves but, if he does, she will 'go out as a missionary to preach liberty to them that are enslaved – your harem inmates amongst the rest. I'll get admitted there, and I'll stir up mutiny'. Jane counters Rochester's possessive sexual orientalism with imagery of resistance to patriarchal, imperial power.

Finally, Gibson suggests, Brontë uses the imagery of 'suttee' (or 'sati'), in which Hindu widows threw themselves onto their husbands' funeral pyres, as a 'figure for Jane's relationship to Rochester and, more seriously, as a prophecy of what her marriage to St. John might entail'.[16] When Rochester sings a ballad about his love dying for him, Jane coolly retorts that 'I had as good a right to die when my time came as he had: but I should bide that time, and not be hurried away in a suttee'. In this and in her final rejection of St John's marriage proposal, which would involve sacrificing herself to being 'grilled alive' in India, Jane identifies with the colonised female, but asserts her right to resist subjection. The discomfiting shadow of female sacrifice and imperial violence, Gibson argues, is, however, never quite erased from *Jane Eyre*; the novel 'stops short of a thorough critique of empire':

■ Despite the consistency of Brontë's metaphors and the power in Jane's rejection of the seraglio and suttee, the conclusion of Brontë's novel is ambiguous [...] In the end, Jane's domestic happiness depends upon her inheritance from the West Indian trade, on Rochester's income drawn partly from the same source, and on the death of Bertha Mason Rochester, who is the Creole shadow of Jane's own oppression and who perishes actually, as Jane herself could have perished metaphorically, in a self-immolating fire.[17] □

Although Jane Eyre, in Gibson's view, cannot shrug off the ties that bind her to the legacy of imperialism, the novel consistently critiques those ties by comparing the subjection she suffers with that of colonized peoples and by championing her resistance to her own enslavement.

PART OF A SYSTEM OF FEMINIST ORIENTALIST DISCOURSE

Joyce Zonana in 'The Sultan and the Slave: Feminist Orientalism and the Structure of Jane Eyre' (1993) agrees that the metaphor of 'the sultan and the slave' is pervasive in *Jane Eyre*, but disputes Gibson's reading of its significance. In her view, Brontë is deploying imagery that by 1847 was an established part of Western feminist discourse, which encouraged British men to accept a degree of female emancipation by associating female repression with 'backward' and 'foreign' Eastern societies:

■ Charlotte Brontë's sultan/slave simile displaces the source of patriarchal oppression onto an 'Oriental,' 'Mahometan' [Muslim] society, enabling British readers to contemplate local problems without questioning their own self-definition as Westerners and Christians [...] in developing her simile throughout her narrative, Jane does not so much criticize (in the words of Mary Ellis Gibson) 'domestic arrangements and British Christianity from the point of view of the "pagan" woman' as define herself as a Western missionary seeking to redeem not the 'enslaved' woman outside the fold of Christianity and Western ideology but the despotic man who has been led astray within it.[18] □

Zonana argues that *Jane Eyre* is embedded in a long literary tradition of depicting Eastern sexual and moral practices as alien and abhorrent that began with travellers' tales in the early eighteenth century and was absorbed into liberal feminist writing in the work of, among others, the early feminist writer Mary Wollstonecraft (1759–97), the poet Elizabeth Barrett Browning (1806–61), and the hospital reformer and nursing pioneer Florence Nightingale (1820–1910):

■ Part of the larger orientalism that Edward Said has shown to inform Western self-representation, the function of these images is not primarily to secure Western domination over the East, though certainly they assume and enforce that domination. Rather, by figuring objectionable aspects of life in the West as 'Eastern,' these Western feminist writers rhetorically define their project as the removal of Eastern elements from Western life.[19] □

Zonana analyses in detail the episode in the silk warehouse following Jane and Rochester's engagement, where Jane feels uncomfortably that she is being treated like a 'doll' and that in loading her with commodities, Rochester is demeaning her. To Zonana, one of the most interesting features of their exchange is that Jane does not inform Rochester that she is inwardly comparing his behaviour to that of a sultan:

■ She simply asks him to stop looking at her 'in that way'. Rochester is astute enough to understand Jane's unspoken reference, suggesting that feminist orientalist discourse is so pervasive as to be accessible to the very men it seeks to change: '"Oh, it is rich to see and hear her!" he exclaimed. "Is she original? Is she piquant? I would not exchange this one little English girl for the Grand Turk's whole seraglio – gazelle-eyes, houri forms, and all!"' – Rochester suggests that he will take Jane instead of a harem, though Jane bristles at the 'Eastern allusion': '"I'll not stand you an inch in the stead of a seraglio"; I said; "so don't consider me an equivalent for one."'[20] □

Unexamined Western assumptions about Eastern polygamy are overwhelmingly negative and Brontë reproduces a standard distaste. Jane's announcement that, if Rochester does attempt to form a harem, she will go out as a missionary to 'preach liberty to them that are enslaved', tie him up, and force him to sign a charter 'the most liberal that despot ever yet conferred' is, in Zonana's view, a playful but pointed assertion of the Western woman's superior, educative role:

■ Jane's comparison of Rochester to a sultan proves to be no exaggeration. The narrative makes plain that it is because she sees him in this way that she later is able to free herself from a degrading relationship with a man who has bought women, is willing to become a bigamist, and acts like a despot. The plot thus validates the figurative language, making of it much more than a figure. This Western man is 'Eastern' in his ways, and for Jane to be happy, he must be thoroughly Westernized.[21] □

In Zonana's reading, feminist and imperialist discourses play into one another's hands in *Jane Eyre*. In *Reaches of Empire: The English Novel from Edgeworth to Dickens* (1991) Suvendrini Perera also observes a complicated intersection between 'feminist, imperialist, and individualist impulses' that defines this text.[22] Comparing the imagery of 'sati' in *Jane Eyre* with similar imagery in Thackeray's *Vanity Fair,* and Jane Austen's *Emma* (1814), Perera concludes that these texts require the vocabulary of 'oriental misogyny' to describe 'the sexual risks faced by the unattached Englishwoman', but while deploying it they must simultaneously reject genuine sisterhood between Western and Eastern women in order to maintain the boundaries that establish Western cultural superiority: 'The vocabulary of oriental misogyny operates in two ways, enabling the articulation of certain feminist concerns, but limiting their application within the constraints of the master discourse of empire.'[23]

Western feminist discourse, of which *Jane Eyre* is part, depends upon the alienation of the Eastern woman as an erotic object in need of salvation.

THE IDEOLOGY OF IMPERIALISM QUESTIONED – AND THEN REAFFIRMED

Susan Meyer in *Imperialism at Home: Race and Victorian Women's Fiction* (1996), sees in *Jane Eyre* a conflict between 'sympathy for the oppressed' and a hostile 'assertion of white racial supremacy'. She considers Gayatri Spivak wrong in maintaining that *Jane Eyre* is characterised by an 'unquestioned ideology' of imperialism: in her view the novel *does* question and criticise imperialist ideology. Ultimately, however, it reaffirms that ideology, retreating from its earlier critique and permitting conventional racial hierarchies to fall back into place.

Meyer argues that throughout her fiction, including her final, unfinished novel *Emma* (1853), which seems to have a black heroine, Charlotte Brontë:

■ uses [...] references to relations between Europeans and races subjected to the might of European imperialism [...] primarily native Americans and African slaves in the West Indies and the United States [...] to represent various configurations of power in British society: female subordination in sexual relationships, female insurrection and rage against male domination, and the oppressive class position of the female without family ties and a middle-class income.[24] □

In Meyer's view, race is thus, importantly, a *metaphor* through which Brontë presents gender and class inequalities in *Jane Eyre*:

■ Throughout the novel, the marginality and disempowerment Jane experiences due to her class and gender are represented through a metaphorical linking between Jane and several of the nineteenth-century's 'dark races'. In the novel's opening scene, she sits in her window seat, exiled from the drawing room, 'cross-legged, like a Turk'. She cries out in rage against Mrs. Reed 'in a savage, high voice', and when she tells Helen that she believes in striking back against injustice, she is told that 'heathens and savage tribes hold that doctrine, but Christians and civilised nations disown it' [...] In Jane's adulthood Rochester sees in her passions that 'may rage furiously, like true heathens, as they are', although held in check by her reason, and he finds in her resolute, wild spirit a 'savage, beautiful creature'. When Jane confronts the angry, passionate Rochester, after the revelation of his previous marriage, she feels, in her attempt to assert control, 'as the Indian, perhaps, feels when he slips over the rapid in his canoe'.[25] □

However, although the novel uses race to present sympathetically the predicament of the lower middle-class woman, it does not extend its sympathies to other dispossessed groups.

Jane Eyre is, Meyer believes, marked by language associated with slave uprisings of the 1820s and the emancipation of British West Indian slaves in 1838. The novel's main action seems to occur before 1838 and both Jane's early rebellion against the Reeds, in which she compares herself with a slave, and Bertha Mason Rochester's torching of Thornfield recall the slave uprisings feared by the British in Jamaica. Brontë's use of this imagery, according to Meyer, is 'an indictment of British imperialism in the West Indies' in which Bertha is associated with the figure of the black slave. (There is some controversy over Bertha's colour, which is not made clear in *Jane Eyre*. She is described as a 'Creole' – a word that has a variety of possible interpretations.) Here, Meyer suggests, 'Creole' connotes that Bertha Mason is a descendant of the forced unions commonplace in the colonies between white plantation owners and their black workers. Emphasis in the novel on Rochester's 'race' being desirable to unite with her wealth hints, Meyer argues, that his contribution to their marriage is racial purity compared with Bertha's darker blood. Rochester's imprisonment of Bertha on the third floor of Thornfield thus replays the British history of imperial domination. When Thornfield burns down, Rochester is appropriately punished for his attempts to enslave both Bertha and Jane and for his colonial spoils. Yet in Bertha, Brontë creates a character 'to use as the vividly embodied signifier of oppression' and then 'has the sign destroy itself'. Her nascent critique of imperialism swallows its own tongue.

There is a further doubling-back in Brontë's portrayal of the Indian imperial mission in the novel. Meyer argues that *Jane Eyre* 'by no means unambiguously endorses' St John's missionary project. St John Rivers, the purest English racial type, with fair hair, blue eyes, and a classical profile, proves to be a cold and haughty man, who treats the 'physically inferior' Jane rather as if she were a 'savage' to be educated and redeemed. The figurative language of the novel associates domination and oppression with the oppressive heat and disease of the regions to which St John is attracted to work. But the novel's final response to such oppression is not to relieve it but to dis-tance it, to keep England 'clean' for its middle-class heroine: to this end, St John's later history is quarantined from the main body of the narrative. Jane achieves an egalitarian marriage, free of the imperial domination that has been used to figure power relations between the sexes in the novel. But she writes her story in Indian ink: the fiction of redistributed wealth and power between the sexes in England is made possible only by the continued exploitation of the colonies. Meyer decides:

■ Like imperialist trade itself, bringing home the spoils of other countries to become commodities in England, such as Indian ink, the use of the racial 'other' as a metaphor for class and gender struggles in England commodi-fies the dark-skinned people of the British empire as they exist in historical actuality and transforms them into East or West Indian ink with which to write a novel about ending injustices within England.[26] □

Jane Eyre, then, is finally complicit in the imperial ideology it begins to interrogate.

JANE AS THE IDEAL VICTORIAN WOMAN OF EMPIRE

In *Allegories of Empire: The Figure of Woman in the Colonial Text* (1993), Jenny Sharpe argues that the simple distinction between 'coloniser' and 'colonised' is insufficiently nuanced to articulate the 'complex system of tropes' through which Jane Eyre constitutes herself in relation to women of other ethnicities and nationalities. Sharpe instead proposes a 'two-part constellation' in which: '(1) the "rebel slave" and "harem woman" are used to articulate the forms of appropriate and inappropri-ate rebellion, and (2) the creole woman and sati rework the doctrine of woman's mission'.[27]

In Sharpe's reading, while *Jane Eyre* uses rhetoric established during the campaign to abolish slavery to win sympathy for Jane's situation in the Reed household, 'the figure of the rebel slave [...] lacks the cognition on which moral agency is based. This is the mark of racial difference, a point of resistance for extending the meaning of the slave rebellions to a female agency predicated on speech'.[28] Jane may initially be *like* a rebel slave in her predicament but, crucially, she has a *different*, educated sense of her own freedom, rights, and autonomy that will enable her to 'channel her desires into a socially acceptable form of self determination'. The story of her growth to adulthood involves Jane negotiating a space between the unacceptably violent, uncontrolled rage of the rebel slave and the equally unacceptable passivity under exploitation of the harem woman.

Again, at Thornfield, Jane's character emerges in the space created between the two poles of extreme female self-indulgence (represented by the Creole, Bertha) and extreme female self-sacrifice (represented by the Hindu widow who commits sati). Sharpe disagrees with Susan Meyer's reading of Bertha as, in essence, black – a representative of the colonised races. In Sharpe's view, Bertha is clearly a female representative of the worst kind of coloniser, the white-identified West Indian 'sugar plantoc-racy'. During the years following the abolition of slavery, Sharpe observes, allusions to this declining and discredited class were deployed as 'a useful shorthand for depravity'.[29] It is not so much Bertha's madness that disgusts Rochester as her debauchery: her excesses and vices cause her to lose con-trol of her mind rather than vice versa. Rochester, however, refuses to use cruelty towards her, a restraint that signals his difference from the colonial slaveholder. In this way, the Creole Bertha serves as a comparative marker for the purity of Rochester's national character as well as a marker for Jane, the 'true English woman', who will succumb neither to the temptations of inappropriate abandon nor of inappropriate submission.

■ The paradox of being an individual in the domestic sphere is resolved by defining the English woman in relation to other women instead of to men. In *Jane Eyre* a domestic form of social agency is established through a national and racial splitting of femininity, with the Creole woman serving as a figure of self-indulgence and the Oriental woman, of self-immolation.[30] □

Brontë uses a variety of images of 'other' women, in Sharpe's reading, both as a foil against which to establish Jane's heroic female autonomy and in order to generate a particular vision of English national charac-ter: Jane 'embodies the new honesty and national pride that will guide England in its overseas mission'.[31]

Other modern critics have also explored the sense in which Jane is 'the ideal Victorian woman of Empire'. In *Rule Britannia: Women, Empire and Victorian Writing* (1995), Deirdre David remarks that, armed with 'physical toughness, moral high-mindedness, and innate bossi-ness', Jane has all the desirable qualities needed to be a good governess, not merely of children, but of Britain's expanding colonial possessions:

■ An assured self-alliance with a national authority is to be found every-where in Jane's thinking. For example, the historical circumstances that sanction her questions to herself – whether it is better 'to be a slave in a fool's paradise at Marseilles [...] or to be a village schoolmistress, free and honest, in a breezy mountain nook in the healthy heart of England' – reside exactly in her sense of being British, of being able rationally to resist Rochester's sexuality (unlike his French, Italian, and German mistresses), of working steadily in the 'healthy heart of England' rather than lounging around in a stifling villa in Marseilles. Jane's values coincide with those prescribed for British imperial womanhood: first, a belief in her own social and cultural superiority to the native; second, recognition that she must sacrifice her physical comfort in the cause of civilizing the native; and third, an acceptance of her ancillary status in the male-dominated business of running the empire.[32] □

As the 'symbolic governess of Empire' Jane, in David's analysis, is a both a ruling subject, whose authority is felt by the erring colonist (Rochester) and the aspiring missionary (Rivers) alike, and a subordinate object, of whom sacrifices are persistently required in the demanding work of writing the nation.

Jane's choice of lovers is also a choice between different kinds of work for empire. She can convert the colonised by going out to India as a missionary with St John, or she can rehabilitate the coloniser, Rochester. David argues that in the colonial politics of the 1830s and 1840s, the latter task was of prime importance. Rochester's West Indian plunders, with the moral corruption they have involved, belong to an older phase of imperialism, one that threatens to infect English society: 'Jane Eyre is about the way Thornfield is not the West Indies and is not India; and it is also about the way that what is in the West Indies and what is in India comes back to invade the metropolitan spaces of empire'.[33]

Jane's thoroughly modern mission, in David's reading, is to reform Rochester, the 'antiquated patriarch whose imaginative affiliation with Eastern sultans places him in the morally tainted stages of colonial governance'.[34] Unlike that of the 'imperious' Blanche Ingram, Jane's sway is reasonable, moderate, and just. Under her responsible govern-ance, Rochester is 'civilised' from his former savage and unchristian ways and becomes fit to represent, with Jane, Britain's new Victorian culture of Empire.[35]

JANE EYRE AND IRELAND

In recent years postcolonial readings of Jane Eyre have considered the novel as a response not only to the relationship between England and its far-flung empire, but also to tensions much closer to home. Patrick Brontë, Charlotte's father, came from Ireland, once a rebellious colony of England and, during Brontë's lifetime, bound to Great Britain by an Act of Union (1800) whose compromised political terms many found unsatisfactory. Relations between England and Ireland were particularly tense during the period of *Jane Eyre*'s composition and publication: the Irish potato famine (1845–49) caused at least a million deaths and forced a million people to emigrate; the end of belated relief efforts in 1847, with the resumption of tax demands from England, brought widespread unrest. In 'White Chimpanzees and Oriental Despots: Racial Stereotyping and Edward Rochester' (1996), Elsie Michie states that: 'Reading *Jane Eyre* in the historical context of Anglo-Irish relations, specifically as a novel written in the aftermath of the potato famine, enables us to identify the oriental despot as an emblem of displaced colonial anxieties'.[36]

In Michie's reading, Rochester has many racial features associated in the Victorian period with the Irish: he is dark, heavy-set, with a 'broad chest almost disproportionate to his length of limb' in contrast to St John Rivers's true 'English' appearance: fair in hair and complexion, tall, with blue eyes and a pure, Classical profile. Rochester's recklessness, morbid sensitivity, and intense personal attachments also conform to contemporary stereotypes of Irish character. The fact that he is persistently associated with the East, as an 'emir', 'sultan', and 'Grand Turk', should not blind us to this Irish connection: Rochester's racial difference is displaced via oriental imagery. Rochester thus embodies a complex amalgam of fears and desires associated with otherness and colonial mastery: he is both rebel Irishman and English colonist, black and white. The power play involved in his courtship of Jane allows Brontë to stage a variety of responses to race and empire – attraction and repulsion, submission and revolt – that, while couched in metaphors associated with India and the Orient, persistently recall Anglo-Irish relations.

Katherine Constable in 'Writing the Minefield: Reflections of Union in Charlotte Brontë's *Jane Eyre* and *Shirley*' (2003) also reads Jane and Rochester's relationship as acting out aspects of the troubled union between England and Ireland. In her analysis, however, Jane represents the figure of Ireland. Constable highlights Charlotte Brontë's early and persistent interest in Anglo-Irish politics and the presence of Irish themes, characters, and vocabulary in her juvenile works such as 'An Adventure in Ireland' (1829):

■ Her chief protagonists were frequently Irish-born, the most important examples being The Duke of Zamorna and the 'divinely Irish' Mina Laury. Mina is frank about her heritage, as Brontë could never be in Haworth: '"Ah," said Mina Laury smiling, "you and I are both Westerns Mr O'Neill – Irish – and we favour our countrymen."' Zamorna, however, is a 'gentleman' of ancient family, a blow-in of old, while Mina is a soldier's daughter. This juxtaposition would eventually merge into the relationship between Jane Eyre and Rochester.[37] □

Constable suggests that not only the potato famine but also the movement to repeal the Act of Union, led by Daniel O'Connell (1775–1847), which split over the issue of non-violence in 1846, is a vital context for reading *Jane Eyre*. At a time when it seemed possible that a Catholic revolt would threaten the Anglo-Irish Union, the story of Jane and Rochester's tempestuous progress toward a marriage of equals has, Constable proposes, an allegorical significance. According to Constable's intriguing allegorical interpretation, Jane (Ireland) is at the beginning of novel in a humiliating and powerless situation, perpetually reminded of her dependent status. She struggles for equality, refusing to be treated as an inferior. Despite nearly being tricked into a fraudulent marriage, she forgives the deception and violence she has suffered and eventually achieves a union based on parity and mutual esteem. Constable judges that 'this alternative spousal configuration can be seen to entail the potential formula for success in the marriage between Ireland and England as represented by Union'.[38]

DO WE NEED A POST-POSTCOLONIAL APPROACH TO *JANE EYRE*?

Have literary critics gone too far in emphasising the significance of race and colonial issues in *Jane Eyre*? Erin O'Connor's polemical article, 'Preface for a post-postcolonial criticism' (2003), argues that they have. O'Connor suggests that the postcolonial narrative of literary history has 'overwritten' the Victorian novel, ignoring the genre's 'thematic subtleties, structural indeterminacies, and genuine intellectual rigor', reducing every work to an 'allegory' for the non-literary processes of imperialism and nation-building.

O'Connor objects that the critical response to Gayatri Spivak's controversial assertion in 1985 that *Jane Eyre* was a prime example of the Victorian imperialist project at work has been 'essentially conciliatory' rather than questioning:

■ No one argues with Spivak's claim about how the novel operates within the ideology of imperialism. What they do dispute is her suggestion that feminist criticism somehow replicates the patterns we see in the nineteenth-century novel. As Jenny Sharpe has noted, *Jane Eyre* has become 'a contested site for establishing the relationship between feminism and imperialism'. The observation is a revealing one. It tells us that *Jane Eyre*'s privileged position as a 'contested site' is not itself contested.[39] □

O'Connor feels that the many studies that have come out in recent years on '*Jane Eyre*'s relationship to Jamaica, to India, to Ireland, and to Africa; to colonialism, to Orientalism, and to racism; to slavery, and to sati' have tended merely to replicate and consolidate Spivak's central contention that to fail to address imperialism in *Jane Eyre* is to be complicit in the prejudice and domination practised by imperialism. Ironically, postcolonial criticism of *Jane Eyre* has itself become a globalised empire with an assimilative ideology, intent on expanding its territory:

■ one could argue that Spivak's essay has done to Victorian studies something very like what she argues the Victorian novel has done to imperialism. Subjecting Jane Eyre to the very sort of 'information retrieval approach' that she accuses politically naïve critics of bringing to the study of third world literature, Spivak may be said to have exchanged one set of oversimplifications for another: in order to produce her account of the nineteenth-century novel's 'worlding', particularly as it relates to questions of feminism, individualism, and empire, she has chosen to simplify, and so objectify, the novel itself.[40] □

O'Connor, controversially, claims that, while *Jane Eyre* has been treated as a 'guide to nineteenth-century literary representations of empire', it actually has little to tell us about the imperial imagination. Bertha's story is a sub-plot, which does not require the level of attention it has recently commanded.[41] We need, in her view, a 'post-postcolonial criticism' that can stop berating the book 'for having bad politics' and browbeating the reader 'by prescribing a properly politicized reading practice'. Such a criticism would be inherently diverse and would begin to address the complexity and uniqueness of *Jane Eyre* and other novels as works of art, rather than subjecting them to paradigmatic readings whose chief purpose is to 'model politicized modes of thought'.

Modern readers, then, face an increasingly detailed map of studies devoted to investigating aspects of race, imperialism, political geography, and cultural self-fashioning in *Jane Eyre*, but the question of whether and how they choose to locate their own critical position on that map remains wide open. The final chapters of this guide look at the most recent developments in *Jane Eyre* criticism and the directions in which future studies might tend.

CHAPTER SIX

New Historicism and The Turn Toward History

Studies of *Jane Eyre* from 1980 to the present have been diverse and wide-ranging, but many are informed by a new interest in the novel's relationship to nineteenth-century social and cultural history. Critics have been at pains to situate *Jane Eyre*, its composition, publication, readership and later forms of transmission such as adaptations for theatre, radio, and cinema, within contexts that illuminate the ideas on which the novel draws, the debates in which it participates, the cultures of which it has been and remains a part.

The New Historicism, an academic approach that defined itself in American and British universities in the 1980s, strongly influenced by the work of Michel Foucault (1926–84), emphasizes the existence of literary works within a social reality that is characterised by political struggle and competition for power. The text cannot be viewed apart from the dynamics of the broader social and ideological contexts to which it necessarily responds and contributes. For new historicists, indeed, there are no dividing lines between text and context, literature and history. As John Brannigan explains:

■ Where many previous critical approaches to literary texts assumed that texts had some universal significance and essential ahistorical truth to impart, new historicist [...] critics tend to read literary texts as material products of specific historical conditions [...] texts of all kinds are the vehicles of politics insofar as texts mediate the fabric of social, political and cultural formations. This view is evident in the work of new historicist critics who read historical context through legal, medical and penal documents, anecdotes, travel writings, ethnological and anthropological narratives and, of course, literary texts [...] They refuse to see literary texts against an overriding background of history or to see history as a set of facts outside the written text.[1] □

New historicists dwell on the 'historicity' of cultural products such as novels: their embeddedness in a specific historical moment and cultural setting, which cannot be recovered but must be acknowledged and imagined, if the social and ideological investments of the text are to be understood.

In nineteenth-century studies, this preoccupation stimulated a new wave of archival research, much of it on materials that had once been disregarded as non-literary. Analysing an expanded range of cultural 'representations' and dismantling traditional hierarchies between them, a new historicist reading might deploy a medical treatise, a visual advertisement, or a popular song alongside a piece of fiction. Canonical hierarchies between literary works also come under critical fire from new historicists, who have described their approach as 'wary', 'sceptical' and even 'adversarial'.[2] Their techniques include 'discovering unexpected discursive contexts for literary works by pursuing their "supplements"[3] rather than their overt thematics' and investigating 'the history of the human body and the human subject'.[4] Importantly, new historicist critics are attentive to 'why and where and within what parameters we ourselves are reading a text', stressing that the linguistic, social, cultural and political dynamics of our own history are constantly at issue in our interpretation. The label 'new historicist' had become less popular by the late 1990s, but recent academic work continues to pursue the project of historicizing nineteenth-century literature, while considering how the politics of our own historicity play into our reading of Victorian representations.

The turn toward history in Brontë criticism has meant that *Jane Eyre* has increasingly been read against other nineteenth-century documents including contemporary autobiographies (which shed light on its unusual style of 'life-writing'), educational prospectuses and primers (which offer interesting comparisons with the curriculum at Lowood), Evangelical sermons, tracts and missionary writings (which help to place Brocklehurst's and St John Rivers's methods), and other Victorian texts on subjects ranging from the treatment of madness to the conduct of governesses.[5] It has also inspired a revisionist, sceptical approach to what is sometimes referred to as 'The Brontë Myth', a set of older stories about the Brontë family and their works, which, historicist critics point out, often owe more to romantic tradition than to considered analysis of the available historical data.[6] The painstaking work of Christine Alexander on the complex array of the Brontës' childhood writings has helped academics to trace the influences, especially of periodical literature, on their early creative world and how this relates to their later fiction. Margaret Smith's scholarly edition of Charlotte Brontë's *Letters* (1995–2004) greatly improved the accuracy and referencing of the texts once available to readers, shedding light on Brontë's own view of *Jane Eyre*. Juliet Barker's landmark 1994 biography, *The Brontës*, likewise opened up new views of the family's place in a nineteenth-century social and cultural milieu.[7] Haworth was romantically portrayed in Elizabeth Gaskell's *Life of Charlotte Brontë* (1857) as a grim and isolated rural backwater. In fact, as Barker among others demonstrates, Haworth was a busy, well-connected, politically and culturally active town in which Charlotte and her siblings had access to a wide variety of books, magazines, ideas and debates that permeate their fiction.

This chapter looks at some readings of *Jane Eyre* since 1980, which in different ways exemplify the turn toward history: the investigation of new contexts and supplements for reading the novel; the adoption of a demystifying, sceptical stance that challenges earlier habits of interpretation and a new interest in reading the body, especially as a site of competition for power. Historicist approaches often interconnect with Marxist, feminist and postcolonial readings; work discussed below in many cases relates to work discussed in earlier chapters.

HISTORICIZING *JANE EYRE*: PHRENOLOGY, PSYCHOLOGY, AND ECONOMICS

Sally Shuttleworth in *Charlotte Brontë and Victorian Psychology* (1996) dismantles the once-traditional view of Charlotte Brontë as an intuitive genius operating in a historical vacuum, arguing that *Jane Eyre*, like Brontë's other novels, is deeply engaged in Victorian debate about psychology, an emergent science closely linked both to the popular science of phrenology and to contemporary medical and economic theories of selfhood and bodily control. As Shuttleworth explains:

■ On publication, *Jane Eyre* was greeted by reviewers as a wonderfully 'natural' and 'real' depiction of emotional life. Its appeal [...] was less that it managed to capture as never before the inner workings of the mind, than that it incorporated into the novel contemporary psychological discourse [...] With the depiction of the heroine's psyche that follows the rise and fall of physiological energies, and of a romantic engagement which is less of a harmonious union between souls than a power struggle that centres on the ability of each partner to read, unseen, the hidden secrets of the other, we are clearly in new novelistic territory. Such terrain was to be found, however, in the context of medical and economic debates, and in the fields of psychiatry and the popular sciences of physiognomy[8] and phrenology. As Foucault has argued, the nineteenth century witnessed the emergence of a new economy of individual and social life, centred on the regulation of the forces of the body and controlled through surveillance. A new interiorized notion of selfhood arose and, concomitantly, new techniques of power designed to penetrate the hidden secrets of this hidden domain. Psychiatry and phrenology emerged as sciences, dedicated to decoding the external signs of the body in order to reveal the concealed inner play of forces which constitute individual subjectivity. Brontë's novels operate within this paradigm.[9] □

Phrenology was a system of reading the human head externally for evidence of its internal character. Based on the work of Franz Joseph Gall in the 1790s, it depended on the idea that the mind was divided into distinct faculties, which were located in different regions of the brain. Phrenologists believed that the relative strength and dominance of different cerebral 'organs', governing abilities such as verbal skill and traits such as benevolence, pride, and vanity, could be detected from analysing the relative prominence of different parts of an individual's skull. Phrenology had a very large following in the nineteenth century – one guide to the subject sold 90,000 copies – and Charlotte Brontë was keenly interested in the subject. There are several explicit references to phrenology in *Jane Eyre*: for example, where Rochester invites Jane to read his forehead, lifting up his hair to show 'a solid enough mass of intellectual organs; but an abrupt deficiency where the suave sign of benevolence should have risen',[10] or the scene where Rochester, disguised as a gypsy, reads Jane's head for signs of her character.

Various critics have considered Brontë's use of phrenology in *Jane Eyre*. In *Eros and Psyche: The Representation of Personality in Charlotte Brontë, Charles Dickens, and George Eliot* (1984), Karen Chase contends that it is part of the 'interior design' of the novel that the workings of the mind are imaged in spatial terms, just as the characters and phases of the novel occupy distinct spatial zones (houses and rooms, as Chase remarks, structure Jane's life experience).[11] This preoccupation with interior space, Chase argues, is characteristic of Brontë's figurative exploration of human psychology and emotional states: an exploration new in the Victorian novel. Sally Shuttleworth goes further. Arguing that phrenology is part of a new mode of thinking about selfhood that cuts across Victorian medical, political and economic discourse, she reads Brontë's use of phrenology in *Jane Eyre* as a politicized act.

Phrenology was a potentially liberating discourse for women and others excluded from social power, Shuttleworth posits, because it identified innate mental capacities that might be possessed by anyone and which could be developed with self-improvement and self-control. Jane Eyre, it is evident in the novel, possesses strong innate capacities which are stifled in her subordinate social role at the Reeds. In contemporary theory, the release of these psychological forces is necessary to individual health; Jane experiences this when she finally tells Mrs Reed what she thinks of her: 'It seemed as if an invisible bond had burst, and that I had struggled out into unhoped-for liberty'. However, phrenology also problematically presented a picture of the individual as the site of conflicting energies and competing faculties: a model of selfhood strikingly similar to contemporary political and economic models, which were moving from ideas of sovereign governance to models of competition, struggle, and flux as the natural human state. *Jane Eyre*, Shuttleworth argues, also embodies this insight from Victorian phrenology and psychology. As Jane herself recognises, she is a 'heterogeneous thing':

> ■ in *Jane Eyre* [...] [Brontë] explores the contradictions at the heart of theories of unified selfhood. Jane dwells repeatedly on her internal divisions, her lack of a unifying, controlling centre of self. In her conversations with Mrs Reed, 'something spoke out of me over which I had no control'. Although constrained grammatically to the use of 'I', Brontë draws attention to the illusory fiction of unified control connoted by that term.[12] □

Jane's narrative, says Shuttleworth, explores a tension that was central to Victorian thinking about economics, politics, and psychology, between the necessity for regulation and control and the necessity to maximise the flow of innate energies for the health of the social body. The passionate child and the hysterical, mad woman were classic models of psychological excess: women were often figured as at the mercy of their physiological urges. Jane has to negotiate these images of what she has been and might become, fighting 'a battle on two fronts: the internal struggle to regulate her own flow of energy, and the external, social fight to wrest control of the power of social definition'.[13] Shuttleworth points out that the language of the novel, with its explosive surges of expression contained within a tense structure of syntactic inversions, enacts this battle, replicating linguistically 'Jane's attempts to transgress social boundaries while remaining within an accepted social framework'.[14]

Jane and Rochester's relationship is also negotiated using the terms and ideas of phrenological discourse. Their courtship consists of a series of episodes in which one attempts to 'read' the propensities of the other while keeping the self unread. Erotic pleasure depends upon the dynamic tension between the release of energy, the penetration of another's self, and the regulation and control that prevent the self from ever fully being penetrated and uniting with another. Where earlier fiction, such as *Pamela* (1740) by Samuel Richardson (1689–1761), had made the heroine's virginity the elusive prize of the narrative's cat-and-mouse manoeuvres, in Brontë it is the inner self whose unveiling is a source of perpetually deferred erotic pleasure.

Shuttleworth suggests that the excitation and regulation of competing energies, with an emphasis on surveillance and the definition of self through opposition, links the new terms of Jane and Rochester's romance to the new paradigm of economic and political discourse in the early Victorian period. Those critics who identify isolated political moments in the novel, notably Jane's outburst on Thornfield's battlements about 'millions [...] in silent revolt', are missing the political ideas that permeate the novel on every level. On the one hand, Jane is a 'heroine of individualism'.[15] Her success is emblematic of the possibilities open to the innately gifted mind that regulates and improves its own capacities, defending its selfhood and achieving social power. On the other hand, Jane's story 'exposes the contradictions of individualist ideology'. Her selfhood, far from being unified, is an assemblage of diverse and conflicting elements, which the novel's ending does not resolve. Indeed, Shuttleworth claims, the 'internal contradictions' of *Jane Eyre* mirror those of Victorian discourses on economics, psychology, and society. The novel strives toward romantic union, but simultaneously presents courtship in terms that strongly resemble the competitive dynamics of the marketplace. It seems to take us into the realm of interiority, while showing that even that realm is socially constructed; and it exposes crucial contradictions at the heart of contemporary models of selfhood and of womanhood.

Mary A. Armstrong, in 'Reading a Head: *Jane Eyre*, Phrenology, and the Homoerotics of Legibility' (2005), extends Shuttleworth's account of phrenology in *Jane Eyre* to incorporate same-sex desire. The erotic pleasure of gazing at and deciphering another's countenance is, in Armstrong's account, not confined to the relationship between Jane and Rochester, but is also a feature of Jane's reading of female heads including Helen Burns's, Blanche Ingram's, and Rosamond Oliver's. This is not to say, Armstrong emphasizes, that Jane Eyre possesses lesbian tendencies (though a few critics have argued that the novel does arouse such tendencies).[16] Rather, because the discourse of phrenology crosses ideological and gender lines – the organs were deemed to lie in the same place in male and female heads – it allows for the expression of erotic pleasure in reading that likewise 'flickers' across heteroerotic and homoerotic boundaries. Such 'flickering' is noticeable in Jane's portrait of Blanche Ingram, which repeatedly turns into a sketch of Rochester. It is also, Armstrong argues, a feature of the scene in which Rochester, dressed as a female gypsy, reads Jane: a 'thinly masked sexual experience'.[17] The temporary de-centring of gender boundaries that such scenes allow us as readers, as well the characters within them, are, in Armstrong's view, typical of the 'spaces for trangressive desires'[18] that the novel opens up, which are all the more tantalising because they are only fleetingly visible.

Reading the Body: *Jane Eyre* and Visuality

Janet Gezari, in *Charlotte Brontë and Defensive Conduct* (1992), also focuses on the body in Brontë's novels, which she portrays as 'the site of social conflict and constraint'.[19] Gezari is particularly interested in

'Brontë's achievement as a writer on the defensive': the ways in which she incorporates cultural conflicts, including those concerning her own writing, into her fiction, via positive strategies of self-defence and self-vindication. Her characters 'define themselves in terms of their accommodation and resistance to hostile circumstances, characters, and readers. For Brontë, defensiveness is not just self-regarding or self-protective but an engaging enterprise of intelligent and imaginative counter-moves'.[20] Defensive strategies are deployed in the physical and in the verbal realm. Gezari argues that the body is an 'organizing motif' in Brontë's fiction and that her preoccupation with physical materiality pervades her language, which wrestles with abstractions, insisting on its continuity with the physical realm it represents.

Jane Eyre, says Gezari, is Brontë's 'defence of vision'. Charlotte began the novel when accompanying her father to Manchester where he underwent surgery to remove cataracts that were blinding him, so eyes would have been at the forefront of her concerns. Also at this time Charlotte was smarting from publishers' rejection of *The Professor*, her first novel: in this regard her own imaginative vision was under attack. Unsurprisingly then, Gezari proposes, references to eyes, sight, and 'vision' in the sense of revelatory imagining, saturate the narrative of *Jane Eyre*, which establishes Jane's view as 'not merely dominant but exclusive'.

Clues to the centrality of sight in *Jane Eyre*, Gezari suggests, are evident in Jane's name. In Brontë's manuscript, Adèle pronounces Jane's surname 'Aïre', which suggests a pronunciation close to 'Eyer' and even to the French verb 'haïr', meaning 'to hate'. Jane is, indeed, a notorious 'eyer', as well as a powerful hater, in the text: she persistently watches others, often from a place where they cannot see her, and resists others' attempts to use exposure and vision as a weapon against her:

■ Seeing in *Jane Eyre* opens up questions of power, property, and propriety in ways that help to explain this novel's eccentric relation to the tradition of the English novel and justify its perennial interest for feminist critics. When, in the compelling opening chapters of Jane Eyre, Jane is denied not only a place within the family circle but the right to look, first at the book she has taken with her into the window-seat, then at her attacker, the punishable impropriety of her so looking deserves more notice than it has had [...] The pictures in Bewick stimulate visions more engaging than those presented by either the interior of Gateshead Hall or the landscape outdoors, and such looking itself resists being kept in one's proper place by appropriating both a book and a prospect.[21] □

The freedom and intensity of Jane's gaze is a marker of her determination to improve her 'prospects' in life. Brocklehurst, like John Reed, attempts to harm her through making her the passive object of others' controlling vision. When he directs the gaze of the other pupils[22] at her, branding her a liar, Jane feels 'their eyes directed like burning-glasses against my scorched skin'. Jane, however, defends her own power of vision against this exposure, both by repudiating his view as false, and by annexing new realms of expression, French and drawing, through which she can make visible to others her own vision.

Gezari observes that one of most remarkable things about *Jane Eyre* is that, throughout the period of courtship, it presents Jane as subject gazing at Rochester, the arousing object of her view. This inverts the usual pattern, identified by feminist critics such as Luce Irigaray, where the woman is the erotic object of the desiring male gaze: '*Jane Eyre* controverts this idea that a woman finds visual pleasure primarily in being visible or that a woman who gazes takes on masculine qualities. "I looked, and had an acute pleasure in looking," Jane says.'[23] Indeed, Gezari argues, the notion of an active subject and passive object of erotic vision fails to define the experience of Jane and Rochester, who look at each other reciprocally. Gezari explores in detail Brontë's 'wonderfully resourceful [...] language of perception' by which she conveys the subtle effects of looking and being looked at in their relationship. The vital literal and figurative importance of visuality in that relationship, Gezari shows, prepares us for Brontë's striking use of visuality to communicate the experience of their aborted marriage, the trauma of their separation, and the restoration of vision that attends their reunion.

On the evening before her wedding, Gezari notes, Jane touches Rochester's hand, which, rhetorically demanding 'is that a dream?', he has placed close to her eyes. Jane, who feels a foreboding sense of unreality, responds 'Yes, though I touch it, it is a dream', putting it 'down from before her face'. This episode symbolically prefigures Rochester's loss of a hand and an eye in the Thornfield fire, a disfigurement which, as various critics, have noted, is also the designated Biblical punishment for adultery. Rochester's maiming is also prefigured in Jane's speech on the morning after the failed wedding, when she says 'Let me be torn away' and Rochester responds 'No, you shall tear yourself away [...] you shall, yourself, pluck out your right eye; yourself cut off your right hand: your heart shall be the victim; and you the priest [...]' Gezari suggests that 'for both Jane and Rochester, then, the events that separate them [...] constitute acts of self-mutilation'. Attending to the parallels between Jane's renunciation of the sight of Rochester and Rochester's partial blinding in the Thornfield fire, we may regard his injuries less as a figurative castration, more as a literalised loss of vision that only Jane can supply. Jane has previously compared Rochester to an eclipse that stands between her and every thought of religion: her visible material world has become more vital than the invisible, spiritual realm.

Gezari argues that the use of 'vision' in the last part of the novel, far from atoning for this idolatry, is equally blasphemous: Jane's telepathic communication with Rochester is described in words that echo those of the Virgin Mary and of Revelations, literalising the language of the Bible in the material realm of the senses. Gezari suggests that Brontë's habit of literalization is part of her defence of the imagination:

■ The truth of imagination is confirmed when it achieves expression in the 'real' world. Rochester's injuries literalize and authenticate the horror of his separation from Jane, and his dependence on her eyes when he has actually lost his own sight literalizes and authenticates his earlier figurative blindness to what she sees [...] The blinding of Rochester [...] also completes the triumphant progress of a heroine who has been denied the right to look and punished by the looks of others [...] In the marriage of Jane and Rochester, Jane's vision becomes the whole of the visible world.[24] □

Although Jane's marriage coopts her vision to serve Rochester and produces a baby whose eyes replicate his, *Jane Eyre* as a whole defends Jane's 'oppositional and proprietary view' and through it female visual pleasure and authority.

Other critics have also explored the significance of visuality in *Jane Eyre*. Peter Bellis, in 'In the Window-Seat: Vision and Power in *Jane Eyre*' (1987), offers a Lacanian reading of the dynamics of looking in the novel, particularly the struggle between Rochester and Jane, arguing that 'sexual and social power is visual power'[25] and discussing the ways in which both Jane and Charlotte Brontë assertively withhold themselves from the reader's critical gaze. More recently, Jane Kromm in 'Visual Culture and Scopic Custom in *Jane Eyre* and *Villette*' (1998) pays particular attention to Jane's unusual paintings which, she argues, resemble in certain respects the dramatic, apocalyptic images of the painter John Martin (1789–1854), who was much admired in the Brontë household. The three paintings that Rochester selects from Jane's portfolio – one of a shipwreck, with a cormorant sitting atop the ship's mast with a bracelet in his mouth plucked from a woman's corpse; one an allegorical vision of 'The Evening Star'; and the third a polar icescape in which a gigantic head rests against an iceberg – have sometimes been read psychoanalytically as images that project aspects of Jane's various traumatic separations (the death of Mr Reed, the departure of Miss Temple and the loss of Helen Burns).[26] Kromm, however, sees the three paintings as a secularized and feminized version of a traditional religious triptych. The fact that the images are neither copied nor assisted work and that they resist interpretive closure is significant, Kromm argues, given the widespread expectation that lady amateur painters confine themselves to meticulously detailed, imitative forms and modes of representation. Kromm suggests that *Jane Eyre*, like Brontë's later novel *Villette*, is attentive to the gender expectations that dominate Victorian visual culture and offers 'a carefully crafted feminist critique of spectatorship and representation'.[27]

HISTORICIZING *JANE EYRE*: EDUCATION AND EVANGELICALISM

Heather Glen's *Charlotte Brontë: The Imagination in History* (2002), like other historicist accounts, argues that we should not be fooled by Charlotte Brontë's declaration in a letter that *Jane Eyre* 'has no learning, no research, it discusses no subject of public interest'.[28] Contemporary readers were alert to the fact that *Jane Eyre* was not merely a universal pipe dream, but dealt with subjects of specific current concern. Once Elizabeth Gaskell had publicized the fact that Lowood was based on the Clergy Daughters School at Cowan Bridge, which the Brontë sisters had attended, and that Mr Brocklehurst was modeled on its Evangelical superintendent, the Reverend Carus Wilson, debate raged in the press between those who defended the education this and similar establishments provided and those who felt Brontë's damning portrayal was accurate.

We cannot understand *Jane Eyre*, Glen proposes, without appreciating its internalisation of and response to evangelical ideology:

> ■ in her depiction of Jane's traumatic childhood Charlotte Brontë is responding to a major social and cultural fact of early nineteenth-century England, which she herself had known in an especially extreme manifestation: that distinctive pedagogy [system of teaching] which had developed out of the evangelical revival of the eighteenth century and which by the nineteenth was enshrined in schools such as those [...] at Cowan Bridge and promulgated in hundreds of tracts and articles, sermons and stories – which had become, indeed, in more or less modified form, probably the most powerful ideology of child-rearing in early Victorian England.[29] □

Evangelicalism was a form of Christian theology that emphasized sin and the need for redemption. The evangelical Christian recognised the world as a temporary and corrupt sphere of existence; the chief purpose of life was to prepare for a devout death, in hope of attaining to the lasting joys of heaven. Evangelical ideas were not confined to a particular sect, but were widespread in Victorian Britain: Patrick Brontë was an evangelical minister and Charlotte grew up with evangelical texts about education, both at home and at school. In the evangelical worldview, the child was born a sinner, whose self-will must be curbed and whose faults, in particular vanity and deceit, must be rooted out through strict vigilance and discipline. Glen comments that the practices described in *Jane Eyre* as prevailing at Lowood Institution are quite typical and by no means extreme when seen in the context of contemporary evangelical teaching as reflected in tracts, primers, and memoirs. 'Mortification' – suppression of self-regarding and worldly impulses to achieve a state where death was welcome – was a cornerstone of this belief system, and impressing upon children the ever-present possibility of their imminent death, as Brocklehurst does when he interviews Jane at Gateshead, was routine. Far from being a private, morbid fantasy of childhood, Glen suggests, the first chapters of *Jane Eyre*, with the dire warnings and grim punishments Jane receives, the rigours and privations of Lowood with its emphasis on surveillance and regimentation, and the portraits of the nature-defying Brocklehurst and self-mortifying Helen Burns, form a 'hostile but realistic portrayal of the ethos of evangelicalism'. Glen continues:

> ■ if [...] the depiction of the Lowood regime amounts to a 'wholesale' attack on the methods of evangelical pedagogy, more subtly, but just as trenchantly, Jane's narrative challenges the values it sought to inculcate. The 'restraint' and 'chastisement' to which she is subjected are opposed by the 'liberty' for which she strains, the 'praise' she longs for; the acceptance and forbearance preached to her by those about her by the 'rebellion and rage' that impels her on. Unmoved by threats of hellfire, and with remarkably little inner struggle, she makes her choice of earthly happiness: a choice whose difference from the path of evangelicalism is emphasized in her narrative's closing contrast between the mutuality of her life with Rochester and St John Rivers's 'undaunted' aspiration towards death.[30] □

Glen acknowledges that certain figures in *Jane Eyre*, such as John Reed, the bully and gambler who is struck down by his own vices and dies horribly, or even Rochester, who is punished for his sins and pardoned only after humbling himself before God, seem akin to the exemplary characters in evangelical writing. The 'providential' aspects of Jane's own plot, where she flees temptation after supernatural prompting and is magically rewarded by finding her family and her fortune, could also be taken to reflect a benign conformity to the evangelical paradigm. Glen, however, submits that these 'configurations of evangelicalism' are used in *Jane Eyre* to 'quite opposite effect'. Rather than a tale of virtue rewarded in which the heroine triumphs over every obstacle, *Jane Eyre* is a novel that is dogged by the darkness of a theological worldview in which the subject is permanently threatened, coerced, insubstantial in the face of the constant fear of death and eternal torment. This atmosphere of terror and insecurity, Glen insists, never truly disperses in the novel: it overhangs the narrative, shrouding Jane's apparent tale of successful self-realisation. Brontë's morbid vision of the self narrowly evading violence, death, and persecution, says Glen, is not the result of feverish fancy: it was a daily reality for many early Victorians, living under the shadow of evangelical teachings that constructed children as sinners whose faults required eradication and women as beings best occupied in the self-abnegating duties of the domestic sphere. In this way, *Jane Eyre* 'articulates a cultural unconscious that the realism of its period could not express,'[31] communicating the bleakness of systems of physical and spiritual control in early nineteenth-century Britain as sharply as Dickens does in his later novels.

Other critics have seen *Jane Eyre*'s relationship to evangelical religion as much more positive.[32] Marianne Thormählen, in *The Brontës and Religion* (1999), argues that the evangelicalism practised in the Brontë household was extremely tolerant and allowed each sister freedom to develop her own, often unorthodox, theological ideas. In Thormählen's view, one of the characteristics of their evangelical practice was the subordination of doctrinal issues to the importance of living a good Christian life, nurturing a personal and loving relationship to God. In this light, Thormählen considers 'the enigma of St John Rivers', who is alternately praised in *Jane Eyre* as a good Christian and implicitly criticized for his aggressive ambition and coldness. She concludes that the presentation of St John is typical of the way in which Brontë allows more than one religious interpretation to stand. St John does not seem to have humbled himself before his Creator, and we have only his own word that he is destined for Heaven, yet Brontë leaves open the possibility that he has achieved salvation:

█ The Brontë fiction as a whole reflects a reliance on Divine forgiveness which transcends the views that prevailed in the authors' time [...] More than anything else, the mixture of extreme qualities that is St John Rivers thus illustrates the radical enquiry into religious thought, feeling and conduct which is so characteristic of all the Brontë works.[33] □

The difference between Glen's and Thormählen's respective accounts of evangelical faith as an oppressive and a liberating force in *Jane Eyre* illustrates the widely divergent interpretive paths that the same historical and contextual material may open up.

PLOTS AND MASKS: *JANE EYRE* AND THE HISTORY OF THE NOVEL

This chapter so far has looked at readings of *Jane Eyre* that consider the novel in various key contexts of social, cultural, and political history. Recent criticism also includes a number of works that place *Jane Eyre* in the history of techniques and strategies deployed by the British novel as a form. Firdous Azim's *The Colonial Rise of the Novel* (1993), argues that *Jane Eyre*, in establishing its heroine's consciousness as central and unified shares strategies of marginalising 'Other' figures in the narrative employed by much earlier novels such as Aphra Behn's *Oroonoko* (1688) and Daniel Defoe's *Roxana* (1724). Alison Case, in *Plotting Women: Gender and Narration in the Eighteenth- and Nineteenth-Century British Novel* (1999), also reads *Jane Eyre* against earlier fiction, asking how it differs from its textual predecessors. Case claims that:

> ■ In the history of female narrative voice in the English novel, *Jane Eyre* stands out as a unique and startling moment [...] the novel conspicuously lacks the deferential, apologetic, and moralizing frames that had been used to downplay the presumption of earlier autodiegetic female narrators [narrators who are also protagonists of the narrative they recount] by stressing the subordination of their story to moral and religious authorities and purposes. Instead, the narrator plunges us directly into her story, presuming and indeed compelling our interest in its heroine on her own terms. While some reviewers clearly noticed (and duly chastised) its subversive potential, the book's massive popularity and subsequent literary influence indicate that its strategies for authorizing its female narrator were largely effective. But Jane Eyre's self-authorization does not occur in a literary vacuum. Throughout the novel, Brontë engages directly and indirectly with the conventions of feminine narration, particularly as figured by Pamela and her narratorial alter ego, the plotting woman.[34] □

Pamela is the heroine and first-person narrator of Samuel Richardson's influential novel *Pamela* (1740), whose plot bears certain important resemblances to *Jane Eyre*'s. Pamela is a young and inexperienced servant in a large house. The master of the property, Mr. B., is attracted to her and tries various tricks and wiles to make her his mistress. Pamela, however, is canny enough to resist his enticements until he finally offers her legitimate marriage, which she accepts. Richardson's novel is mentioned in *Jane Eyre* as one of the sources of the stories that Bessie tells Jane as a child.

Case considers the ways in which *Jane Eyre* engages with the model provided by Richardson's *Pamela*, but rejects the narrative technique that Richardson adopts and its implications. In *Pamela*, the youthful heroine reports the events that have recently befallen her in the form of 'letters' to her family. The narrative events thus appear to be occurring moment by moment, without the narrator having much opportunity to reflect upon them or to shape the story she tells. Indeed, the narrative strategy of *Pamela* works to disavow the heroine's agency in producing the plot: she is constantly the object of Mr B.'s machinations and the credulous reader trembles for her vulnerability, wondering whether she will continue to succeed in evading others' designs upon her. As Case observes, the mature Jane Eyre, in her retrospective narrative, insistently asserts the personal agency that Pamela disclaims: she shows how she has acted deliberately and decisively to change her situation throughout her history. However, Case suggests, Jane, in telling us her story, still has to deploy strategies to counter the negative associations conventionally attached to women who plot – in the linked senses of 'scheme manipulatively' and 'produce narrative'.

The first such strategy that Jane Eyre adopts is to stress, in the account of her childhood, that her thoughts and actions are generally unpremeditated, even involuntary. She recalls, for example: 'I was oppressed, suffocated: endurance broke down – I uttered a wild, involuntary cry'; 'I cried out suddenly and without at all deliberating on my words'; 'it seemed as if my tongue pronounced words without my will consenting to their utterance'. The Reeds accuse Jane of being an 'artful, noxious child'. Her own narrative contradicts this charge. Jane constantly evokes the difficulties children have in analysing and articulating their experience, remarking that 'Children can feel, but they cannot analyze their feelings; and if the analysis is partially effected in thought, they know not how to express the result of the process in words'. In the section of *Jane Eyre* devoted to Jane's childhood, says Case, 'the narrator makes Jane's youth itself a guarantee of her artlessness'.[35] Jane gains credibility and the reader's sympathy. In the Lowood section of *Jane Eyre*, Jane moves beyond this model of unselfconscious artlessness toward one of ethical self-awareness. We see Jane tell her story to Miss Temple with self-conscious moderation and claim public authority for her account, when the doctor, Mr Lloyd, corroborates her version of events at Gateshead and the stigma of being branded a liar is publicly erased.

In the Thornfield section, Case argues, *Jane Eyre* engages most explicitly with the model of Richardson's *Pamela*. The story generates a similar sexual energy from 'the heroine's verbal resistance to her employer'. But, rather than presenting male encroachment and female rebuff as a circumstantial hazard that the woman can only endure, Jane acknowledges her part and her pleasure in alternately irritating and soothing Rochester. In Case's reading: 'Jane moves beyond the opposition between sinister artfulness and virtuous artlessness to the practice of a mutually acknowledged artistry'.[36] While Pamela's repartee with Mr. B. ceases after her engagement to him, when she submits willingly to his authority, Jane is at her most provoking once engaged to Rochester, demonstrating a self-control in the face of his and her own desire that highlights her own power and her own restraint as a narrator.

The negative figure of the 'plotting woman' is not wholly absent from *Jane Eyre*: her shadow appears in the shape of Bertha, who is both cunning and wanton. In order to escape the opprobrium that attaches to women who plot, Case proposes, Jane as a narrator must constantly present herself in a different light. At key moments – when she advertises for a job, when she flees Thornfield, and when she returns – Jane depicts herself as being prompted by an unseen, supernatural agency. This prevents the reader from seeing Jane as a character who is, chillingly, always in control: it emphasizes her vulnerability. Ultimately, Case concludes:

> ■ *Jane Eyre* succeeds in creating a female character whom we can also accept as an authoritative narrator because it makes room for the kind of self-knowledge and purposive action that thus far had been the prerogative of both male characters and narrators. Perhaps the most important difference between Jane and the literary heroine-narrators who preceded her is her willingness to choose a course of action solely [...] on the basis of its calculated effect on another person. That she is able to do so without becoming morally suspect as a manipulator in the process is a tribute to Brontë's skill in working self-consciously within and against the conventions of feminine narration.[37] □

In *Caught in the Act: Theatricality in the Nineteenth-century English Novel* (1992), Joseph Litvak, while also placing *Jane Eyre* within a developmental history of earlier and later fiction, takes a different and more caustic view of Jane as a narrator. His reading, as he admits, is not 'celebratory' but deliberately 'demystifying' of a novel which has been 'deadeningly pasteurized and homogenized for absorption into the collective unconscious'.[38]

Litvak argues that *Jane Eyre* is a highly theatrical novel, not merely in the sense that certain incidents in the plot are melodramatic, but in the way that the text manages a process of evasion and exposure, masking and unmasking, that dramatizes the difference between interior and exterior experience, public and private behaviour. *Jane Eyre*'s preface promises that the novel will 'pluck the mask' from the face of social hypocrisy; the text seems to offer a new forthrightness, openness, access to the inner feelings of its heroine. Yet, Litvak contends, that promise of unveiling is teasing and illusory.

> ■ For where the narrative of sensation or detection typically enacts a linear movement toward transparency and closure, the plots of Brontë's novels notoriously refuse the comforts of linearity, intensifying the demand for demystification precisely by frustrating it. For all their vaunted commitment to direct communication, and despite their author's reputation as one who 'pours forth her feelings [...] without premeditation,' these novels virtually institutionalize the obstacles to unmediated and unpremeditated expression and understanding. If they stand out as emblematic demonstrations of the will to unveil, they do so because they install

opacity as a permanent fixture of the novelistic world. In the veritable theatre of self-fashioning that they constitute, theatricality-as-display and theatricality-as-deception articulate the conflictual masquerade of the modern novel, which seems, in its cult of interiority, to have left its theatrical prehistory far behind. Brontë's novels stand as memorials to the process whereby the novel as cultural production absorbs and covers over its *supplementary*[39] relation to the theatre [...] In the nineteenth century, the novel becomes a crypt in which theatricality lies concealed, but only half-concealed, since this very encrypting bespeaks an intrinsically theatrical subterfuge.[40] □

Jane Eyre, then, camouflages its theatricality, denying it by internalizing it. Jane is carefully distinguished from the showy and self-conscious Blanche Ingram, the flagrantly dramatic Bertha Mason Rochester, and from Rochester's French mistress, Céline Varens, whose career in the theatre is emblematic of her performative, fickle, and deceitful qualities. Yet Jane herself, as Mrs Reed recognises, is a 'precocious actress' – all the more effective because she consistently presents herself in the opposite role of spectator, criticising the bad acting of other women. Litvak suggests that Jane's frequent position behind a curtain, watching others, is intended to signify her anti–theatricality: where others feign and simper, plain Jane is characterised by intimate candour and emotional restraint. This seeming containment and self-control, however, only intensifies Jane's histrionic qualities: repression and expression prove to be very similar forms of self-dramatizing excitement.[41]

By staging herself as trusted intermediary between the Gothic, anti-social inwardness of Bertha and the worldly, shallow outwardness of Blanche, Jane constructs her own subjectivity as reasonable and reliable but, Litvak argues, we should distrust her ideological role as placeholder between the 'personal' and the 'social' realms and recognise the play of power and performance, suspicion and surveillance in which she operates. Interestingly, Litvak suggests that the academic critic may be more like Jane than s/he is willing to admit. While appearing to strip away masks from literary texts, the critic also inevitably wears a mask. Like Jane's narrative, the critic's narrative frequently claims restraint and candour while covertly expressing 'his or her desire to "out-governess them all"',[42] exercising a power of surveillance and judgement that is both aggressive and performative. In his Foucauldian emphasis on the power relations encoded in texts and in society, and his sense of both as spheres of performance in which identity is never natural but always constructed, Litvak's sceptical and self-reflexive reading is typical of approaches to *Jane Eyre* influenced by post-structuralism and the more adversarial aspects of new historicism.

The Limits of History? Why Dating
Jane is Dangerous

John Sutherland's *Can Jane Eyre Be Happy? More Puzzles in Classic Fiction* (1997) is a light-hearted approach to the question of history in *Jane Eyre*. Sutherland uses a detective approach to determine what the likely dates are for Jane and Rochester's courtship and marriage and then uses these to make inferences about Rochester's behaviour and his motives. One of the few concrete date markers in *Jane Eyre* is an allusion to the new publication of Sir Walter Scott's poem *Marmion*, which St John Rivers presents as a gift to Jane during her time as the local schoolmistress. *Marmion* was first published in 1808 – but this makes little sense as a date for the novel's action. Adèle announces that she came over from France in a steam ship: these were not performing the Channel crossing before the 1820s. Various other details suggest that the novel's action is occurring some time after the Napoleonic Wars. It is more likely, Sutherland concludes, that the 'new publication' of *Marmion* to which the novel refers is the popular 'Magnum Opus' edition of 1834, affordably priced at 6 shillings, whose purchase was an exciting event in the Haworth parsonage when Charlotte Brontë was 19.[43] If Rochester and Jane's aborted wedding, then, takes place in the early 1830s, it predates the English Marriage Act of 1835, which stated that marriage with a mad spouse could not be dissolved if the spouse was sane at the time of the ceremony. Rochester, then, has reasonable legal grounds for believing that his marriage with Bertha is null and void. Why doesn't he put Bertha in a humane asylum, get a good lawyer to pronounce the first marriage invalid, and then lead Jane to the altar with a clear conscience? Sutherland suggests that it is Rochester's cruel Bluebeard tendencies that cause him to mistreat Bertha, try to marry Blanche Ingram until Mrs Fairfax foils his plans, and marry Jane only when there is no available alternative. Can Jane be happy with such a man? Surely not, says Sutherland: as readers we should fear for her future.

Sutherland's account is tongue-in-cheek, but it raises some serious questions about the pursuit of historical evidence as a tool for approaching *Jane Eyre*. Analysis that interprets the novel on the basis of the events, ideas, and norms of the historical period that forms a loose backdrop for its action may produce readings that, while logically sound, run counter to the imaginative experience most readers have of the text as fiction. Millions of readers have, after all, felt that Jane Eyre *is* happy with Rochester and that they are happy with the inconsistencies and improbabilities of the plot that unites them. How we can best use historical evidence to interpret *Jane Eyre* remains a live and controversial topic.

This chapter has explored the 'turn toward history' in criticism of *Jane Eyre* from the 1980s to the present day. The influence of the 'New

Historicism' on critical practice in universities in the 1980s and 1990s encouraged commentators to consider Brontë's novel anew in the social, ideological and cultural context of the nineteenth century, uncovering previously submerged debates in the text about contemporary sciences such as psychology, phrenology, and economics but also dialogues with the ideology of evangelical religion and contemporary educational methods. The turn toward history led to new archival research and an interest in reading *Jane Eyre* on equal terms with cultural artefacts that had once been deemed of little literary importance such as religious tracts, missionary writings, advertisements and educational prospectuses. Critics inspired by the work of Michel Foucault increasingly began to look at the text and the society of which it was part as sites of struggle and competition for power: they discuss the power dynamics of the body in *Jane Eyre*, of how Jane sees and is seen by others, how she performs on the social stage and discredits others' performances in order to fashion a 'self' that may appear natural and unitary, but is in fact a shifting and fragile construct. The preoccupation with 'historicity', the embeddedness of all discourse in a particular historical moment, also led critics to reflect more openly on the historicity of their own practice and on the ways in which earlier interpretations of the Brontës had perpetuated myths about their lives and works, often interweaving them. Critics strove to demystify *Jane Eyre*, presenting challenging readings that reacted against its 'pasteurised', overfamiliar status as a classic romance.

In recent years, heightened interest in *Jane Eyre* and history has also stimulated new investigation of *Jane Eyre*'s 'afterlives': translations, reworkings and adaptations of Brontë's novel from cinema to comic book, opera to science fiction. In the last chapter of this Guide, I discuss some of these adaptations and the critical issues they raise.

CHAPTER SEVEN

Jane Eyre Adapted

Modern criticism has become increasingly attentive not only to the way in which *Jane Eyre* is embedded in the particular history of its time of writing and first publication, but also to the way in which each adaptation and rewriting of Brontë's novel relates to the social, ideological, and cultural life of its age. Once regarded as inferior bridesmaids, following and imitating the original text, adaptations of *Jane Eyre* have recently enjoyed their own trip down the literary studies aisle, as critics espouse the fascinations of *Jane Eyre*s set in India, Italy, and America, and consider the possibilities of prequels, sequels, and rewritten plot-lines in which Jane works in a soup kitchen; marries her clergyman cousin and has six children; or even becomes a generator maintenance technician on the isolated planet Fieldspar in outer space.[1]

Each version of *Jane Eyre*, such studies recognise, is itself a critical reading of the novel. The inflections of setting, plot, and characterisation; the emphases and omissions created by staging and direction; the possible addition of musical and other effects, interpret Brontë's text in new and potentially revealing ways, engaging in dialogue with a narrative that has come to exist, even for those who have never read the book, as a cultural artefact. The modern concepts of iterability, a text's infinite capacity to be re-read and rewritten with plural meanings, and intertextuality – the notion that no text is a closed structure, but 'a mosaic of quotations: any text is the absorption and transformation of another'[2] – problematize the very idea that there is a recoverable, 'original' *Jane Eyre* that can be studied in isolation. It is not now possible to respond to Brontë's novel without acknowledging the multiple forms of transmission through which it has been and continues to be mediated.

STAGE ADAPTATIONS OF *JANE EYRE*

Patsy Stoneman's *Brontë Transformations: The Cultural Dissemination of Jane Eyre and Wuthering Heights* (1996) was one of the first critical studies to uncover and discuss the versions and adaptations of *Jane Eyre* that have proliferated from the 1840s to the present day.

As Stoneman points out, *Jane Eyre* was immediately seized upon by dramatists, becoming a stage play in 1848, only three months after the novel's publication, whereas *Wuthering Heights* took much longer to be adapted into other media. The speed and ease with which *Jane Eyre* translated into a play suggests that producers immediately saw and exploited the theatrical elements already present in the book. However, in 'returning' the plot to its melodramatic roots, nineteenth-century dramatists produced readings of the novel that highlighted the social conflict between the lowly but quick-witted governess and the high-born but mean-spirited Reeds, Brocklehursts and Ingrams while tending to underplay Brontë's contentious depiction of gender roles and social transgression in Jane and Rochester's courtship. Stoneman explains:

■ The stage melodrama versions of *Jane Eyre* which appeared almost immediately after the novel's publication [...] altered the emphasis of the novel in two, almost opposite ways. On the one hand, they gave exaggerated vocal expression to Jane's sense of class oppression and victimization; on the other, they recuperated the radical implications of her relationship with Rochester into conventional comic nuptials [weddings].[3] □

Melodrama (literally 'music drama') was a popular form of theatre that in the early nineteenth century was typically performed on stages less genteel than those of Covent Garden and Drury Lane, the only two London theatres licensed to stage 'legitimate' drama, which involved only the spoken word. It made the most of its alternative attractions, often including not only music but spectacular visual tableaux and other thrilling effects. Melodrama had a long history of voicing anti-aristocratic and anti-employer sentiment, but its indignation at wicked and exploitative authority figures co-existed with an acceptance of existing structures embodied in its traditionally happy ends. This combination of qualities is evident in the 'readings' of *Jane Eyre* provided by John Courtney's early stage version *Jane Eyre or The Secrets of Thornfield Manor* (1848) and *Jane Eyre* (1849) by the American dramatist John Brougham (1810–80). In Courtney's play, the first speakers are servants, who complain about the harsh conditions at Lowood Institution. Jane is interestingly aligned with this group of domestics, who threaten to lay about Brocklehurst with a broom. In Brougham's *Jane Eyre*, by contrast, comic class warfare is achieved in a scene where Jane is left with the Ingram family before Rochester's arrival. Jane shows them up for a bunch of dim and ill-spoken rogues – who, in the case of the men, make passes at her in a way that they would never do with women of their own class. As Stoneman notes in her recent academic edition of these plays, they:

> ■ simplify and narrow the novel's focus. In place of a subtly ambiguous Jane we have the stereotypes of melodrama – orphan victim, spotless maiden, 'astounding woman' [...] These changes of focus, however, can play a temporary spotlight on aspects of the novel which might not otherwise seize our attention. When Courtney aligns his heroine with the servants, it diminishes her individuality, and distorts the realities of class stratification, but its exaggeration of Jane's lowly status emphasizes her class effrontery in daring to claim equality with the gentry. It is intriguing to speculate whether Lady Eastlake (who wrote her famous review of *Jane Eyre* in the same year as this play) took fright at the story's popularity at the Victoria Theatre, a known Chartist hotbed [...] Her denunciation has seemed laughably extreme to modern ears, but Courtney's play, with its comically insolent subversion of authority, shows us how the novel might be read in this way.[4] □

Late nineteenth-century and early twentieth-century theatrical adaptations were increasingly sympathetic toward the character of Bertha. Some stage versions also created sub-plots that gave a new spin to the questions of sexual morality present in the narrative. James Willing's *Jane Eyre* (1879) had John Reed seduce and then abandon Blanche Ingram, who returns 'a cast off mistress – a woman of the streets' and seeks Jane's charity. When Blanche says to Jane 'then you too, have been deceived?', she gestures pointedly at the possibility that Jane, like her, might have fallen victim to a fatal sexual snare. As Stoneman remarks, the reading this play offers is newly critical of Rochester's moral status. Jane adopts the fallen Blanche as a 'sister' and offers to share her legacy with her: hinting at a new solidarity between the fortunate woman who can claim, as Jane does in this play, 'I am my own mistress', and the unfortunate woman who is deceived into becoming a man's mistress and faces the consequences in poverty, disease, and shame.

REWORKINGS OF THE *JANE EYRE* PLOT IN FICTION

Later Victorian treatments of the 'governess novel', a genre heavily indebted to *Jane Eyre*, often push their plots in directions that develop themes that are present but submerged in Brontë's text. In the wildly popular novel *East Lynne* (1861) by Ellen Wood (1814–87), Lady Isabel Vane, the wife of Archibald Carlyle, runs away from her husband and children to join a new lover. She is reported to have been killed in a railway accident, but in fact returns, unrecognisable because disfigured, to become governess to her own children. Her husband, meanwhile, has remarried. Isabel, in *East Lynne*, fascinatingly combines the threat of female sexual promiscuity and unhappiness concealed within the domestic realm (Bertha) and the threat of the new governess who elides the role of female employee, mistress and mother (Jane). Bigamy here, as in many late Victorian sensation novels, is a reality rather than merely a potentiality, as it is in *Jane Eyre*. In the famous novella *The Turn of the Screw* (1898) by Henry James (1843–1916), the protagonist of the recounted tale is a governess, whose experience of teaching two young children in an isolated country house is haunted by threats of terror and madness. The ingredients of the plot resemble and deliberately allude to those of *Jane Eyre*. But James's treatment of the story, which constantly casts doubt on the governess's first-person account of events, creates an atmosphere of deep unease, a suspicion of sexual trauma hovering between children and adults, and a narrative mode of painfully unresolved tension that plumbs the darkest reaches of the shadow side of Brontë's original.

Reworkings of *Jane Eyre* in early twentieth-century fiction frequently produce a commentary on the stifled but still powerful persistence of Victorian patterns in twentieth-century life. Vestiges of the *Jane Eyre* plot thus, like Bertha Mason Rochester in *Jane Eyre*, become emblems of the repressed past that may return with a vengeance. As Patsy Stoneman shows, women writers between the First and Second World Wars draw on the model of *Jane Eyre* to produce novels that expose the lingering spectre of nineteenth-century gender and class relations in modern marriage. In *Vera* (1921) by Elizabeth Von Arnim (1866–1941), *South Riding* (1936) by Winifred Holtby (1898–1935), and *Rebecca* (1938) by Daphne Du Maurier (1907–89), the older man who introduces a young woman to the country house he once shared with his first wife proves to be a troubling figure. In *Vera*, Everard Wemyss, whose first wife Vera died after falling from the house's third storey, is a domestic tyrant. His second wife, Lucy, feels increasingly close to the dead Vera as she realises the true horror of the man she has married. The second Mrs De Winter in *Rebecca* similarly finds herself at first intimidated by the legacy of her husband's first wife and then suspicious of the possibility that she, like Rebecca – the first Mrs De Winter – may be maddened and even killed by the combination of marriage, the great house Manderley, and her choleric husband Maxim. Although the first wife in these books no longer represents a technical obstacle, she continues to represent a psychological barrier: a mirror in which the new wife sees her own doom. Stoneman comments:

> ■ When the young heroine of *Rebecca* first speaks the words, 'your wife', she feels as if she had said 'something heinous and appalling', just as Mr Rochester makes the word sound like an insult when he points to Bertha and says, 'That is my *wife*'. The repetition of words, both within and between texts, implies that the suffering in these stories comes, not from

individual actions, but from social structures – the institution of marriage as it is lived in the country house which allots to men and women separate spheres and imposes on both, but especially the women, the duty to repeat the lives of previous generations. Du Maurier's novel links past, present and future only to suggest that nothing really changes.[5] □

These novels reflect a growing feminist persuasion that the real threat to 'Jane' is not a bigamous union but a different kind of entrapment in an outdated paradigm of femininity and an outdated class structure. Winifred Holtby solves the conundrum by killing off the Rochester-figure and converting the country house into a home for disabled children: her heroine, Sarah, must face the future alone.

FILM AND TELEVISION ADAPTATIONS OF *JANE EYRE*

By contrast, as critics such as Kate Ellis and Ann Kaplan have observed, early twentieth-century film versions of *Jane Eyre* were extremely conservative in their reading of the novel's gender politics.[6] In the 1934 adaptation directed by Christy Cabanne (1888–1950) starring Colin Clive (1878–1937) and Virginia Bruce (1910–82), Adèle is not Rochester's probable illegitimate daughter but his niece – and we learn that he is seeking a legal annulment of his first marriage, which has almost arrived when the blonde and beautiful Jane bumps into the mad but mild-mannered Bertha. Both Rochester's gruff temper and his moral culpability are considerably diluted. In the 1944 adaptation directed by Robert Stevenson (1905–86), featuring Orson Welles (1915–85) as Rochester and Joan Fontaine (born 1917), who had lately starred in *Rebecca*, as Jane, the governess is a quiet and submissive figure: Ellis and Kaplan comment that 'Rochester comes and goes, commands and manages, orders Jane's presence as he wishes'.[7] Donna Marie Nudd in 'Rediscovering *Jane Eyre* through its adaptations' (1992) remarks on the differences between Brontë's handling of Jane and Rochester's first meeting, in which he falls from his horse, and the way in which this scene is presented in Stevenson's film. Nudd considers Brontë's 'horse scene [...] both typically romantic and undeniably feminist'. Rochester may enter like a romantic hero but he is 'a middle-aged grump' whose 'first action is to fall from the horse and swear'. He is brought to Jane's level and requires her assistance to remount – a situation that prefigures the 'spiritual equality' of their later relationship. In Stevenson's *Jane Eyre*, however, the heroine is never permitted to hobble Rochester's masculine power:

■ The filmmakers have emphasized the Gothic, romanticized images while censoring Brontë's radical notion of Jane and Rochester as 'spiritual equals.' Indeed, virtually every sound or image in the scene serves to underscore Rochester's power: the bell tolls an eerie warning, the horns blare as if announcing a king's arrival, the horse's hooves thunder. Moreover, we never actually *see* Rochester fall down; instead, a magnificent steed is reined up an instant before its hooves would have crushed the hapless governess. And then the wayward steed rises from the mist – a herald, as it were, of the caped figure, her savior, who shoots up from the dry ice like Thor from the thundering clouds. We note the differences between the novel's Rochester, who moves haltingly to the stile and sits through the initial conversation, and the film's hero, who looms over the diminutive Jane. The clip ends with Rochester easily mounting his horse and galloping into the night; whereas, in the novel, Rochester leans 'with some stress' on Jane's shoulder, limps to his horse, and then springs to his saddle 'grimacing grimly as he made the effort, for it wrenched his sprain' [...] the filmmakers have edited out the adult Jane Eyre's feminism in this scene and chosen instead to highlight only the Gothic romance.[8] □

Notably, in Stevenson's 1944 *Jane Eyre* the Rivers family is omitted completely. Jane, after her aborted marriage, returns to Gateshead, where she is sitting in the conservatory when she hears Rochester's mysterious summons. This omission of much of the final section of Brontë's novel has a significant impact on how we 'read' Jane's history. Since she does not become a schoolteacher at Morton or contemplate becoming a missionary, the possibility of an alternative career for her that does not involve marriage is never broached. And since she does not wander starving and homeless on the moors, a religious reading of her principled flight from potential adultery at Thornfield and providential discovery of her family is not available to the viewer. The 'Gothic' paraphernalia of the 1944 *Jane Eyre*, with its spectacular castle setting and abundant swirling dry ice, link it, as Stoneman concludes, to an older tradition of stage melodrama, while its treatment of the narrative is by no means as daring as many of those Victorian theatrical predecessors.

More recent cinema adaptations and TV serialisations of *Jane Eyre* raise a variety of topics that have stimulated scholarly criticism, including the treatment of childhood and the portrayal of Rochester's Byronic qualities.[9] In general, screen adaptations value fidelity to certain aspects of historical detail: costumes, carriages, and cookware are lovingly reproduced to model those of the period in which the drama is set. Interestingly, however, that period is rarely the period in which the novel is set. *Jane Eyre*, although published in 1847, is clearly set in a pre-Victorian time frame: though dates are never spelled out, various allusions suggest that Jane and Rochester's romance occurs in the 1830s. The fact that so many adaptations prefer a mid-Victorian setting testifies to the seepage between treatment of the lives of the Brontës and the content of their novels that we have noted as a feature of much twentieth-century Brontë criticism.

Recent film and TV version of *Jane Eyre* likewise tend to lean toward a 'realistic' treatment of the narrative, omitting or offering rational explanations for its more magical and supernatural elements. Thus in the 1995 film of *Jane Eyre* by Franco Zeffirelli (born 1923), Jane is already acquainted with her cousin St John Rivers and his sister, whom she has met during Mrs Reed's last illness. Rather than wandering famished on the moor, when she flees Thornfield she simply takes a carriage to their door. In the 2006 BBC television serialisation of *Jane Eyre*, we are prepared for Rochester's 'telepathic' communication with Jane by the introduction of identical twins to Rochester's house party, who comment on their ability to communicate with one another even when miles apart. In this adaptation, Rochester is an amateur scientist with a framed collection of dragonflies, who invites Jane to join him by the lake for some mutual indulgence in natural history. It is worth considering that, ironically, in producing these 'realistic' and 'historically accurate' period dramas, scriptwriters and directors may still be radically unfaithful to the novel – altering the period setting, secularising plot elements that have a religious framework, and truncating or omitting key scenes in ways that change our sense of what Jane's story means. In the 2006 BBC TV serialisation, Jane's entire history before she arrives at Thornfield is dealt with as a 'flashback': for many stage and screen adaptors and their audiences *Jane Eyre* **is** the romance between Jane and Rochester. This, however, constitutes a partial reading of the novel that, like all versions, speaks as much of the desires and prejudices of its own time as it does of the narrative it re-presents.

It is noticeable that many modern stage and screen adaptations of *Jane Eyre* treat Bertha Mason Rochester as a central rather than a tangential figure, according her scenes and forms of expression that are not shown in Brontë's novel. This development parallels the heightened regard for Bertha in late twentieth-century feminist and postcolonial criticism. In Zeffirelli's 1995 film, for example, Bertha, played by the attractive actress Maria Schneider, develops a pathetic reliance upon Grace Poole. When Grace falls to her death as a stairway collapses during the Thornfield fire, we see Bertha elect to plunge after her. The reinvention of this scene gives Bertha a degree of agency and a tragic denouement, where the novel prefers to present Bertha's death, via reported speech, in terms that leave her motives unclear. In Polly Teale's 1997 stage version of *Jane Eyre*, Bertha and Jane are interpreted as different sides of the same person. Both actresses are continuously, simultaneously on stage and the actress playing Bertha acts out with her body the anger and desire that Jane is unable to express due to social constraints. As Teale explains in her production notes:

■ Central to the adaptation is the idea that hidden inside the sensible, frozen Jane exists another self who is passionate and sensual. Bertha (trapped in the attic) embodies the fire and longing which Jane must lock away in order to survive in Victorian England. At the beginning of the story, Jane reads a book about foreign lands. Bertha plays out Jane's secret imaginings, conjuring up the pictures she sees in her head. Bertha becomes wild and abandoned as Jane allows her inner world to take over. This is only possible because Jane is alone and can let down her guard. When John Reed enters the room Jane struggles to control and conceal Bertha until the point where Bertha breaks free, springing forward and attacking John Reed. From this moment to the end of Scene One, where Jane forces Bertha back into the red room and locks her in, there is a struggle between the inner and the outer self for control. In leaving Bertha behind, Jane has chosen to lock away the side of herself which is unacceptable to others. From this point onwards Bertha can no longer speak. Although they are now separated, Bertha continues to express the feelings that Jane is trying to conceal. She does this through movement and sound. These movements should affect Jane's body as if Bertha were a force inside her.[10] □

Teale's 1997 stage adaptation gives physical expression to a reading of Bertha as Jane's repressed self that, as we saw in chapter three, was espoused in the late 1970s by academic critics including Elaine Showalter, Sandra Gilbert and Susan Gubar. Similarly, the two-act opera *Jane Eyre* (2000), by Michael Berkeley with a libretto by David Malouf, allows Bertha a central role, where she screams, laughs, and dances. Bruno Lessard, in 'The Madwoman in the Classic: Intermediality, Female Subjectivity, and Dance in Michael Berkeley's *Jane Eyre*' (2007) argues that inter-musical references to *Lucia di Lammermoor* (1835), an opera by Gaetano Donizetti (1797–1848), in which a madwoman takes centre stage, and to *Bluebeard's Castle* (1918), an opera by Béla Bartók (1881–1945), which dramatises the plight of the betrayed wife, encourage the listener/viewer to understand Bertha's story as a major rather than a minor element in the opera's grand narrative.[11] These instances illustrate the ideological choices that writers, directors, and performers constantly make when they interpret *Jane Eyre* and the relationship that can exist between developments in critical theory and physical readaptation of the text.

Accounts and reworkings of a 'classic' text create their own traditions, influencing one another. It is striking that artists in many different illustrated editions of *Jane Eyre* choose to depict the same scenes, forming a visual memory of the novel as a sequence of key tableaux. The concrete nature of visual representation requires that artists, directors, and viewers make choices and reach conclusions (for example about Bertha's complexion) where the novel allows doubt to remain. These choices over time and with repetition acquire their own authority. As Carol M. Dole has observed, cinema–goers now expect to *see* the Thornfield fire, which they 'remember' as a scene in *Jane Eyre*, though in the novel it is described only at second-hand.[12] Since many people do not read the novel or do so only after encountering the story via other media, the question arises 'what is *Jane Eyre* now'? Might we regard the name as a brand that, in an increasingly corporate world, is prized for the ideas it connotes as much as the literary content of the novel that launched it?

The editors of the recent essay collection *A Breath of Fresh Eyre: Intertextual and Intermedial Reworkings of Jane Eyre* (2007) note that in China there is a 'Jane Eyre' factory producing digital albums for photo studios. The factory advertises on the internet with a specimen wedding photograph, an icon that, they observe, might seem:

■ a somewhat unsuitable choice [...] considering that Jane's own wedding in white was interrupted by a charge of bigamy, but splendid proof of Umberto Eco's claim that in order to transform a work into a cult object one must be able to break, dislocate, unhinge it so that one can remember only parts of it irrespective of their original relationship to the whole.[13] □

Jane Eyre, as they and other modern critics underline, has been since its appearance in 1847 not only a novel but a set of ideas that others have transformed. The extraordinary success and persistence of Brontë's text has paradoxically depended on its susceptibility to adaptation. This process of remaking and reinterpreting *Jane Eyre* is constantly evolving and you are a part of it. In reading this Guide and reflecting on its contents, you, too, are participating in the ongoing history of critical response to a novel that, since its first publication, has never ceased to be in print, in demand, and in debate.

Conclusion

Where will criticism of *Jane Eyre* go next? It is difficult to forecast the critical future of a text that, as this Guide has shown, has already generated such a rich history of literary response from critics in so many different camps. Two predictions can, however, be made with some confidence. The first is that new technologies will continue to expand the range of ways in which an ever-growing audience encounters and debates *Jane Eyre*. The second is that future approaches to *Jane Eyre* will continue to expand the range of cultural products they address.

As we have seen, a growing trend in Brontë studies is to look at the novels' metamorphoses into a multiplicity of different forms. These include translations, literary adaptations for adults and children, stage plays, musicals, films, television serials, visual artworks, and novels that are prequels, sequels, or involve transposed versions of the plot. Much critical work remains to be done in this area to understand how *Jane Eyre* has functioned in different historical, geographical, and social contexts and the many fascinating interpretations of the novel offered by representations in different media. The growing body of work on *Jane Eyre*'s 'afterlives' intersects with continuing critical interest in questions of class, gender, race, and nation in Victorian culture. Sue Thomas's *Imperialism, Reform and the Making of Englishness in Jane Eyre* (2008), for example, includes an account of an 1859 Caribbean reworking of *Jane Eyre* as well as considering the politics of the 1848 staging of John Courtney's theatrical adaptation of the novel at the Victoria Theatre in London.

Another area of exploration that seems likely to prove fruitful is the study of how and by whom *Jane Eyre* has been read. It may seem at first glance as if we already have a great deal of evidence on this subject: this *Guide* testifies to the range of readers and responses *Jane Eyre* has gleaned over time. However, as a cursory flick back through the previous chapters will tell you, most of the readers whose views are represented occupy a particular social position and come from a broadly similar social background. In the nineteenth century, they are mostly well-educated professional writers; in the twentieth century, they are mostly professional academics. This sample can tell us a great deal about the literary estimate and analysis of *Jane Eyre* and about ideas and methodologies current amongst middle-class, university-educated readers. It tells us remarkably little, however, about the views of millions of working-class readers who have consumed and commented upon *Jane Eyre*. Jonathan Rose in *The Intellectual Life of the British Working Classes* (2001) begins to piece together some of the frequently disregarded data that tell us, for example, that *Jane Eyre* – alongside other Victorian classics – was a staple of Miners' Libraries, and was persistently borrowed. Rose also looks at texts such as the letters and diaries of Ruth Slate (1884–1953), a packer who rose to become a clerk, and Eva Slawson (1882–1917), a domestic servant who became a typist. Their private musings reveal the ways in which Charlotte Brontë's writings, and also those of George Eliot, framed their own debates on the rival paths of 'marriage and motherhood' and 'intellectual freedom'.[1] Kate Flint in *The Woman Reader 1837–1914* (1993) also considers the question of the significance of *Jane Eyre* to women, asking both how Victorian fiction was read by women and how it depicted the female reader.[2] Kathleen Tillotson in *Novels of the Eighteen-Forties* (1954) reports personal acquaintance with daughters of the later nineteenth century who were prohibited from reading volume three of *Jane Eyre* (from the aborted wedding to Jane and Rochester's reunion) until after marriage or middle age and hearing of one lady, Elizabeth Malleson (1828–1916), a friend of George Eliot, who read *Jane Eyre* aloud to her children and carefully missed out the mad wife.[3] Such significant aspects of informal social commentary on the novel have, alas, often been lost to scholarship. Recent electronic, open-access, web-based initiatives such as the Reading Experience Database created by the UK Open University, which gathers written data about reading experiences in history, will continue to add to our knowledge of a wide range of responses to *Jane Eyre* that have been previously unavailable to students.

As well as offering a new, accessible medium for academic criticism, the internet has produced its own range of popular commentaries on *Jane Eyre*, which cannot be ignored. The internet is also an insistent reminder of the material and commercial world in which the Brontë novels and their authors continue to be marketed across the globe. A recent search for Brontë products led me to a site advertising a T-shirt depicting 'Tarzan and Jane Eyre'. In the picture, Tarzan, in his trademark loincloth and sitting in a tree, is deep in study of a copy of Brontë's novel, which he is holding between his feet. When an early twentieth-century literary character who is now best known as a visual icon of unreconstructed masculinity is depicted puzzling over a nineteenth-century novel whose heroine is an icon of independent femininity, we confront a curious cultural intertext. Has Jane Eyre replaced the Jane who is normally Tarzan's mate, inspiring him to move from vine-swinging and monosyllabic commands to the more civilised pleasures of literature? Or should we infer that the heroes invented by men and the heroines invented by women ultimately can't speak to one another: they exist in different textual and sexual worlds? Wearing such a T-shirt, the male or female body becomes a message board that carries a sign inviting interpretation. It calls attention to *Jane Eyre* as a sign that itself continues to travel, perpetually acquiring new contexts and new meanings.

Notes

Introduction

1. Queen Victoria, Journal for 23 November 1880 repr. Christopher Hibbert, *Queen Victoria in her Letters and Journals* (London: Penguin, 1984), p. 265.
2. Emily Dickinson, *The Letters of Emily Dickinson* ed. Thomas H. Johnson and Theodora Ward 3 vols (Cambridge MA: Harvard University Press, 1986) vol. 3, p. 775.
3. Prince D. S. Mirsky 'The Brontës through foreign eyes' (1923) in The Brontë Society ed., *The Brontës Then and Now* (Shipley: Outhwaite, 1947), p. 44.
4. Sir William Haley, 'Three Sisters' (1947) in *The Brontës Then and Now*, p. 10.
5. Anon, *Era* (14 November 1847), p. 9.
6. Anon, *'Jane Eyre; an Autobiography'*, *Atlas* (23 October 1847), p. 719.
7. Elizabeth Rigby, 'Vanity Fair – and Jane Eyre', *Quarterly Review* (December 1848), pp. 173–4.
8. E.P. Whipple, 'Novels of the Season', *North American Review* (October 1848), pp. 356–7.
9. Angela Carter, Introduction to *Jane Eyre* (London: Virago, 1990), p. vi.
10. Lucasta Miller, *The Brontë Myth* (London: Vintage, 2002), p. 12.
11. Doreen Roberts, *'Jane Eyre* and "The Warped System of Things"' in *Reading the Victorian Novel: Detail into Form* ed. Ian Gregor (London: Vision Press, 1980), p. 144.

1 Victorian Responses: Power and Popularity; Coarseness and Criticism

1. T.Wemyss Reid, *Charlotte Bronte. A Monograph* (London: Macmillan, 1877), p. 8.
2. William Thackeray, Letter to W.S. Williams, 23 October 1847, *The Letters and Private Papers of W.M. Thackeray* 4 vols ed. Gordon N. Ray (London: Oxford University Press, 1945), vol. 2, pp. 318–19. This and many of the other nineteenth-century critical responses to *Jane Eyre* discussed in this chapter are reproduced, usually in abridged form, in Miriam Allott, *The Brontës: the Critical Heritage* (London: Routledge, 1974), which is an invaluable resource for students. I have preferred here to cite the original reviews and my selections occasionally differ from Allott's.
3. One rumour was that *Jane Eyre* had been penned by a discarded mistress of William Thackeray, whose character had also formed the basis for his portrayal of Becky Sharp, in *Vanity Fair*. This spurious piece of scandal was inspired by the coincidence (unknown to Charlotte Brontë) that Thackeray's wife, like Rochester's, was confined due to insanity and by Charlotte's admiring dedication of the second edition of *Jane Eyre* to Thackeray.
4. G.H. Lewes, *Westminster Review* (January 1848), p. 581.
5. Anon, *Critic* (30 October 1847), pp. 277–8.
6. In particular, Rochester refers to Blanche Ingram as 'a real strapper [...] big, brown, and buxom'.
7. 'Nervous diction' here means 'vigorous and powerful expression of ideas in words'.
8. Anon, *'Jane Eyre; an Autobiography'*, *Atlas* (23 October 1847), p. 719.
9. See, for example, A.W. Fonblanque, 'The Literary Examiner', *Examiner* (27 November 1847), p. 756: *'Jane Eyre* is a very clever book. Indeed it is a book of decided power.'

10. H.F. Chorley, 'Our Library Table', *Athenaeum* (23 October) 1847, p. 1100.
11. Anon, *Era* (14 November 1847), p. 9.
12. *Era* (1847), p. 9.
13. A.W. Fonblanque, 'The Literary Examiner', *Examiner* (27 November 1847), p. 756.
14. Fonblanque (1847), p. 756.
15. George Eliot, Letter to Charles Bray 11 June 1848, repr. *The George Eliot Letters* ed. Gordon S. Haight 9 vols (New Haven: Yale University Press, 1978), vol. 1, p. 268. Eliot remarks of Jane refusing to be Rochester's mistress that 'all self-sacrifice is good – but one would like it to be in a somewhat nobler cause than that of a diabolical law which chains a man soul and body to a putrefying carcase. However, the book *is* interesting – only I wish the characters would talk a little less like the heroes and heroines of police reports'.
16. G.H. Lewes, 'Recent Novels: French and English', *Fraser's Magazine* (December 1847), p. 691.
17. Lewes (1847), p. 693.
18. Lewes (1847), p. 693.
19. Anon, 'Jane Eyre', *The Spectator* (6 November, 1847), pp. 1074–5.
20. *Spectator* (1847), pp. 1074–5.
21. Charlotte Brontë, Letter to Messrs Smith and Elder 13 November 1847, *The Letters of Charlotte Brontë* ed. Margaret Smith 3 vols (Oxford: Clarendon, 1995) vol. 1, p. 563.
22. Charlotte's combative preface of January 1848, in which she asserted that 'Conventionality is not morality, Self-righteousness is not religion', was not calculated to appease unfriendly critics.
23. Anne Mozley, 'Jane Eyre: An Autobiography', *Christian Remembrancer*, April 1848, pp. 396–7.
24. Mozley (1848), p. 397.
25. Mozley (1848), p. 401.
26. Elizabeth Rigby, 'Vanity Fair – and Jane Eyre', *Quarterly Review* (December 1848), pp. 173–4.
27. Rigby (1848), p. 173.
28. E.P. Whipple, 'Novels of the Season', *North American Review* (October 1848), pp. 356–7.
29. James Lorimer, 'Noteworthy Novels', *North British Review* (August 1849), p. 486.
30. Brontë (1995), vol. 2, p. 140.
31. Eugène Forçade, *Revue des Deux Mondes* (31 October 1848), tome 24, pp. 473–5. I am indebted to Dr David Evans of the School of Modern Languages at the University of St Andrews for this fresh translation of the original text.
32. Forçade (1848), pp. 493–4.
33. Whipple (1848), p. 357.
34. Margaret Sweat, 'Charlotte Bronte and the Bronte Novels', *North American Review* 177 (October, 1857), p. 316.
35. Émile Montégut, *Revue des Deux Mondes* (1 July 1857), tome 4, pp. 139–84, repr Allott, *Critical Heritage* p. 372. This is Allott's translation.
36. Margaret Oliphant, 'Modern Novelists – Great and Small', *Blackwood's Edinburgh Magazine* 77 (May 1855), p. 557.
37. Oliphant (1855), p. 557.
38. Oliphant (1855), pp. 558–9.
39. George Campbell, *The Infidelity of our Current Literature; with special reference to Charlotte Brontë and Tennyson* (Aberdeen: Wagrell, 1861), p. 12.
40. Margaret Oliphant, 'Novels', *Blackwood's Edinburgh Magazine* 102 (September 1867), p. 258.
41. Anon, 'Belles Lettres and Art', *Westminster Review* n.s. 13 (January–April 1858), pp. 297–8.

42. Bret Harte, *Condensed Novels* (London: Routledge, 1873), p. 103.
43. Reid (1877), p. 233.
44. Reid (1877), pp. 9–10.
45. Algernon Swinburne, *A Note on Charlotte Brontë* (London: Chatto and Windus, 1877), p. 7.
46. Swinburne (1877), pp. 26–8.
47. Swinburne (1877), pp. 69–70.
48. Swinburne (1877), p. 73.
49. Leslie Stephen, 'Hours in a Library No. XVII: Charlotte Brontë', *Cornhill Magazine* (December 1877), p. 726, p. 739.
50. Stephen (1877), p. 727.
51. Stephen (1877), p. 737.
52. Peter Bayne, *Two Great Englishwomen: Mrs Browning and Charlotte Brontë, with an Essay on Poetry* (London: Clarke, 1881), p. 290.
53. Bayne (1881), pp. 291–2.
54. Mary [Mrs Humphry] Ward ed. *Jane Eyre* in *The Life and Works of Charlotte Brontë and her Sisters* (Smith, Elder, 1899), pp. x, xiii.
55. Ward (1899), p. xxxviii.
56. Ward (1899), p. xxxvii.
57. See also William Wright, *The Brontës and Ireland* (London: Hodder & Stoughton, 1893) and Cathal O'Byrne, *The Gaelic Source of the Brontë Genius* (Edinburgh and London: Sands, 1933).
58. Ward (1899), p. xix.
59. Erin O'Connor, 'Preface for a post-postcolonial criticism', *Victorian Studies* 45 (Winter 2003), p. 237.

2 Jane Eyre's 'I': From Humanism to Deconstruction

1. David Cecil, *Early Victorian Novelists* (London: Constable, 1934), p. 116.
2. Cecil (1934), pp. 125, 130.
3. Walter Allen, *The English Novel* (London: Penguin, 1958), p. 190.
4. F.R. Leavis, *The Great Tradition* (London: Chatto and Windus, 1948), p. 27.
5. Tom Winnifrith, *The Brontës* (London: Macmillan, 1977), p. 3.
6. Q.D. Leavis, Introduction to *Jane Eyre* (London: Penguin, 1966) repr. in *Q.D. Leavis: Collected Essays* 3 vols (Cambridge: Cambridge University Press, 1983), vol. 1, p. 177.
7. W.G. Clark, 'New Novels', *Fraser's Magazine* 40 (December 1849), p. 692.
8. Heather Glen, *Charlotte Brontë: The Imagination in History* (Oxford: OUP, 2002), p. 57.
9. Glen (2002), p. 58.
10. Cecil (1934), p. 112.
11. Kathleen Tillotson, *Novels of the Eighteen-Forties* (Oxford: Clarendon, 1954).
12. Alice Foley, *A Bolton Childhood* (Manchester: Manchester University Extra-Mural Dept., 1973), p. 55.
13. Philip Inman, *No Going Back* (London: Williams and Norgate, 1952), p. 46.
14. Ernest Dimnet, *The Brontë Sisters* [*Les Soeurs Brontë*] translated by Louise Morgan Sill (London, Jonathan Cape: 1927), p. 143. This book was first published in France in 1910.
15. Dimnet (1927), p. 144.
16. Virginia Woolf, *The Common Reader* (London: Hogarth Press, 1929), p. 196. The book announces that Woolf's essay, '"Jane Eyre" and Wuthering Heights"' was written in 1916.
17. Woolf (1929), p. 197.
18. Woolf (1929), p. 198.
19. Woolf (1929), p. 199.
20. Cecil (1934), p. 112.

21. Cecil (1934), p. 3.
22. Cecil (1934), p. 110.
23. Cecil (1934), p. 120.
24. Cecil (1934), p. 122.
25. Cecil (1934), p. 125.
26. Cecil (1934), p. 130.
27. Cecil (1934), p. 132.
28. Cecil (1934), p. 143.
29. May Sinclair, introduction to *Jane Eyre* in *The Novels of Charlotte, Emily and Anne Brontë* (London and Toronto: Dent, 1922), p. v. The tradition of regarding Charlotte Brontë as free of literary influence predates Sinclair. See Henry H. Bonnell, *Eliot, Jane Austen: Studies in their Works* (New York: Longman, 1902), p. 11: 'there never was author of highest rank so uninfluenced by, because there never was one so unconscious of, literary models.'
30. Woolf (1929), p. 200.
31. F.R. Leavis, *The Great Tradition* (London: Chatto and Windus, 1948), p. 27.
32. Leavis (1948), p. 27.
33. Tillotson (1954), p. 257.
34. Tillotson (1954), pp. 259–60.
35. Robert B. Heilman, 'Charlotte Brontë's "New" Gothic' in *From Jane Austen to Joseph Conrad* ed. by Robert C. Rathburn and Martin Steinmann (Minneapolis: University of Minnesota Press, 1958), p. 131.
36. Heilman (1958), p. 131 .
37. Heilman (1958), p. 121.
38. Heilman (1958), p. 121.
39. Heilman (1958), pp. 122–3.
40. Robert Martin, *The Accents of Persuasion: Charlotte Brontë's Novels* (London: Faber,1966), p. 19.
41. Q.D. Leavis (1983), vol. 1, pp. 178–9.
42. Q.D. Leavis (1983), vol. 1, p. 177.
43. David Lodge, *The Language of Fiction* (London: Routledge, 1966), p. 115.
44. Lodge (1966), p. 120. 'Objective correlative' is a term coined by T.S. Eliot in his 1920 essay 'Hamlet and His Problems'.
45. Karl Kroeber, *Styles in Fictional Structure: the Art of Jane Austen, Charlotte Brontë, George Eliot* (Princeton NJ: Princeton University Press, 1971), p. 3, p. 10.
46. Kroeber (1971), p. 192.
47. Margot Peters, *Charlotte Brontë: Style in the Novel* (Madison, Wisconsin: University of Wisconsin Press, 1973), p. 23.
48. Peters (1973), p. 40.
49. Lodge (1966), p. 134.
50. Peters (1973), p. 41.
51. See Eric Solomon, '*Jane Eyre*: Fire and Water', *College English*, 25 (December 1963), pp. 215–17; Donald Erickson, 'Imagery as Structure in *Jane Eyre*', *Victorian Newsletter* 30 (Autumn 1966), pp. 18–22 and Cynthia A. Linder, *Romantic Imagery in the Novels of Charlotte Brontë* (London: Macmillan, 1978).
52. W.A. Craik, *The Brontë Novels* (London: Methuen, 1968), p. 72.
53. Doreen Roberts, '*Jane Eyre* and "The Warped System of Things"' in *Reading the Victorian Novel: Detail into Form* ed. by Ian Gregor (London: Vision Press, 1980), p. 131.
54. Roberts (1980), pp. 137–8.
55. Roberts (1980), p. 133.
56. Roberts (1980), p. 133.
57. Roberts (1980), p. 134.
58. Roberts (1980), p. 135.
59. Roberts (1980), p. 135.

60. Roberts (1980), p. 144.
61. Roberts (1980), p. 147.
62. Roberts (1980), p. 144.
63. Annette Tromly, *The Cover of the Mask: The Autobiographers in Charlotte Brontë's Fiction* (Victoria, B.C.: University of Victoria Press, 1982), p. 14.
64. Tromly (1982), p. 15.
65. Tromly (1982), p. 44.
66. Lawrence Jay Dessner, *The Homely Web of Truth: A Study of Charlotte Brontë's Novels* (The Hague: Mouton, 1975), p. 73.
67. Tromly (1982), pp. 48–9.
68. Carol Bock, *Charlotte Brontë and the Storyteller's Audience* (Iowa City: University of Iowa Press,1992), p. 102.
69. Lisa Sternlieb, 'Jane Eyre: "Hazarding Confidences"' *Nineteenth-Century Literature* 53 (March 1999), p. 454.
70. Charlotte Brontë, *Jane Eyre* ed. Jane Jack and Margaret Smith (Oxford: Clarendon Press, 1969), pp. 166–7.
71. Sternlieb (1999), p. 454.
72. Sternlieb (1999), p. 474.
73. Sternlieb (1999), p. 470.
74. Peter Allan Dale, 'Charlotte Brontë's "Tale Half-Told": the Disruption of Narrative Structure in *Jane Eyre*', *Modern Language Quarterly* 47 (1986), pp. 108–29, repr *New Casebooks: Jane Eyre* ed. Heather Glen (Basingstoke: Macmillan, 1997), p. 209.
75. Peter Allan Dale (1986), p. 214.
76. Peter Allan Dale (1986), p. 224.
77. Mark M. Hennelly, '*Jane Eyre*'s Reading Lesson', *English Literary History* 51 (1984), p. 709.
78. Hennelly (1984), p. 709.
79. Hennelly (1984), p. 706.
80. Karen Chase, *Eros and Psyche: The Representation of Personality in Charlotte Brontë, Charles Dickens, and George Eliot* (New York and London: Methuen, 1984), pp. 73–4.
81. Chase (1984), p. 74.
82. Chase (1984), p. 76.
83. Glen (2002), p. 64.
84. Jerome Beaty, *Misreading Jane Eyre: A Postformalist Paradigm* (Columbus, Ohio: Ohio State University Press, 1996).
85. Beaty (1996), p. 220.

3 An Iconic Text: Feminist and Psychoanalytic Criticism

1. Harriet Martineau, *Autobiography* ed. Gaby Weiner 2 vols (London: Virago, 1983) vol. 2, p. 324.
2. Margaret Oliphant, 'Modern Novelists – Great and Small', *Blackwood's Edinburgh Magazine* 77 (May 1855), p. 557.
3. Peter Bayne, *Two Great Englishwomen: Mrs Browning and Charlotte Brontë, with an Essay on Poetry* (London: Clarke, 1881), pp. 290–2.
4. Charlotte Brontë, *Jane Eyre* ed. Jane Jack and Margaret Smith (Oxford: Clarendon Press, 1969), pp. 132–3. Woolf does not quote the same selection from this passage as I have done here. Cora Kaplan in *Sea Changes: Culture and Feminism* (London: Verso, 1986), p. 172 suggests that Woolf deliberately omits sentences from the passage that do not suit her own aesthetic, missing the linkage between class rebellion and women's revolt and Brontë's positive assertion that even a confined and restless state can produce 'many and glowing' visions.
5. Virginia Woolf, *A Room of One's Own* (Oxford: Oxford University Press, 2000), p. 90.
6. Robert Martin, *The Accents of Persuasion: Charlotte Brontë's Novels* (London: Faber, 1966), p. 93.

7. Martin (1966), p. 81.
8. Martin (1966), p. 94.
9. Q.D. Leavis, Introduction to *Jane Eyre* repr. in Q.D. *Leavis: Collected Essays*, vol. 1, p. 177.
10. Inga-Stina Ewbank, *Their Proper Sphere: A Study of the Brontë Sisters as Early Victorian Female Novelists* (London: Arnold, 1966), pp. xv–xvi.
11. Brontë (1995), vol. 2, p. 66.
12. Ewbank (1966), pp. 157, 160.
13. Ewbank (1966), p. 197.
14. Ewbank (1966), pp. 199–200.
15. Brontë (1995), vol. 2, p. 235.
16. Kate Millett, *Sexual Politics* (London: Abacus, 1972), p. 147.
17. Millett (1972), p. 144.
18. Patricia Meyer Spacks, *The Female Imagination: A Literary and Psychological Investigation of Women's Writing* (London: Allen and Unwin, 1976), p. 36.
19. Spacks (1976), p. 63.
20. Adrienne Rich, 'Jane Eyre: The Temptations of a Motherless Woman' repr. in *On Lies, Secrets and Silence: Selected Prose 1966–1978* (London: Virago, 1980), p. 89.
21. Rich (1980), p. 90.
22. Rich (1980), p. 91.
23. Rich (1980), p. 106.
24. Richard Chase, 'The Brontës, or; Myth Domesticated', in *Forms of Modern Fiction* ed. by William Van O'Connor (Minneapolis, The University of Minnesota Press, 1948), p. 108. Chase continues (p. 110) that 'obviously Jane Eyre is a feminist tract, an argument for the social betterment of governesses and equal rights for women. But we have to see this propaganda and other explicit elements of the Brontë novels in comprehensive mythical images before we can begin to understand their full significance'.
25. Rich (1980), p. 105.
26. Helene Moglen, *Charlotte Brontë: The Self Conceived* (New York: Norton, 1976), pp. 142–3.
27. Maurianne Adams, 'Jane Eyre: Women's Estate' in *The Authority of Experience: Essays in Feminist Criticism* ed. Arlyn Diamond and Lee R. Edwards (Amherst: University of Massachusetts Press, 1977), p. 139.
28. Adams (1977), p. 144.
29. Adams (1977), p. 148.
30. Adams (1977), p. 145.
31. Adams (1977), p. 146.
32. Elaine Showalter, *A Literature of their Own: British Women Novelists from Brontë to Lessing* (London: Virago, 1978), p. 13.
33. Showalter (1978), pp. 112–13.
34. Showalter (1978), p. 115.
35. Showalter (1978), p. 117.
36. Showalter (1978), p. 118.
37. Showalter (1978), p. 124.
38. Sandra Gilbert and Susan Gubar, *The Madwoman in the Attic: The Woman Writer and the Nineteenth-Century Literary Imagination* (New Haven and London: Yale University Press, 2000), p. 339.
39. Gilbert and Gubar (2000), p. 341.
40. Gilbert and Gubar (2000), p. 78.
41. Angela Carter, Introduction to *Jane Eyre* (London: Virago, 1990), p. vi.
42. Gilbert and Gubar (2000), pp. 343–4.
43. Margaret Homans, *Bearing the Word: Language and Female Experience in Nineteenth-Century Women's Writing* (Chicago: University of Chicago Press, 1986), pp. 85–6.
44. Homans (1986), p. 90.

45. Patricia Yaeger, *Honey-Mad Women: Emancipatory Strategies in Women's Writing* (New York: Columbia University Press, 1988), pp. 35–6.

46. Yaeger (1988), p. 36.

47. Carolyn Williams, 'Closing the Book: The Intertextual End of *Jane Eyre*' in *Victorian Connections* ed. Jerome McGann (Charlottesville: University Press of Virginia, 1989), p. 63.

48. Sigmund Freud, father of psychoanalysis, posited that, like the Greek tragic protagonist Oedipus, boys sexually desire their mothers; girls sexually desire their fathers. Both sexes must pass through a childhood struggle with the other parent before achieving mature sexual selfhood.

49. Williams (1989), p. 77.

50. Williams (1989), p. 82.

51. Jean Wyatt, *Reconstructing Desire: The Role of the Unconscious in Women's Reading and Writing* (Chapel Hill: University of North Carolina Press, 1990), p. 23. For a different oedipal reading of *Jane Eyre* see Dianne F. Sadoff, 'The Father, Castration, and Female Fantasy in *Jane Eyre*' in Beth Newman ed. *Jane Eyre* (New York: St Martin's, 1996), pp. 518–34.

52. Wyatt (1990), pp. 39–40.

53. Mary Poovey, *Uneven Developments: The Ideological Work of Gender in Mid-Victorian England* (Chicago: University of Chicago Press, 1989), p. 127.

54. Poovey (1989), p. 141.

55. Susan Fraiman, *Unbecoming Women: British Women Writers and the Novel of Development* (New York: Columbia University Press, 1993), p. 94.

56. Cora Kaplan, *Sea Changes: Culture and Feminism* (London: Verso, 1986), p. 172.

57. Laura Donaldson, *Decolonizing Feminisms: Race, Gender and Empire-Building* (London: Routledge, 1993), p. 31.

58. Penny Boumelha, *Charlotte Brontë* (London: Harvester Wheatsheaf, 1990), p. 77.

59. Jane Lazarre, '"Charlotte's Web": Reading *Jane Eyre* Over Time' in *Between Women* ed. Carol Ascher, Louise DeSalvo, Sara Ruddick (New York and London: Routledge, 1993), p. 223.

60. Carla Kaplan, *The Erotics of Talk: Women's Writing and Feminist Paradigms* (New York and Oxford: Oxford University Press, 1996), p. 98.

4 Caste Typing: Marxist and Materialist Criticism

1. Elizabeth Rigby, 'Vanity Fair – and Jane Eyre', *Quarterly Review* (December 1848), pp. 173–4.

2. For Lockhart's report see Brontë, *The Letters of Charlotte Brontë* (Oxford: Clarendon, 1995), vol. 2, p. 67.

3. Raymond Williams, *The English Novel From Dickens to Lawrence* (London: Chatto and Windus, 1970), pp. 60–1.

4. Williams (1970), pp. 11–12.

5. Williams (1970), p. 63.

6. Terry Eagleton, *Myths of Power: A Marxist Study of the Brontës* (London: Macmillan, 1975), p. 4.

7. Eagleton (1975), p. 26.

8. Eagleton (1975), p. 15.

9. Eagleton (1975), pp. 30–1.

10. Nancy Pell, 'Resistance, Rebellion, and Marriage: The Economics of *Jane Eyre*', *Nineteenth-Century Fiction* 31 (March 1977), pp. 399–400.

11. Pell (1977), p. 405.

12. Eagleton (p. 15) also considers this dialogue between Helen and Jane, but concludes that Helen's 'vacillation' between an appreciation of 'essential reformist change' and 'a spirited Romantic conservatism' reflects Charlotte Brontë's own ambivalence.

13. Pell (1977), p. 406.

14. Carol Ohmann, 'Historical Reality and "Divine Appointment" in Charlotte Brontë's Fiction', *Signs* 2 (Summer 1977), p. 757.

15. Ohmann (1977), p. 763.

16. Igor Webb, *From Custom to Capital: The English Novel and the Industrial Revolution* (Ithaca and London: Cornell University Press, 1981), p. 86.

17. Jina Politi, 'Jane Eyre Class-ified' *Literature and History* 8:1 (1982), pp. 56–66 repr. in *New Casebooks: Jane Eyre* ed. Heather Glen (Basingstoke: Macmillan, 1997), p. 90.

18. Politi (1997), p. 84.

19. Politi (1997), p. 78.

20. Susan Fraiman, *Unbecoming Women: British Women Writers and the Novel of Development* (New York: Columbia University Press, 1993), p. 94.

21. Fraiman (1993), p. 97.

22. Fraiman (1993), p. 94.

23. Brontë (1969), p. 132.

24. Cora Kaplan, *Sea Changes: Culture and Criticism* (London: Verso, 1986), p. 173.

25. Fraiman (1993), p. 112.

26. The result of interbreeding between two different races or ethnic groups. Fraiman suggests Jane Eyre is miscegenated because her parents came from different classes.

27. Fraiman (1993), p. 120.

28. Sally Shuttleworth, *Charlotte Brontë and Victorian Psychology* (Cambridge: Cambridge University Press, 1996), p. 148.

29. Shuttleworth (1996), p. 149.

30. Brontë, Letter to W.S. Williams 12 May 1848 repr. *Letters*, vol. 2, p. 66.

31. Sharon Marcus, 'The Profession of the Author: Abstraction, Advertising, and Jane Eyre' *PMLA* 110:2 (March, 1995), p. 207.

32. Marcus (1995), pp. 208–9.

33. For a significant discussion of *Jane Eyre* and the politics of pseudonymous publication in the Victorian book market see Catherine A. Judd, 'Male Pseudonyms and Female Authority in Victorian England' in *Literature in the Marketplace: Nineteenth-century British Reading and Publishing Practices* ed. John O. Jordan and Robert L. Patten (Cambridge: Cambridge University Press, 1995).

34. Chris Vanden Bossche, 'What did Jane Eyre do? Ideology, agency, class and the novel' *Narrative* 13 (January 2005), p. 47.

35. Vanden Bossche (2005), p. 55.

5 Bertha's Savage Face: Postcolonial Concerns

1. Among the many concerns postcolonial criticism frequently highlights is the academic tendency to write as if literature were the primary vehicle of communication, ignoring the cultural centrality of oral discourses such as song and storytelling, both of which feature prominently in *Jane Eyre* and in *Wide Sargasso Sea*.

2. In *Wide Sargasso Sea*, Antoinette is crucially both colonial and colonised subject. Her father was a plantation owner with multiple children of various ethnicities. After his death and the end of slavery, Antoinette lives in poverty with her mother until the latter's remarriage to Mr Mason. She is white-skinned but, ethnically, she is neither 'quite white' nor brown nor black and belongs to neither black nor white community.

3. Jean Rhys, *Wide Sargasso Sea* (London: Penguin, 1979), pp. 88, 42. Jaques Tourneur's film 'I Walked with a Zombie' (1943) forms an interesting comparison with Rhys's novel. It relocates the framework of the Jane Eyre story to a Caribbean sugar plantation. The Canadian Betsy Connell (the equivalent of Jane) goes out there as a nurse and falls in love with her employer, the plantation owner, whose mad wife wanders the estate at night. The mad wife appears to be a 'zombie', a living-dead woman, and the characters in the film debate whether

it is marital infidelity, her husband's behaviour, or a voodoo curse that is responsible. The film picks up on unanswered questions about 'Bertha''s madness and implicitly compares the fraught relationship between Rochester and his first wife to that between coloniser and colonised.

4. Gayatri Spivak, 'Three Women's Texts and A Critique of Imperialism' *Critical Inquiry* 12 (Autumn 1985), p. 243.

5. Charlotte Brontë, *Jane Eyre* ed. Jane Jack and Margaret Smith (Oxford: Clarendon Press, 1969), p. 370.

6. Brontë (1969), pp. 393–4. In quoting this passage, Spivak italicises 'I have a right'.

7. Spivak (1985), p. 248.

8. Spivak (1985), p. 249.

9. Firdous Azim, *The Colonial Rise of the Novel* (London: Routledge, 1993), p. 183.

10. Azim (1993), pp. 178–9.

11. Azim (1993), p. 172.

12. Mary Ellis Gibson, 'The Seraglio or Suttee: Brontë's *Jane Eyre*' *Postscript* 4 (1987), p. 1.

13. Gibson (1987), p. 2.

14. Gibson (1987), p. 5.

15. The Roman Emperor Claudius (b. 10 BC, d. 54 A.D.; emperor 41–54 A.D.) had four wives. Messalina, his third wife, was executed, reputedly after a career of political intrigue and sexual promiscuity.

16. Gibson (1987), p. 5.

17. Gibson (1987), p. 7.

18. Joyce Zonana, 'The Sultan and the Slave: Feminist Orientalism and the Structure of *Jane Eyre*', *Signs*, 18 (Spring 1993), p. 593.

19. Zonana (1993), p. 594. Zonana refers here to Said's influential study *Orientalism* (1978), which identifies a long and pervasive prejudice in Eurocentric culture against Arabo-Islamic peoples and cultures, which are associated with a mythical 'East' that inspires desire and disgust.

20. Zonana (1993), p. 596.

21. Zonana (1993), p. 597.

22. Suvendrini Perera, *Reaches of Empire: The English Novel from Edgeworth to Dickens* (New York: Columbia University Press, 1991), p. 79.

23. Perera (1991), p. 84.

24. Susan Meyer, *Imperialism at Home: Race and Victorian Women's Fiction* (Ithaca and London: Cornell University Press, 1996), p. 63. An earlier version of this chapter, to which Sharpe (below) responds, was published as 'Colonialism and the Figurative Strategy of *Jane Eyre*' *Victorian Studies* 33 (Winter 1990), pp. 247–68.

25. Meyer (1990), p. 74.

26. Meyer (1990), p. 94.

27. Jenny Sharpe, *Allegories of Empire: The Figure of Woman in the Colonial Text* (Minneapolis: University of Minnesota Press, 1993), p. 30.

28. Sharpe (1993), p. 42.

29. Sharpe (1993), p. 45.

30. Sharpe (1993), p. 47.

31. Sharpe (1993), pp. 46–7.

32. Deirdre David, *Rule Britannia: Women, Empire and Victorian Writing* (Ithaca and London: Cornell University Press, 1995), p. 79.

33. David (1995), p. 91.

34. David (1995), p. 97.

35. A similar reading of Jane as representative of English national health runs through Alan Bewell's '*Jane Eyre* and Victorian Medical Geography' (1996) in which he links Jane 'Air' with the healthy mountain breeze that characterises England's defence against the

contaminating fevers of an empire whose moral lassitude and insalubrious climate were linked in contemporary medical theory.

36. Elsie Michie, 'White Chimpanzees and Oriental Despots: Racial Stereotyping and Edward Rochester' in *Case Studies in Contemporary Criticism: Jane Eyre* ed. Beth Newman (New York: St Martin's Press, 1996), pp. 596–7. Another version of this essay is printed in Michie's book, *Outside the Pale: Cultural Exclusion, Gender Difference, and the Victorian Woman Writer* (Ithaca: Cornell UP, 1993).

37. Kathleen Constable, 'Writing the Minefield: Reflections of Union in Charlotte Brontë's *Jane Eyre* and *Shirley*' in *Writing Irishness in Nineteenth-century British Culture* ed. Neil McCaw (Aldershot: Ashgate, 2004), p. 102.

38. Constable (2004), p. 105.

39. Erin O'Connor, 'Preface for a post-postcolonial criticism', *Victorian Studies* 45 (Winter 2003), p. 224.

40. O'Connor (2003), p. 228.

41. For an earlier sceptical view of the critical ink spilled in discussing Bertha, see Laurence Lerner, 'Bertha and the critics', *Nineteenth-century Literature* (December 1989), pp. 273–300.

6 New Historicism and The Turn Toward History

1. John Brannigan, *New Historicism and Cultural Materialism* (Basingstoke: Macmillan, 1998), p. 3.

2. Catherine Gallagher and Stephen Greenblatt, *Practicing New Historicism* (Chicago: University of Chicago Press, 2000), p. 9.

3. Gallagher is here drawing on the French word 'supplément', which can mean both 'addition' and 'substitute'. Jacques Derrida in 'Of Grammatology' (1967), a key work of post-structuralist criticism, notices that Jean-Jacques Rousseau, whose work he is analysing, uses 'supplément' consciously in one sense, but that the other meaning is always necessarily also present. This is emblematic of the way in which a text always exceeds its author's intentions and control. Pursuing the 'supplements' of the text, then, involves producing a reading that is attentive not only to the author's designed verbal manoeuvres and meanings, but also to textual patterns and preoccupations that emerge outside and beyond the author's command.

4. Gallagher and Greenblatt (2000), p. 17.

5. For criticism that sets *Jane Eyre* in the context of Victorian women's autobiography see Linda H. Peterson, *Traditions of Victorian Women's Autobiography* (Charlottesville: University of Virginia Press, 1999); for use of contemporary missionary writing see Sue Thomas, *Imperialism, Reform, and the Making of Englishness in Jane Eyre* (Basingstoke: Palgrave, 2008); for discussion of *Jane Eyre* in relation to Victorian evangelical and educational writings see Heather Glen, *Charlotte Brontë: the Imagination in History* (Cambridge: Cambridge University Press, 2002), discussed below.

6. See Lucasta Miller, *The Brontë Myth* (London: Vintage, 2002) and Patsy Stoneman, 'The Brontë Myth' in Heather Glen ed. *The Cambridge Companion to the Brontës* (Cambridge: Cambridge University Press, 2002).

7. Barker's authoritative biography set a new standard for reading the Brontës' lives in the nineteenth-century historical context. However, while rescuing Patrick and Branwell Brontë from centuries of undeserved blame, Barker produces a portrait of Charlotte Brontë that is often acerbic.

8. Physiognomy, an ancient art, held that a person's visual appearance corresponded to their moral condition and character. It was revived in the eighteenth century by the Swiss pastor Johann Kasper Lavater. Like phrenology, it proposed a method of 'reading' the outer body for signs of its internal life, but unlike phrenology it was an essentialist doctrine which posited absolute correspondences, where phrenology suggested mixed and conflicting propensities, which could be developed or suppressed by the individual.

9. Sally Shuttleworth, *Charlotte Brontë and Victorian Psychology* (Cambridge: Cambridge University Press, 1996), p. 3. The texts by Michel Foucault to which she alludes here are *Discipline and Punish: The Birth of the Prison* (1979) and *The History of Sexuality*, vol. 1 (1981).

10. Charlotte Brontë, *Jane Eyre* ed. Jane Jack and Margaret Smith (Oxford: Clarendon Press, 1969), p. 161.

11. Karen Chase, *Eros and Psyche: The Representation of Personality in Charlotte Brontë, Charles Dickens, and George Eliot* (New York and London: Methuen, 1984), pp. 54–65.

12. Shuttleworth (1996), p. 155.

13. Shuttleworth (1996), p. 153.

14. Shuttleworth (1996), p. 152.

15. Shuttleworth (1996), p. 176.

16. Mary A. Armstrong, 'Reading a Head: *Jane Eyre*, Phrenology, and the Homoerotics of Legibility' *Victorian Literature and Culture* 33 (2005), p. 122. For a reading of Jane's love for Helen as specifically Sapphic see Lisa Moore, *Dangerous Intimacies: Toward a Sapphic History of the British Novel* (Durham NC: Duke University Press, 1997).

17. Armstrong (2005), p. 120.

18. Armstrong (2005), p. 127.

19. Janet Gezari, *Charlotte Brontë and Defensive Conduct* (Philadelphia: University of Pennsylvania Press,1992), p. 3.

20. Gezari (1992), p. 4.

21. Gezari (1992), pp. 62–3.

22. Gezari draws attention to this pun, present in *Jane Eyre*, between the pupils (scholars) of Lowood and pupils (the centre of the eyes).

23. Gezari (1992), p. 68.

24. Gezari (1992), p. 88.

25. Peter J. Bellis, 'In the Window-Seat: Vision and Power in *Jane Eyre*' *ELH* 54 (Autumn 1987), p. 639.

26. See M.B. McLaughlin, 'Past and Future Landscapes: Pictures in *Jane Eyre*' *The Victorian Newsletter* 41 (1972), pp. 22–4. For other accounts of the pictures in *Jane Eyre*, see Barabara T. Gates, '"Visionary Woe" and its Revisions: Another Look at Jane Eyre's Pictures' *Ariel* 7 (Winter 1976), pp. 36–49 and Paul Pickrel, 'Jane Eyre: The Apocalypse of the Body' *ELH* 53 (1986), pp. 165–82.

27 Jane Kromm, 'Visual Culture and Scopic Custom in *Jane Eyre* and *Villette*' *Victorian Literature and Culture* 26 (1998), p. 369.

28. Brontë', Letter to W.S. Williams 28 October 1847 repr. *Letters*, vol. 1, p. 554.

29. Heather Glen, *Charlotte Brontë: The Imagination in History* (Oxford: Oxford University Press, 2002), p. 68.

30. Glen (2002), p. 78.

31. Glen (2002), p. 95.

32. For further discussion of the religious aspects of *Jane Eyre* see Barry V. Qualls, *The Secular Pilgrims of Victorian Fiction: The Novel as Book of Life* (Cambridge: Cambridge University Press, 1982); Thomas Vargish, *The Providential Aesthetic in Victorian Fiction* (Charlottesville: University of Virginia Press, 1985); and J. Jeffrey Franklin, 'The Merging of Spiritualities: Jane Eyre as Missionary of Love' *Nineteenth-Century Literature* 49 (March 1995), which argues (pp. 459–60) that 'in one sense *Jane Eyre* is quite representative of its time in showing a multiplicity of competing spiritual discourses *within* Christianity (Brocklehurst's versus St. John Rivers's versus Helen Burns's, for instance); in another sense the novel troubles Christianity itself by introducing spiritual discourses from *outside* orthodox doctrines'.

33. Marianne Thormählen, *The Brontës and Religion* (Cambridge: Cambridge University Press, 1999), p. 219.

34 Alison Case, *Plotting Women: Gender and Narration in the Eighteenth- and Nineteenth-Century British Novel* (Charlottesville: University of Virginia Press, 1999), p. 90.

35. Case (1999), p. 93.
36. Case (1999), p. 99.
37. Case (1999), p. 106.
38. Joseph Litvak, *Caught in the Act: Theatricality in the Nineteenth-century English Novel* (Berkeley: University of California Press,1992), p. 32.
39. See footnote 3 above, for an explanation of the 'supplément' in post-structuralist criticism and new historicist commitment to pursuing the supplements of the text.
40. Litvak (1992), p. 31.
41. For a further exploration of this idea, see John Kucich, *Repression in Victorian Fiction: Charlotte Brontë, George Eliot, and Charles Dickens* (Berkeley: University of California Press, 1987), whose influence Litvak acknowledges.
42. Kucich (1987), p. 73.
43. John Sutherland, *Can Jane Eyre Be Happy? More Puzzles in Classic Fiction* (Oxford: Oxford University Press, 1997), pp. 73–4.

7 *Jane Eyre* Adapted

1. In the 1934 Monogram Pictures film of *Jane Eyre*, Jane is working in a soup kitchen and just about to marry St John Rivers when a servant from Thornfield pops up and tells her about the fire and Bertha's death. In Emma Jane Warboise's *Thornycroft Hall* (1864), a religious re-write of *Jane Eyre*, the heroine marries her cousin, who is a nonconformist minister. Sharon Shinn's *Jenna Starborn* (2002), a science fiction novel, re-locates the *Jane Eyre* plot in outer space.
2. Julia Kristeva, *The Kristeva Reader* ed. Toril Moi (Oxford: Blackwell, 1986), p. 37.
3. Patsy Stoneman, *Brontë Transformations: The Cultural Dissemination of Jane Eyre and Wuthering Heights* (London: Harvester Wheatsheaf, 1996), pp. 8–9.
4. Patsy Stoneman, *Jane Eyre on Stage, 1848–1898* (Aldershot: Ashgate, 2007), pp. 15–16.
5. Stoneman, *Brontë Transformations*, p. 100.
6. Kate Ellis and Ann Kaplan, 'Feminism in Brontë's *Jane Eyre* and its Film Versions' in Michael Klein and Gillian Parker eds *The English Novel and the Movies* (1981), p. 83. See also Sumiko Higashi, '*Jane Eyre*: Charlotte Brontë vs. the Hollywood Myth of Romance' *Journal of Popular Film* 6 (1977) pp. 13–31.
7. Ellis and Kaplan, 'Feminism in Brontë's *Jane Eyre*', p. 89.
8. Donna Marie Nudd, 'Rediscovering *Jane Eyre* through its adaptations' in Diane Hoeveler and Beth Lau eds *Approaches to Teaching Jane Eyre* (New York: MLA, 1992), pp. 141–2.
9. For recent discussions of *Jane Eyre* on film see Elizabeth Atkins, '*Jane Eyre* Transformed' *Literature/Film Quarterly* 21:1 (1993) pp. 54–60; Lisa Hopkins 'The Red and the Blue: *Jane Eyre* in the 1990s' in Deborah Cartmell, I.Q. Hunter, Heidi Kaye and Imelda Whelehan eds *Classics in Film and Fiction* (London: Pluto, 2000); Lisa Hopkins, *Screening the Gothic* (Austin: University of Texas Press, 2005); and Margarete Rubik and Elke Mettinger-Schartmann eds *A Breath of Fresh Eyre. Intertextual and Intermedial Reworkings of Jane Eyre* (Amsterdam: Rodopi, 2007).
10. Polly Teale, *Jane Eyre: adapted from Charlotte Brontë's novel by Polly Teale for Shared Experience* (London: Nick Hern, 1998), p. 3.
11. Bruno Lessard, 'The Madwoman in the Classic: Intermediality, Female Subjectivity, and Dance in Michael Berkeley's *Jane Eyre*' in Rubik and Mettinger-Schartmann eds *A Breath of Fresh Eyre*, p. 334.
12. Carol M. Dole, 'Children in the *Jane Eyre* Films' in *A Breath of Fresh Eyre*, p. 247.
13. Margarete Rubik and Elke Mettinger-Schartmann, *A Breath of Fresh Eyre*, p. 10. They quote Umberto Eco, '*Casablanca*: Cult movies and intertextual collage' in *Modern Criticism and Theory: A Reader* ed. David Lodge (Harlow: Longman, 2000) p. 447.

Conclusion

1. Jonathan Rose, *The Intellectual Life of the British Working Classes* (New Haven and London: Yale University Press, 2001), pp. 250, 215–16.
2. Kate Flint, *The Woman Reader 1837–1914* (Oxford: Clarendon Press, 1993), p. 232.
3. Kathleen Tillotson, *Novels of the Eighteen-Forties* (Oxford: Clarendon Press, 1954), p. 57.

A Brief Guide to Further Reading

A banquet of critical resources is available to the student of *Jane Eyre*. Below I offer a tasting menu of books and articles, indicative of different periods and approaches. Full publication details are provided in the bibliography. Endnotes to individual chapters (above) suggest more detailed further reading on each of the themes treated in this Guide.

EDITIONS OF *JANE EYRE*

Charlotte Brontë, *Jane Eyre* (eds) Jane Jack and Margaret Smith (Clarendon, 1969, rept. with corrections 1975) is the standard library edition for reference. Among paperback editions, Richard J. Dunn ed., *Jane Eyre. By Charlotte Brontë,* 2nd ed (Norton, 1987) and Beth Newman ed. *Case Studies in Contemporary Criticism: Jane Eyre* (St Martin's, 1996) both supply useful critical essays in addition to the novel. The Oxford World's Classics *Jane Eyre* ed. Margaret Smith, with an introduction and notes by Sally Shuttleworth (2008) and the Penguin *Jane Eyre* ed. Stevie Davies (2006) are also recommended.

REFERENCE WORKS

The Letters of Charlotte Brontë ed. Margaret Smith 3 vols (1995–2004) are an invaluable resource for gaining insight into Brontë's world and ideas. R. W. Crump, *Charlotte and Emily Brontë: A Reference Guide* 3 vols (1982) provides a helpful, year-by-year listing and brief description of critical works on *Jane Eyre* from 1847 onward.

BIOGRAPHIES OF CHARLOTTE BRONTË

Elizabeth Gaskell's *Life of Charlotte Brontë* (1857) set the tone for Brontë's posthumous reception and should be read for its historical colour, but with a more modern biography as a counterweight. Winifred Gérin's *Charlotte Brontë: The Evolution of Genius* (Oxford: Clarendon, 1967) was for years the standard account but Juliet Barker's landmark collective biography, *The Brontës* (1994), makes telling use of more recent research.

ANTHOLOGIES OF CRITICISM

Miriam Allott, *Jane Eyre and Villette: A Casebook* (London: Macmillan, 1973) remains useful. Good modern anthologies include Harold Bloom ed., *Modern Critical Interpretations: Charlotte Brontë's Jane Eyre* (New York: Chelsea, 1987); Diane Hoeveler and Beth Lau (eds) *Approaches to Teaching Jane Eyre* (New York: MLA, 1992); Heather Glen ed., *New Casebooks: Jane Eyre* (Basingstoke: Macmillan, 1997); and Elsie Michie, *Charlotte Brontë's Jane Eyre: A Casebook* (Oxford: Oxford University Press, 2006).

NINETEENTH-CENTURY READINGS
OF *JANE EYRE*

Miriam Allott, *The Brontës: The Critical Heritage* (1974) and Eleanor McNees, *The Brontë Sisters: Critical Assessments* vol. 3 (1996) reproduce a variety of nineteenth-century responses. G.H. Lewes, 'Recent Novels: French and English', *Fraser's Magazine* (December 1847) and Elizabeth Rigby, '*Vanity Fair* – and *Jane Eyre*', *Quarterly Review* (December 1848) demonstrate the division between early enthusiasts and detractors. Algernon Swinburne, *A Note on Charlotte Brontë* (1877) and Leslie Stephen, 'Hours in a Library No. XVII: Charlotte Brontë', *Cornhill Magazine* (December 1877) provide a later pair of contrasting views.

EARLY TWENTIETH-CENTURY READINGS

Virginia Woolf's essay on '*Jane Eyre* and *Wuthering Heights*' in *The Common Reader* (1925) is still lively and provocative. David Cecil's *Early Victorian Novelists* (1934) captures the mixture of affection and disdain *Jane Eyre* inspired amongst intellectuals at this time. Richard Chase, 'The Brontës, or Myth Domesticated', in *Forms of Modern Fiction* (1948) stimulated many replies, while Kathleen Tillotson, *Novels of the Eighteen-Forties* (1954) broke new ground in its scholarly use of contextual material.

Robert B. Heilman's essay, 'Charlotte Brontë's "New" Gothic' (1958) was highly influential and is widely anthologised, as is David Lodge's 'Fire and Eyre: Charlotte Brontë's War of Earthly Elements' (1966), usefully read alongside Q.D. Leavis's introduction to the Penguin *Jane Eyre* (1966). Robert Martin, *The Accents of Persuasion: Charlotte Brontë's Novels* (1966), W.A. Craik, *The Brontë Novels* (1968) and Earl Knies, *The Art of Charlotte Brontë* (1969) all demonstrate the academic rehabilitation of *Jane Eyre* as a formal work of art. Margot Peters, *Charlotte Brontë: Style in the Novel* (1973) provides detailed technical analysis, while Doreen

Roberts, 'Jane Eyre and "The Warped System of Things"' (1980) offers a polemical stylistic critique.

FEMINIST CRITICISM

Virginia Woolf's comments on Charlotte Brontë in *A Room of One's Own* (1929) are important, as later feminists frequently debate Woolf's position. Among numerous influential feminist readings are Adrienne Rich 'Jane Eyre: The Temptations of a Motherless Woman' (1973), Maurianne Adams '*Jane Eyre*: Women's Estate' (1977), Elaine Showalter, *A Literature of their Own: British Women Novelists from Brontë to Lessing* (1978); Sandra Gilbert and Susan Gubar, *The Madwoman in the Attic: The Woman Writer and the Nineteenth-Century Literary Imagination* (1979); Mary Poovey, *Uneven Developments: The Ideological Work of Gender in Mid-Victorian England* (1989); Penny Boumelha, *Charlotte Brontë* (1990); and Susan Fraiman, *Unbecoming Women: British Women Writers and the Novel of Development* (1993).

PSYCHOANALYTIC CRITICISM

For a range of works that make use of psychoanalytic theory in approaching *Jane Eyre*, see Robert Keefe, *Charlotte Brontë's World of Death* (1979); Dianne F. Sadoff, *Monsters of Affection: Dickens, Eliot, and Brontë on Fatherhood* (1982); Margaret Homans, *Bearing the Word: Language and Female Experience in Nineteenth-Century Women's Writing* (1986); Patricia Yaeger, *Honey-Mad Women: Emancipatory Strategies in Women's Writing* (1988); Carolyn Williams, 'Closing the Book: The Intertextual End of *Jane Eyre*' (1989); and Jean Wyatt, *Reconstructing Desire: The Role of the Unconscious in Women's Reading and Writing* (1990).

MARXIST AND MATERIALIST CRITICISM

The first Marxist accounts of *Jane Eyre* were in Raymond Williams's *The English Novel From Dickens to Lawrence* (1970) and Terry Eagleton's *Myths of Power: A Marxist Study of the Brontës* (1975). Subsequent essays that draw on these debates include: Carol Ohmann, 'Historical Reality and "Divine Appointment" in Charlotte Brontë's Fiction' (1977); Nancy Pell, 'Resistance, Rebellion, and Marriage: The Economics of *Jane Eyre*' (1977); Jina Politi, 'Jane Eyre Class-ified' (1982); Sharon Marcus, 'The Profession of the Author: Abstraction, Advertising, and Jane Eyre' (1995) and Chris Vanden Bossche, 'What did Jane Eyre do? Ideology, agency, class and the novel' (2005).

POSTCOLONIAL CRITICISM

The seminal academic critique is Gayatri Spivak, 'Three Women's Texts and A Critique of Imperialism' (1985). Subsequent accounts include: Mary Ellis Gibson, 'The Seraglio or Suttee: Brontë's *Jane Eyre*' (1987), Suvendrini Perera, *Reaches of Empire: The English Novel from Edgeworth to Dickens* (1991); Firdous Azim, *The Colonial Rise of the Novel* (1991); Joyce Zonana, 'The Sultan and the Slave: Feminist Orientalism and the Structure of *Jane Eyre*' (1993); Jenny Sharpe, *Allegories of Empire: The Figure of Woman in the Colonial Text* (1993); and Susan Meyer, *Imperialism at Home: Race and Victorian Women's Fiction* (1996). Erin O'Connor, 'Preface for a post-postcolonial criticism' (2003) offers a dissenting voice.

APPROACHES INFLUENCED BY THE NEW HISTORICISM

This is a loose category, which includes Janet Gezari, *Charlotte Brontë and Defensive Conduct* (1992); Sally Shuttleworth, *Charlotte Brontë and Victorian Psychology* (1996), Linda H. Peterson, *Traditions of Victorian Women's Autobiography* (1999); and Heather Glen, *Charlotte Brontë: the Imagination in History* (2002).

POSTSTRUCTURALIST APPROACHES

Again, most late twentieth-century criticism bears the legacy of post-structuralist thought. But explicitly deconstructive readings can be found in Patricia Yaeger, *Honey-Mad Women: Emancipatory Strategies in Women's Writing* (1988); Laura Donaldson, *Decolonizing Feminisms: Race, Gender and Empire-Building* (1993); and Nina Schwartz 'No Place Like Home: The Logic of the Supplement in *Jane Eyre*' in Beth Newman ed. *Jane Eyre* (1996).

ACCOUNTS OF *JANE EYRE* ADAPTATIONS

This constantly expanding field was charted by Patsy Stoneman, *Brontë Transformations: The Cultural Dissemination of Jane Eyre and Wuthering Heights* (1996). See also Donna Marie Nudd, 'Rediscovering *Jane Eyre* through its adaptations' in Diane Hoeveler and Beth Lau (eds) *Approaches to Teaching Jane Eyre* (1992); Lisa Hopkins, 'The Red and the Blue: *Jane Eyre* in the 1990s' (2000) and Margarete Rubik and, Elke Mettinger-Schartmann (eds) *A Breath of Fresh Eyre: Intertextual and Intermedial Reworkings of Jane Eyre* (2007).

Select Bibliography

Adams, Maurianne, 'Jane Eyre: Women's Estate' in *The Authority of Experience: Essays in Feminist Criticism* ed. Arlyn Diamond and Lee R. Edwards (Amherst: University of Massachusetts Press, 1977).

Alexander, Christine, *The Early Writings of Charlotte Brontë* (Oxford: Blackwell, 1983).

Allen, Walter, *The English Novel* (London: Penguin, 1958).

Allott, Miriam, *The Brontës: The Critical Heritage* (London: Routledge & Kegan Paul, 1974).

Allott, Miriam, *Jane Eyre and Villette: A Casebook* (London: Macmillan, 1973).

Anon, 'Belles Lettres and Art', *Westminster Review* n.s. 13 (January–April 1858), 297–8.

Anon, 'Jane Eyre; an Autobiography', *Atlas* (23 October 1847), 719.

Anon, 'Fiction', *Critic* (30 October 1847), 277–8.

Anon, 'Our Library', *People's Journal* (November 1847), 269–72.

Anon, 'Jane Eyre', *Spectator* (6 November 1847), 1074–5.

Anon, 'Literature', *Era* (14 November 1847), 9.

Armstrong, Mary A., 'Reading a Head: *Jane Eyre*, Phrenology, and the Homoerotics of Legibility' *Victorian Literature and Culture* 33 (2005), 107–32.

Armstrong, Nancy, *Desire and Domestic Fiction* (Oxford: Oxford University Press, 1987).

Armstrong, Nancy, 'Captivity and Cultural Capital in the English Novel' *Novel* 31 (1998), 373–98.

Atkins, Elizabeth, '*Jane Eyre* Transformed' *Literature/Film Quarterly* 21:1 (1993), 54–60.

Auerbach, Nina, *Romantic Imprisonment: Women and Other Glorified Outcasts* (New York: Columbia University Press, 1985).

Azim, Firdous, *The Colonial Rise of the Novel* (London: Routledge, 1993).

Barker, Juliet, *The Brontës* (London: Weidenfeld and Nicolson, 1994).

Bayne, Peter, *Two Great Englishwomen: Mrs Browning and Charlotte Brontë, with an Essay on Poetry* (London: Clarke, 1881).

Beaty, Jerome, '*Jane Eyre* and Genre' *Genre* 10 (1977), 619–54.

Beaty, Jerome, *Misreading Jane Eyre: A Postformalist Paradigm* (Columbus, Ohio: Ohio State Up, 1996).

Beer, Patricia, *Reader, I Married Him: A Study of the Women Characters of Jane Austen, Charlotte Brontë, Elizabeth Gaskell and George Eliot* (London: Macmillan, 1974).

Bellis, Peter J., 'In the Window-Seat: Vision and Power in *Jane Eyre*' *ELH* 54 (1987), 639ñ52.

Berman, Carolyn Vellenga, *Creole Crossings: Domestic Fiction and the Reform of Colonial Slavery* (Ithaca: Cornell University Press, 2006).

Bewell, Alan, '*Jane Eyre* and Victorian Medical Geography' *ELH* 63 (1996), 773–808.

Björk, Harriet, *The Language of Truth: Charlotte Brontë, The Woman Question, and the Novel* (Lund: Gleerup, 1974).

Bloom, Harold ed., *Modern Critical Interpretations: Charlotte Brontë's Jane Eyre* (New York: Chelsea, 1987).

Bock, Carol, *Charlotte Brontë and the Storyteller's Audience* (Iowa City: University of Iowa Press, 1992).

Bodenheimer, Rosemarie, 'Jane Eyre in Search of her Story', *Papers on Language and Literature* 16 (1980), 387–402 reprt. in Harold Bloom ed., *Modern Critical Interpretations: Charlotte Brontë's Jane Eyre* (New York: Chelsea, 1987).

Bonnell, Henry H., *Eliot, Jane Austen: Studies in their Works* (New York: Longman, 1902).

Boumelha, Penny, *Charlotte Brontë* (London: Harvester Wheatsheaf, 1990).

Brontë, Charlotte, *Jane Eyre* ed. Jane Jack and Margaret Smith (Oxford: Clarendon, 1969, reprt. with corrections 1975).

Brontë, Charlotte, *Jane Eyre* ed. Stevie Davies (London: Penguin, 2006).

Brontë, Charlotte, *Jane Eyre* ed. Margaret Smith with an intro and notes by Sally Shuttleworth (Oxford: Oxford University Press, 2008).

Brontë, Charlotte, *The Letters of Charlotte Brontë* ed. Margaret Smith 3 vols (Oxford: Clarendon, 1995–2004).

Campbell, George, *The Infidelity of our Current Literature; with special reference to Charlotte Brontë and Tennyson* (Aberdeen: Wagrell, 1861).

Carter, Angela, Introduction to *Jane Eyre* (London: Virago, 1990).

Case, Alison, *Plotting Women: Gender and Narration in the Eighteenth- and Nineteenth-Century British Novel* (Charlottesville: University of Virginia Press, 1999).

Cecil, David, *Early Victorian Novelists* (London: Constable, 1934).

Chase, Karen, *Eros and Psyche: The Representation of Personality in Charlotte Brontë, Charles Dickens, and George Eliot* (New York and London: Methuen, 1984).

Chase, Richard, 'The Brontës, or; Myth Domesticated', in *Forms of Modern Fiction* ed. O'Connor, William Van (Minneapolis, The University of Minnesota Press, 1948).

Chorley, H. F., 'Our Library Table', *Athenaeum* (23 October 1847), 1100–1.

Chow, Rey, 'When Whiteness Feminizes … Some Consequences of a Supplementary Logic' *Differences* 11 (1999–2000), 137–68.

Clark, W.G., 'New Novels', *Fraser's Magazine* 40 (December 1849), 691–94.

Constable, Kathleen, 'Writing the Minefield: Reflections of Union in Charlotte Brontë's *Jane Eyre* and *Shirley*' in *Writing Irishness in Nineteenth-century British Culture* ed. Neil McCaw (Aldershot: Ashgate, 2004).

Craik, W.A., *The Brontë Novels* (London: Methuen, 1968).

Crump, R.W, *Charlotte and Emily Brontë: A Reference Guide* 3 vols (Boston: Hall, 1982).

Dale, Peter Allan, 'Charlotte Brontë's "Tale Half-Told": the Disruption of Narrative Structure in *Jane Eyre*', *Modern Language Quarterly* 47 (1986), 108–29 reprt. *New Casebooks: Jane Eyre* ed. Heather Glen (1997).

David, Deirdre, *Rule Britannia: Women, Empire and Victorian Writing* (Ithaca and London: Cornell University Press, 1995).

Delamotte, Eugenia C., *Perils of the Night: A Feminist Study of Nineteenth-Century Gothic* (Oxford: Oxford University Press, 1990).

Dessner, Lawrence Jay, *The Homely Web of Truth: A Study of Charlotte Brontë's Novels* (The Hague: Mouton, 1975).

Dimnet, Ernest, *The Brontë Sisters* [*Les Soeurs Brontë*] translated by Louise Morgan Sill (London, Jonathan Cape: 1927).

Donaldson, Laura, *Decolonizing Feminisms: Race, Gender and Empire-Building* (London: Routledge, 1993).

Dunn, Richard J. ed., *Jane Eyre. By Charlotte Brontë* 2nd ed (New York: Norton, 1987).

Eagles, John, 'A Few Words About Novels', *Blackwood's Edinburgh Magazine* (October 1848), 459–74.

Eagleton, Terry, *Myths of Power: A Marxist Study of the Brontës* (London: Macmillan, 1975).

Erickson, Donald, 'Imagery as Structure in *Jane Eyre*', *Victorian Newsletter* 30 (Autumn 1966).

Ewbank, Inga-Stina, *Their Proper Sphere: A Study of the Brontë Sisters as Early Victorian Female Novelists* (London: Arnold, 1966).

Fonblanque, A. W., 'The Literary Examiner', *Examiner* (27 November 1847), 756–7.

Forçade, Eugène, *Revue des deux mondes* (31 October 1848), tome 24, 471–94.

Fraiman, Susan, *Unbecoming Women: British Women Writers and the Novel of Development* (New York: Columbia University Press, 1993).

Franklin, J. Jeffrey, 'The Merging of Spiritualities: Jane Eyre as Missionary of Love' *Nineteenth-Century Literature* 49 (March 1995), 456–82.

Gaskell, Elizabeth, *The Life of Charlotte Brontë* [1857] repr. (Oxford: Oxford University Press, 1974).

Gates, Barbara T. '"Visionary Woe" and its Revisions: Another Look at Jane Eyre's Pictures' *Ariel* 7 (October 1976), 36–49.

Gérin, Winifred, *Charlotte Brontë: The Evolution of Genius* (Oxford: Clarendon, 1967).

Gezari, Janet, *Charlotte Brontë and Defensive Conduct* (Philadelphia: University of Pennsylvania Press, 1992).

Gibson, Mary Ellis, 'The Seraglio or Suttee: Brontë's *Jane Eyre*' *Postscript* 4 (1987), 1–8.

Gilbert, Sandra and Gubar, Susan, *The Madwoman in the Attic: The Woman Writer and the Nineteenth-Century Literary Imagination* [1979] reprt. with a new intro (New Haven and London: Yale University Press, 2000).

Glen, Heather ed., *New Casebooks: Jane Eyre* (Basingstoke: Macmillan, 1997).

Glen, Heather, *Charlotte Brontë: the Imagination in History* (Cambridge: Cambridge University Press, 2002).

Glen, Heather ed., *The Cambridge Companion to the Brontës* (Cambridge: Cambridge University Press, 2002).

Harrison, Frederic, *Charlotte Brontë's Place in Literature* (London: Arnold, 1895).

Harte, Bret, 'Miss Mix' in *Condensed Novels* (London: Routledge, 1873).

Heilman, Robert B., 'Charlotte Brontë's "New" Gothic' in *From Jane Austen to Joseph Conrad* ed. Robert C. Rathburn and Martin Steinmann (Minneapolis: University of Minnesota Press, 1958).

Heilman, Robert B., 'Charlotte Brontë, Reason, and the Moon', *Nineteenth-Century Fiction* 14 (1960), 283–302.

Hennelly, Mark M., 'Jane Eyre's Reading Lesson', *ELH* 51 (1984), 693–717.

Higashi, Sumiko, 'Jane Eyre: Charlotte Brontë vs. the Hollywood Myth of Romance' *Journal of Popular Film* 6 (1977), 13–31.

Hoeveler, Diane and Lau, Beth eds, *Approaches to Teaching Jane Eyre* (New York: MLA, 1992).

Homans, Margaret, *Bearing the Word: Language and Female Experience in Nineteenth-Century Women's Writing* (Chicago: University of Chicago Press, 1986).

Hopkins, Lisa, 'The Red and the Blue: *Jane Eyre* in the 1990s' in Deborah Cartmell, I.Q. Hunter, Heidi Kaye and Imelda Whelehan eds, *Classics in Film and Fiction* (London: Pluto, 2000).

Hopkins, Lisa, *Screening the Gothic* (Austin: University of Texas Press, 2005).

Judd, Catherine A., 'Male Pseudonyms and Female Authority in Victorian England' in *Literature in the Marketplace: Nineteenth-century British Reading and Publishing Practices* ed. John O. Jordan and Robert L. Patten (Cambridge: Cambridge University Press, 1995).

Kaplan, Carla, *The Erotics of Talk: Women's Writing and Feminist Paradigms* (New York and Oxford: Oxford University Press, 1996).

Kaplan, Cora, *Sea Changes: Culture and Feminism* (London: Verso, 1986).

Keefe, Robert, *Charlotte Brontë's World of Death* (Austin: University of Texas Press, 1979).

Klein, Michael and Parker, Gillian eds, *The English Novel and the Movies* (New York, Ungar, 1981).

Knies, Earl, 'The "I" of *Jane Eyre*', *College English* 27 (April 1966), 546–56.

Knies, Earl, *The Art of Charlotte Brontë* (Athens: Ohio University Press, 1969).

Kreilkamp, Ivan, 'Unuttered: Withheld Speech and Female Authorship in *Jane Eyre* and *Villette*' *Novel* 32 (1999), 331–54.

Kroeber, Karl, *Styles in Fictional Structure: the Art of Jane Austen, Charlotte Brontë, George Eliot* (Princeton NJ: Princeton University Press, 1971).

Kromm, Jane, 'Visual Culture and Scopic Custom in *Jane Eyre* and *Villette*' *Victorian Literature and Culture* 26 (1998), 369–94.

Kucich, John, *Repression in Victorian Fiction: Charlotte Brontë, George Eliot, and Charles Dickens* (Berkeley: University of California Press, 1987).

Lazarre, Jane, '"Charlotte's Web": Reading *Jane Eyre* Over Time' in *Between Women* ed. Carol Ascher, Louise DeSalvo, Sara Ruddick (New York and London: Routledge, 1993).

Leavis, F.R., *The Great Tradition* (London: Chatto and Windus, 1948).

Leavis, Q.D., Introduction to *Jane Eyre* (London: Penguin, 1966) reprt. in *Q.D. Leavis: Collected Essays* 3 vols (Cambridge: Cambridge University Press, 1983), vol. 1.

Lerner, Laurence, 'Bertha and the Critics', *Nineteenth-Century Literature* (December 1989), 273–300.

Levine, Caroline, '"Harmless Pleasure": Gender, Suspense, and *Jane Eyre*' *Victorian Literature and Culture* (2000) 275–86.

Lewes, G.H., 'Recent Novels: French and English', *Fraser's Magazine* 36 (December 1847), 689–95.

Lewes, G.H., 'Jane Eyre: An Autobiography', *Westminster Review* 48 (January 1848) 581–84.

Linder, Cynthia A., *Romantic Imagery in the Novels of Charlotte Brontë* (London: Macmillan, 1978).

Litvak, Joseph, *Caught in the Act: Theatricality in the Nineteenth-century English Novel* (Berkeley: University of California Press, 1992).

Lodge, David, 'Fire and Eyre: Charlotte Brontë's War of Earthly Elements' in *The Language of Fiction* (London: Routledge, 1966).

Lorimer, James, 'Noteworthy Novels', *North British Review* 11 (August 1849), 475–93.

Marcus, Sharon, 'The Profession of the Author: Abstraction, Advertising, and Jane Eyre' *PMLA* 110 (March 1995), 206–19.

Martin, Robert, *The Accents of Persuasion: Charlotte Brontë's Novels* (London: Faber, 1966).

Matus, Jill, '"Strong family likeness": *Jane Eyre* and *The Tenant of Wildfell Hall*' in Heather Glen ed., *The Cambridge Companion to the Brontës* (Cambridge: Cambridge University Press, 2002).

Maynard, John, *Charlotte Brontë and Sexuality* (Cambridge: Cambridge University Press, 1984).

McLaughlin, M.B., 'Past and Future Landscapes: Pictures in *Jane Eyre*' *The Victorian Newsletter* 41 (1972), 22–4.

McNees, Eleanor, *The Brontë Sisters: Critical Assessments* vol. 3 (Mountfield: Helm, 1996).

Meyer, Susan, *Imperialism at Home: Race and Victorian Women's Fiction* (Ithaca and London: Cornell University Press, 1996).

Michie, Elsie, 'White Chimpanzees and Oriental Despots: Racial Stereotyping and Edward Rochester' in *Case Studies in Contemporary Criticism: Jane Eyre* ed. Beth Newman (1996).

Michie, Elsie, *Outside the Pale: Cultural Exclusion, Gender Difference, and the Victorian Woman Writer* (Ithaca: Cornell UP, 1993).

Michie, Elsie, *Charlotte Brontë's Jane Eyre: A Casebook* (Oxford: Oxford University Press, 2006).

Miller, Lucasta, *The Brontë Myth* (London: Cape, 2001).

Millett, Kate, *Sexual Politics* (London: Abacus, 1972).

Moers, Ellen, *Literary Women* (London: Allen, 1977).

Moglen, Helene, *Charlotte Brontë: The Self Conceived* (New York: Norton, 1976).

Montégut, Émile, 'Miss Brontë: Sa Vie et Ses Oeuvres', *Revue des Deux Mondes* 10 (July 1857), 139–84, 423–65.

Moore, Lisa, *Dangerous Intimacies: Toward a Sapphic History of the British Novel* (Durham NC: Duke University Press, 1997).

Mozley, Anne, 'Jane Eyre: An Autobiography', *Christian Remembrancer* 15 (April 1848), 396–409.

Nestor, Pauline, *Female Friendships and Communities: Charlotte Brontë, George Eliot, Elizabeth Gaskell* (Oxford: Clarendon, 1985).

Newman, Beth ed., *Case Studies in Contemporary Criticism: Jane Eyre* (New York: St Martin's Press, 1996).

Nudd, Donna Marie, 'Rediscovering *Jane Eyre* through its adaptations' in Diane Hoeveler and Beth Lau eds, *Approaches to Teaching Jane Eyre* (New York: MLA, 1992).

O'Connor, Erin, 'Preface for a post-postcolonial criticism', *Victorian Studies* 45 (Winter 2003), 217–46.

Ohmann, Carol, 'Historical Reality and "Divine Appointment" in Charlotte Brontë's Fiction', *Signs* 2 (Summer 1977), 757–78.

Oliphant, Margaret, 'Modern Novelists – Great and Small', *Blackwood's Edinburgh Magazine* 77 (May 1855), 557–9.

Oliphant, Margaret, 'Novels', *Blackwood's Edinburgh Magazine* 102 (September 1867), 257–80.

Pell, Nancy, 'Resistance, Rebellion, and Marriage: The Economics of *Jane Eyre*', *Nineteenth-Century Fiction* 31 (March 1977), 397–420.

Perera, Suvendrini, *Reaches of Empire: The English Novel from Edgeworth to Dickens* (New York: Columbia University Press, 1991).

Peters, Margot, *Charlotte Brontë: Style in the Novel* (Madison, Wisconsin: University of Wisconsin Press, 1973).

Peterson, Linda H., *Traditions of Victorian Women's Autobiography* (Charlottesville: University of Virginia Press, 1999).

Pickrel, Paul, 'Jane Eyre: The Apocalypse of the Body' *ELH* 53 (1986), 165–82.

Politi, Jina, 'Jane Eyre Class-ified' *Literature and History* 8 (1982), 56–66 reprt. in *New Casebooks: Jane Eyre* ed. Heather Glen (Basingstoke: Macmillan, 1997).

Poovey, Mary, *Uneven Developments: The Ideological Work of Gender in Mid-Victorian England* (Chicago: University of Chicago Press, 1989).

Qualls, Barry V., *The Secular Pilgrims of Victorian Fiction: The Novel as Book of Life* (Cambridge: Cambridge University Press, 1982).

Rhys, Jean, *Wide Sargasso Sea* (London: Penguin, 1979).

Rich, Adrienne, 'Jane Eyre: The Temptations of a Motherless Woman' [1973] reprt. in *On Lies, Secrets and Silence: Selected Prose 1966–1978* (London: Virago, 1980).

Rigby, Elizabeth, '*Vanity Fair* – and *Jane Eyre*', *Quarterly Review* 84 (December 1848), 153–85.

Rigney, Barbara Hill, *Madness and Sexual Politics in the Feminist Novel* (Madison: University of Wisconsin Press, 1978).

Roberts, Doreen, 'Jane Eyre and "The Warped System of Things"' in *Reading the Victorian Novel: Detail into Form* ed. Ian Gregor (London: Vision Press, 1980).

Roy, Parama, 'Unaccommodated Woman and the Poetics of Property in *Jane Eyre*' *Studies in English Literature* 29 (Autumn 1989), 713–27.

Rubik, Margarete and Mettinger-Schartmann, Elke eds, *A Breath of Fresh Eyre. Intertextual and Intermedial Reworkings of Jane Eyre* (Amsterdam: Rodopi, 2007).

Sadoff, Dianne F., *Monsters of Affection: Dickens, Eliot, and Brontë on Fatherhood* (Baltimore: Johns Hopkins University Press, 1982).

Sadoff, Dianne F., 'The Father, Castration, and Female Fantasy in *Jane Eyre*' in Beth Newman ed., *Case Studies in Contemporary Criticism: Jane Eyre*.

Schacht, Paul, 'Jane Eyre and the History of Self-Respect' *Modern Language Quarterly* 52 (1991), 423–53.

Schwartz, Nina, 'No Place Like Home: The Logic of the Supplement in *Jane Eyre*' in Beth Newman ed., *Case Studies in Contemporary Criticism: Jane Eyre*.

Sharpe, Jenny, *Allegories of Empire: The Figure of Woman in the Colonial Text* (Minneapolis: University of Minnesota Press, 1993).

Showalter, Elaine, *A Literature of their Own: British Women Novelists from Brontë to Lessing* (London: Virago, 1978).

Showalter, Elaine, *The Female Malady: Women, Madness, and Culture in England, 1830–1980* (New York: Pantheon, 1985).

Shuttleworth, Sally, *Charlotte Brontë and Victorian Psychology* (Cambridge: Cambridge University Press, 1996).

Sinclair, May, *The Novels of Charlotte, Emily and Anne Brontë* (London and Toronto: Dent, 1922).

Solomon, Eric, '*Jane Eyre*: Fire and Water', *College English* 25 (December 1963).

Spacks, Patricia Meyer, *The Female Imagination: A Literary and Psychological Investigation of Women's Writing* (London: Allen and Unwin, 1976).

Spivak, Gayatri, 'Three Women's Texts and A Critique of Imperialism' *Critical Inquiry* 12 (Autumn 1985), 243–61.

Stephen, Leslie, 'Hours in a Library No. XVII: Charlotte Brontë', *Cornhill Magazine* (December 1877), 723–39.

Sternlieb, Lisa, '*Jane Eyre*: "Hazarding Confidences"' *Nineteenth-Century Literature* 53 (March 1999), 452–79.

Stoneman ,Patsy, *Brontë Transformations: The Cultural Dissemination of Jane Eyre and Wuthering Heights* (London: Harvester Wheatsheaf, 1996).

Stoneman, Patsy, *Jane Eyre on Stage, 1848–1898* (Aldershot: Ashgate, 2007).

Sutherland, John, *Can Jane Eyre Be Happy? More Puzzles in Classic Fiction* (Oxford: Oxford University Press, 1997).

Sweat, Margaret J., 'Charlotte Brontë and the Brontë Novels', *North American Review* 85 (October 1857), 293–329.

Swinburne, Algernon, *A Note on Charlotte Brontë* (London: Chatto and Windus, 1877).

Teale, Polly, *Jane Eyre: adapted from Charlotte Brontë's novel by Polly Teale for Shared Experience* (London: Nick Hern, 1998).

Tillotson, Kathleen, *Novels of the Eighteen-Forties* (Oxford: Clarendon, 1954).

Thomas, Sue, *Imperialism, Reform, and the Making of Englishness in Jane Eyre* (Basingstoke: Palgrave, 2008).

Thormählen, Marianne, *The Brontës and Religion* (Cambridge: Cambridge University Press, 1999).

Tromly, Annette, *The Cover of the Mask: The Autobiographers in Charlotte Brontë's Fiction* (Victoria, B.C.: University of Victoria Press, 1982).

Vanden Bossche, Chris, 'What did Jane Eyre do? Ideology, agency, class and the novel' *Narrative* 13 (January 2005), 46–66.

Vargish, Thomas, *The Providential Aesthetic in Victorian Fiction* (Charlottesville: University of Virginia Press, 1985).

Ward, Mary [Mrs Humphrey] ed., *Jane Eyre* in *The Life and Works of Charlotte Brontë and her Sisters* (Smith, Elder, 1899).

Webb, Igor, *From Custom to Capital: The English Novel and the Industrial Revolution* (Ithaca and London: Cornell University Press, 1981).

Wemyss Reid, T., *Charlotte Bronte. A Monograph* (London: Macmillan, 1877).

Whipple, E.P., 'Novels of the Season', *North American Review* 67 (October 1848), 354–69.

Williams, Carolyn, 'Closing the Book: The Intertextual End of *Jane Eyre*' in *Victorian Connections* ed by Jerome McGann (Charlottesville: University Press of Virginia, 1989).

Williams, Raymond, *The English Novel From Dickens to Lawrence* (London: Chatto and Windus, 1970).

Winnifrith, Tom, *The Brontës and their Background* (New York: Barnes and Noble, 1973).

Winnifrith, Tom, *The Brontës* (London: Macmillan, 1977).

Woolf, Virginia, *The Common Reader* [1925] reprt. (London: Hogarth, 1929).

Woolf, Virginia, *A Room of One's Own* [1929] reprt. (Oxford: Oxford University Press, 2000).

Wright, William, *The Brontës and Ireland* (London: Hodder & Stoughton, 1893).

Wyatt, Jean, *Reconstructing Desire: The Role of the Unconscious in Women's Reading and Writing* (Chapel Hill: University of North Carolina Press, 1990).

Yaeger, Patricia, *Honey-Mad Women: Emancipatory Strategies in Women's Writing* (New York: Columbia University Press, 1988).

Zlotnick, Susan, 'Jane Eyre, Anna Leonowens, and the White Woman's Burden: Governesses, Missionaries, and Maternal Imperialists in Mid-Victorian Britain' *Victorians Institute Journal* 24 (1996), 27–56.

Zonana, Joyce, 'The Sultan and the Slave: Feminist Orientalism and the Structure of *Jane Eyre*', *Signs* 18 (Spring 1993), 592–617.

FILM AND TELEVISION ADAPTATIONS OF *JANE EYRE*

There were many earlier versions, but these are not widely available.

Jane Eyre. Dir. Christy Cabanne. With Colin Clive and Virginia Bruce. Monogram Pictures, 1934.

Jane Eyre. Dir. Robert Stevenson. With Joan Fontaine and Orson Welles. Twentieth-century Fox, 1944.

Jane Eyre. Dir. Delbert Mann. With Susannah York and George C. Scott. British Lion, 1970.

Jane Eyre. Dir. Julian Aymes. With Zelah Clarke and Timothy Dalton. BBC, 1983.

Jane Eyre. Dir Franco Zeffirelli. With Charlotte Gainsbourg and William Hurt. Rochester Films, 1995.

Jane Eyre. Dir Susanna White. With Ruth Wilson and Toby Stephens. BBC, 2006.

Students of the Brontës may also wish to visit the Internet site of the Brontë Society, which manages the Haworth Parsonage Museum and organises exhibitions and educational workshops on aspects of the Brontës' lives and work: http://www.bronte.info

Index

Adams, Maurianne, 71–3
Austen, Jane, 25, 35, 38, 68–9, 117
Azim, Firdous, 112–13, 137

Bakhtin, Mikhail, 48, 60
Bayne, Peter, 23, 26–7, 62–3
Beaty, Jerome, 48, 59–61
Bertha
    and adaptations of *Jane Eyre*, 145, 149–50
    as Jane's double, 68, 73–7, 112–13, 140,
        146, 149–50
    and racial typology, 22–3, 85, 101,
        109–13, 118–20
    readings of her laughter, 63–5, 72–3,
        75, 103
Bewick, Thomas
    History of British Birds, A, 43, 45, 53, 131
Bildungsroman as form of *Jane Eyre*, 44, 51,
    69, 75, 113
biographical criticism, 17–19, 25, 34–8, 40–1
Blackwood's Edinburgh Magazine, 14–15,
    19, 53
Bock, Carol, 33, 53–4
Brontë, Anne, 5, 17, 38, 41, 92
    Agnes Grey, 5, 10, 13
    Tenant of Wildfell Hall, The, 13–14
Brontë, Branwell, 17–18, 41
Brontë, Charlotte
    Professor, The, 5, 19, 51, 97, 131
    relationship between biography and *Jane
        Eyre*, 11, 17–18, 27–8, 34–6, 92–3,
        131, 134–6
    and religion, 134–6
    and revolution, 96–7, 104–5
    Shirley, 19, 97, 122
    views on the 'Woman Question', 65–7
    Villette, 19, 20, 38, 51, 68, 133
Brontë, Emily, 5, 17, 25, 30, 38, 41, 92
    Wuthering Heights, 5, 10, 13–14, 25,
        78–80, 92, 143–4
Brontë, Patrick, 17–18, 41, 93, 134
Brontë Society and Haworth Parsonage
    Museum, The, 23, 30, 178

Bunyan, John
    Pilgrim's Progress, The, 43, 56, 81–3, 112
Burns, Helen
    debates with Jane, 43, 96, 161–2
    feeblest character in *Jane Eyre*, 11
    as female archetype, 70–1, 74, 76
Byron, George Gordon, Lord, 37, 148

Carter, Angela, 2, 77–8
Case, Alison, 137–9
Cecil, David, Lord, 1, 30, 32, 36–9, 44, 61
Chartism, 1, 10, 12, 91, 101
Chase, Karen, 58–9, 128
class struggle and *Jane Eyre*, 85–7, 90–105,
    107–8, 117–18
Coleridge, Samuel Taylor, 44
Cowan Bridge School, 11, 17, 134

Dale, Peter Allan, 48, 55–7
Dickens, Charles, 8, 40, 44, 92, 136

Eagleton, Terry, 93–5, 101, 106, 112
education in *Jane Eyre*, 43–4, 69–70, 80–1,
    96, 134–6
Eliot, George, 8, 23–4, 38, 46, 68–9,
    73–4
ending of *Jane Eyre*, 56–7, 81–3
Ewbank, Inga-Stina, 65–7
Eyre, resonances of the name, 43, 45, 80–1,
    100, 131

fairy tale echoes in *Jane Eyre*, 77–8, 141
feminist criticism, 20, 26, 61, Chapter
    three *passim*, 95, 103–6, 112, 116–17,
    127, 170
films of *Jane Eyre*, 33–4, 147–52
Forçade, Eugène, 15–17, 91
formalist criticism, 2, 32, 39–45, 47
Foucault, Michel, 125, 127, 142, 165
Fraiman, Susan, 86–7, 96, 101–4
France as an influence on and a subject in
    Jane Eyre, 25, 27–8, 80–1, 99–101
Freudian analysis, 50, 76–8, 82–4, 161

Gaskell, Elizabeth, 50, 92
  Life of Charlotte Brontë, 6, 17–18, 127
genre and *Jane Eyre*, 60–1, 88, 99–100
Gezari, Janet, 130–3
Gibson, Mary Ellis, 87, 113–15
Gilbert, Sandra and Gubar, Susan
  Madwoman in the Attic, The, 3, 67, 73,
    75–7, 102, 150
Glen, Heather, 31–2, 59, 61, 134–6
Godwin, William, 8
Gothic, 41–2, 74–5, 147–8
governesses, 85–6, 92, 104–5, 120–1, 140,
  145–6

Harte, Bret, 22–3
Heilman, Robert, 41–2
Hennelly, Mark M., 47, 57–8
Homans, Margaret, 78–80

influence of *Jane Eyre* on subsequent novels,
  19–22, 40, 145–7
intertext, *Jane Eyre* as, 48, 81–3, 143,
  150–1
Ireland, 28, 121–4

James, Henry, 38, 69, 146
Jane
  as an artist, 52–3, 133–4
  and class origins, 93–104, 118
  as Everywoman, 68–89
  and motherhood, 68–70, 78–80
  reader's identification with, 8–9, 31–2,
    49–51, 88–9
  relationship with Rochester, 63, 66–7,
    70–6, 83–5, 88–9, 94–5, 97, 104,
    114–15, 127, 129, 132–3, 141

Kristeva, Julia, 48, 78, 81

Lacan, Jacques, 78, 105, 133
Lawrence, D.H., 38, 42
Leavis, F. R., 2, 30–1, 38–9, 46
Leavis, Q. D., 31, 43–4, 51, 65, 69
Lewes, George Henry, 5, 8–9
Lodge, David, 44–5, 48, 61

Martin, Robert, 42–3, 65
Martineau, Harriet, 40, 62, 66
Marxist criticism, 3, 85–6, Chapter four
  passim, 112, 127, 170

Meyer, Susan, 117–19
Moglen, Helene, 71–3
Mozley, Anne, 10–12

narrative voice of *Jane Eyre*, Chapter two
    passim
  compelling, 3, 20, 31, 35–6
  complex, 57–60, 129
  expressionistic, 51, 58–9
  as a medium for winning control, 53–5,
    137–40
  unreliable, 51–5, 139–41
New Critics, 39, 45
New Historicism, 3, 125–36, 140, 171

Oliphant, Margaret, 19–22, 62

Peel, Robert, Sir, 16, 91
Peters, Margot, 45–7, 49–50
phrenology, 127–30
Politi, Jina, 99–101
political tendencies of *Jane Eyre*, 10–13,
    15–17, 19, 91–108, 121–4, 128–30
Poovey, Mary, 85–6, 104
postcolonial criticism, 23, 85, 87, Chapter
    five *passim*, 127, 171
poststructuralist criticism, 2, 48, 56–60,
    140, 171
prose style of *Jane Eyre*, 5, 8–9, 45–7,
    49–51, 129
psychoanalytic criticism, 9, 58–9, 73–85,
    170

reader response theory, 47, 49–51,
    57–8
readership of *Jane Eyre*, 4, 33–4,
    152–3
reading as a trope in *Jane Eyre*, 43, 55–8,
    129–34
religious tendencies of *Jane Eyre*, 10–13,
    20–1, 55–7, 81–3, 132–3, 134–6
Revue des Deux Mondes, 15–19
Rhys, Jean
  Wide Sargasso Sea, 77, 110–11
Rich, Adrienne, 63, 65, 68–73
Richardson, Samuel
  Pamela, 129, 137–8
Rigby, Elizabeth (Lady Eastlake), 10,
    12–13, 24, 91, 98
Rivers, Diana and Mary, 57, 70, 86

Rivers, St John
   as missionary, 112, 115, 119, 121, 136
   as representative of patriarchal power,
      78, 81–3, 95–6, 114
   an unsuccessful character, 4, 24
Roberts, Doreen, 3, 33, 47–51, 61
Rochester, Edward
   and debate over masculinity, 24–5, 88, 130
   loss of hand and eye, 70–1, 98, 132–3
   as oedipal father-figure, 83–5
   as villain, 54–5
   romanticism and *Jane Eyre*, 24, 28, 37, 44,
      57, 93

Sand, George, 25, 28
Scott, Walter, Sir, 8, 24, 53, 141
sensation novels, 6, 19–23, 145–6
Showalter, Elaine, 73–5, 88, 102, 150
Shuttleworth, Sally, 104–5, 127–30
slavery, 87, 96, 109, 114–20
Spivak, Gayatri, 85, 110–13, 117, 123–4
Stephen, Leslie, 25–7, 34–5
Stoneman, Patsy, 143–8
structuralist criticism, 33, 48, 55–7
stylistic analysis, 45–7, 49
supernatural motifs in *Jane Eyre*, 42, 59, 72,
   74–5, 100, 110

Swinburne, Algernon, 23–5, 27
symbolism in *Jane Eyre*, 41–5, 58–9, 72–80,
   132–3

Thackeray, William Makepeace,
   4, 24, 40
   Vanity Fair, 4, 12, 104–5, 117
theatre adaptations of *Jane Eyre*, 143–5,
   149–50, 152
theatricality in *Jane Eyre*, 139–41, 144
Tillotson, Kathleen, 32, 39–41, 153
Tolstoy, Leo, 35–6, 69
Tromly, Annette, 33, 51–4

Ward, Mary Augusta (Mrs Humphry
   Ward), 27–9, 34
Whipple, E. P., 13–14
Williams, Carolyn, 48, 81–3
Williams, Raymond, 91–3, 96
Woolf, Virginia, 25, 32, 46, 69, 72
   Common Reader, The, 34–6, 38
   Room of One's Own, A, 63–5
Wyatt, Jean, 83–5

Yaeger, Patricia, 65, 80–1

Zonana, Joyce, 87, 115–17

Printed and bound by CPI Group (UK) Ltd, Croydon, CR0 4YY